ORGANIZING AMERICA

ORGANIZING AMERICA

WEALTH, POWER, AND THE ORIGINS
OF CORPORATE CAPITALISM

Charles Perrow

PRINCETON UNIVERSITY PRESS

PRINCETON AND OXFORD

Library of Congress Cataloging-in-Publication Data

Perrow, Charles.

    Organizing America : wealth, power, and the origins of corporate capitalism /
Charles Perrow.

      p. cm.

    Includes bibliographical references and index.

    ISBN 0-691-08954-X (alk. paper)

    1. Organizational behavior — United States — History — 19th century.   2. Big
business — United States — History — 19th century.   3. Social change — United
States — History — 19th century.   I. Title.

HD58.7 .P464 2002

302.3'5 — dc21   2001055196

British Library Cataloging-in-Publication Data is available

This book has been composed in Sabon

Printed on acid-free paper. ∞

www.pup.princeton.edu

Printed in the United States of America

10 9 8 7 6 5 4 3 2 1

CONTENTS

ACKNOWLEDGMENTS   ix

CHAPTER 1
Introduction   1
  Some Central Concepts   3
    Density and concentration   3
    Size and small-firm networks   4
    Organizations or capitalism   6
    Noneconomic organizations   7
    Power   8
    Culture and other shapers of society   9
    Organizations as the independent variable   10
  What Do Organizations Do?   12
  What Kind of Organizations?   16
  Alternative Theories   17
  Conclusion   19

CHAPTER 2
Preparing the Ground   22
  Communities, Markets, Hierarchies, and Networks   22
    Community   23
    The market direction   25
    Toward hierarchy and networks   28
  The Legal Revolution that Launched Organizations   31
    Fear of corporations   33
    What organizations need to be able to do   35
    Making capitalism corporate   36
  Capitalism to Corporate Capitalism   40
  Lawyers: "The Shock Troops of Capitalism"   43

CHAPTER 3
Toward Hierarchy: The Mills of Manayunk   48
  Getting the Factory Going: The Role of Labor Control   48
    The first mill — a workhouse   50
    To mechanize or not?   51
  Social Consequences   53
  Labor Policies and Strikes   58
  Organizations and Religion   60
  From Working Classes to a Working Class   61
    The politics of class   62
  Conclusion   63

CHAPTER 4
Toward Hierarchy and Networks   65
  Lowell and the Boston Associates   65
    Wage dependence and labor control   65
    Lowell I: The benign phase   67
    Profits and market control   69
    Lowell II: The exploitive phase   70
  Explaining the First Modern Business   75
    Structural constraints   77
  The Slater Model   79
  Toward Networks with the Philadelphia Model   81
    When capital counts   82
    Philadelphia's large mills   84
    Size and technology   86
  Networks of Firms   88
    Labor conflict   90
    Externalities   90
  The Decline of Textile Firms   92
  Summary   94

CHAPTER 5
Railroads, the Second Big Business   96
  Railroads in France, Britain, and the United States:
  The Organizational Logic   102
    France   104
    Britain   108
    The importance of the railroads   111
  Why Were the Railroads Unregulated and Privatized?   113
    The efficiency argument   115
    Historical institutionalism   117
    Historical institutionalism assessed   122
    The neoinstitutionalist account   123
    The organization interest account   127
    The details   129
    Self-interested opposition to the railroads   139
  Corruption Observed but Not Interpreted   141
    Evidence from the public record, and the outcry   144
    Scholars explain corruption   151
  Summary and Conclusions   157

CHAPTER 6
The Organizational Imprinting   160
  Making the Railroads Work   160
    Divisionalization   161

Finance takes charge   162
Inevitable, or a chance path?   165
Contracting out   166
Leadership Style and Worker Welfare   173
Work in general   175
Nationalization and Centralization: The Final Spike   179
Organizational versus political interpretations   180
Where did the money come from?   183
Regionalization versus Nationalization   186
The debate over the ethos   187
A political or an organizational interpretation of the struggle?   192
Was Regionalism Viable?   195
Concentrating Capital and Power   196
The corporate form triumphs   197
Explaining the arrival of the corporate form   201
An organizational agency account   204
Summary and Conclusions   212

CHAPTER 7
Summary and Conclusions   217

Appendix Alternative Theories Where Organizations Are the Dependent Variable   229

Notes   237

Bibliography   243

Index   251

ACKNOWLEDGMENTS

A GREAT MANY COLLEAGUES have contributed helpful readings of drafts or responses to presentations of this book. Louis Galambos was very helpful and encouraging with comments on an early draft, as was Philip Scranton with his extensive comments and suggestions on not only the textile chapters but also others as well. John Campbell gave the first draft a critical, encouraging, and helpful reading; so did Karen Merrill, Steven Arons, and other members of a year-long seminar on business and history at the Davis Center for Historical Research at Princeton, where a fellowship released me from teaching duties at Yale. An informal workshop at the Institute for Advanced Study, where I had a study that year, provided helpful comments from Eric Johnson, Susan Nalle, Alan Wells, and Roumen Daskalov; similarly, a workshop in the Sociology Department at Princeton yielded encouraging comments from Lee Clarke, Paul DiMaggio, Frank Dobbin, Miguel Centeno, Michèle Lamont, and others. Jason Kaufman, a graduate student in the department at the time, was an excellent research assistant. A two-month faculty seminar I gave at the Hong Kong University of Science and Technology put some drafts to the test. The chapter on the railroads benefitted from the comments of a seminar jointly conducted with Marc Schneiberg at the University of Arizona in spring 1998. Finally, extensive, challenging, and extremely helpful publisher's reviews came from William Roy, Frank Dobbin, Mark Mizruchi, and two anonymous readers; they were tough and exemplary. A lovely spring at the Center for Advanced Study in the Behavioral Sciences in Stanford, California, made coping with the reviews more pleasant. My late first wife, Edith, saw the project begin, and my present wife, Barbara, saw it end; without their love and support it would not have been full of passionate intensity, but would have lacked all conviction.

ORGANIZING AMERICA

Chapter 1

INTRODUCTION

THIS BOOK SEEKS to tell us how and why it happened that the most important feature of our social landscape is the large organization, public or private. Americans celebrate individualism and entrepreneurship, and some see organizations as getting smaller or more decentralized; so concern with bigness and bureaucracy may have abated. But we should be reminded that today, well over 90 percent of the work force works for someone else—as wage and salary employees—up from 20 percent in 1800; over half of the gainfully employed people in the country work for organizations with 500 or more employees, up from 0 percent in 1800. Today, although establishments have an average size of about thirty employees, organizations can own and control many separate establishments. And control is the important factor, not the size of the branch bank or the factory site or the fast food outlet or the service franchise. The truly big organizations, public and private, have come to define and even absorb much of our society.

Despite all the talk of downsizing, our organizational population has not become perceptibly thinner; the Fortune 500 industrials have declined in size by about 8 percent in a decade, but their average size changed little, from about 3,000 employees in 1979, the peak year, to 2,750 in 1993. That is still very big. Meanwhile, the average size of the 500 largest service corporations rose from 1,700 in 1982 to 2,750 in 1993, making them as big as the industrials (Useem 1996, 165). Even with the government contracting out many activities to private firms (generally large ones), government has not shrunk appreciably.

The American population increases, and so does the number of big organizations. More and more they have come to constitute societies in themselves, providing, on their own terms, the cradle-to-grave services that communities and small organizations used to provide. We could not have our level of affluence without organizations, of course, and some of them, including certain government organizations such as the armed forces or the social security administration, are bound to be huge.

But most do not need to be very large, and their size and power is troubling. Our economic organizations—business and industry—concentrate wealth and power; socialize employees and customers alike to meet their needs; and pass off to the rest of society the cost of their pollution, crowding, accidents, and encouragement of destructive life styles. In the vaunted "free market" economy of the United States, regulation of business and industry to prevent or mitigate this market failure is relatively ineffective, as compared to that enacted by other industrialized countries.

Big noneconomic organizations also trouble me. Big churches and school systems and local, state, and federal governments also centralize power, socialize employees to bureaucratic values, "de-skill" them unnecessarily, and generate their own "externalities" — the costs of doing their business that are shifted onto a fragile environment or fragile groups within the polity.

Increasingly, especially since the mid-twentieth century, politicians and government leaders have tried to ameliorate these problems, saying that we need big organizations but that they need to be more responsive to citizens. In this area we have made some progress. But perhaps not enough. Antitrust enforcement has waxed and waned; conceptions of unfair competition are relaxed; big organizations and their masters dominate campaign financing and shape regulatory procedures. Cleaning up after the economic organizations has generated more big organizations to do the clean up, and they bring more externalities, and more incorporation of social functions that once were filled by small groups, families, neighborhoods, and small local governmental units. Elsewhere I have explored the possibilities, faint but real, for networks of small firms that can drive innovation and also distribute wealth and power more equitably (Perrow 1992). Networks of small firms have appeared in some parts of the industrialized world, such as Northern Italy, the Scandinavian countries, Japan and Taiwan to some extent, and even in parts of the United States (Sabel and Zeitlin 1997). An economy that allowed extensive use of small-firm networks was a possibility in the United States in the nineteenth century, and I will explain why that possibility disappeared.

Why did the United States grow big organizations and come to accept them? I will start with the early days of the Republic, with the first mass-production organizations using "wage dependent" labor, the textile mills, and the legal revolution that made big organizations possible before they even appeared. Until the Civil War there were few organizations large enough to matter and they did little shaping of the society, but it is important to examine the first ones because they prefigured future forms. Two types of textile mills developed, one with the attributes and the social consequences of our large mass-production firms, the other resembling small-firm networks that persisted until the end of the century. Then I will examine the second big business in the United States, the railroads, because they created the corporate form we now use.

This book ends with the decade 1910. In future work I intend to show how the organizational revolution that the railroads effected spread to government, schools, and religious and voluntary organizations in subsequent decades. But by 1910 or so, the organizational mold was set. Big bureaucratic organizations were turned out in all sectors in society, making it the form of choice for public and private problem solving by the end of World War II. The relevance of family, friendship groups, neighborhood associations, and small independent business and social service organizations conversely waned. Their vital functions, once a right of citizenship rather than of employment status, were increasingly absorbed by large organizations, creating a "society of organizations" rather than communities. The centralization of wealth and power increased in the nineteenth century as a result of the growth of large organizations. Not until the 1930s was it checked, as a result of steady, if mild, redistributive efforts over the next forty years by the federal government and by a variety of political and voluntary organizations. But centralization surged again in the 1970s and continued through the end of the century, as large private organizations grew, and wealth was further concentrated.

Only two things are more basic to the structure of our society than organizations: basic demographic forces and cognitive structures of the mind. Acknowledging these, I will make the following grand claim for organizations:

> Bureaucratic organizations are the most effective means of unobtrusive control human society has produced, and once large bureaucracies are loosed upon the world, much of what we think of as causal in shaping our society — class, politics, religion, socialization and self-conceptions, technology, entrepreneurship — becomes to some degree, and to an increasing degree, and a largely unappreciated degree, shaped by organizations.

This book will investigate the origins of large bureaucratic organizations in the nineteenth-century United States.

SOME CENTRAL CONCEPTS

Density and Concentration

Of course, large organizations have been necessary at least since the pyramids were built, and some, such as the Catholic Church, have been with us for a very long time. It is their sheer number and size, their *density* and *concentration* that is new since the nineteenth century. Density — the proportion of productive workers working for wages and salaries under an explicit employment contract—has been very low for most of human history. Wage labor was rare, organizations employing people on contract were few. Density increased a bit in the eighteenth century as the first industrial revolution gained speed. Most estimates put the percentage of economically active people working for salary or wages at 20 percent at the beginning of the nineteenth century in the United States, over 50 percent at the end—enough density to make a difference even in large cities—and over 90 percent today. As we shall see in textile towns in Pennsylvania, having as little as 20 percent of the work force working for wages can affect the social structure of the town if the majority are employed by one or two large organizations. Concentrating the wage workers under one management gives that management power, not only over the lives of the workers, but over the community as a whole.

A factory of 100 employees was big in the first half of the nineteenth century, because most people worked on farms, in small trades, or in tiny organizations. Density may not have had much of an impact on society when these were all *small* organizations. In a typical mid-century American town, 50 percent of the gainfully employed worked in small organizations, and the rest worked on farms or in family businesses or were craftsmen and artisans and shopkeepers. Organizations of five or twenty people had little impact as organizations, per se. But if the employment in organizations was highly concentrated, that is, if a few of the organizations had 100 or 200 employees, they had concentrated power to shape the community. They could set wages, withstand strikes, ignore industrial accidents, control the school system, select religious denominations, block infrastructure improvements such as water supply and street paving, and fire employees who did not vote correctly. When 75 percent of the citizens of a city depend upon wages for a living, this high density increases the power that flows from concentration.

In the nation as a whole, large organizations became really important only in the last quarter of the century, when density and concentration were significant nationally, but the dynamics of their concentration of wealth and power appeared early in local settings, where it was recognized and opposed. Our story has to begin at the beginning, about 1820, as something historically novel appeared: a combination of a high density of wage workers and their concentration in a few organizations.

Size and Small-Firm Networks

The case of the textile mills in the nineteenth century United States will provide us with an effective example of the role of organizational size.

We will find that two models coexisted through much of the century: highly centralized, absentee-owned, and very large mass-production mills in New England (the "Lowell" model), and a network of quite small, decentralized specialty producers in Philadelphia. Once the former were in place little technological innovation occurred in the New England firms, whereas Philadelphia firms were consistently innovative. When the labor shortage disappeared in New England as the Irish victims of the potato famine arrived, the firms exploited labor and let the mill towns decay. In Philadelphia, the firms exploited workers less and invested in the infrastructure to make functioning communities. In the New England firms, wealth became highly concentrated, and their local and national power was great. In Philadelphia, simply because there were so many firms, profits were spread over many more people and families, and they were locally invested and locally spent, enriching the communities.

It should be noted that small firms can exploit workers and the environment just as much as big firms, but if the small firms are linked together in a network, sharing workers, space, capital, and technical knowledge, they are likely to come to realize that they share a common fate and must cooperate as well as compete, investing in labor and its skills rather than exploiting workers. Without the networking that can balance competition with cooperation, small firms are likely to exploit labor. Networks of large firms balance competition with cooperation, too, but their concentrated power is far more likely to produce negative social externalities than networks of small firms with dispersed power. Finally, to complicate things further, there are instances of small-firm networks supplying a few large firms without being exploited by them. The small firms are encouraged, or even required, to have multiple customers. The large firms want the small suppliers to survive even if they do not buy from a particular one in a particular year, since large firms ultimately benefit from cross-fertilization among many small firms.

We will discover these dynamics of size in other areas and even in the unlikely case of the railroads. It might seem inevitable that railroads would become big and national, but their size and reach was a matter of national debate. We will discover the innovative role of a small regional railroad, and the efficiency of decentralization through subcontracting in operating and maintaining the lines. Though the innovations in subcontracting were soon abandoned, they will illustrate that even in this prototype of large organizations some alternatives appeared to be more efficient for society.

Let me repeat that small organizations can exploit labor and produce unnecessary costs for society, but much evidence now exists suggesting that where they are interdependent — linked together in networks of exchange — they are less exploitive than large organizations, and their externalities (from degree of pollution to wealth distribution) are more positive. Nor are they inefficient; networks of small firms can achieve economies of scale that match those of large organizations. They also appear to be more innovative (Perrow 1992; Sabel and Zeitlin 1997; Sabel 1989; Sabel and Zeitlin 1985). Large organizations tend to be socially responsive when appropriate governmental regulation is imposed on all competitors. If regulation is not universal, those who pay the added costs typically associated with socially responsive practices will lose out to their more "efficient" competitors who avoid these costs, at least in the short run. Small firms will be unresponsive to social needs if they do not identify a community of interests that realizes the long-run advantages of cooperation and social infrastructure investment. They will also be unresponsive if they depend completely on one large firm for their business; in such cases, they are price takers, ruthlessly competing with other small firms that want to sell to the large, monopsonistic buyer.

Responsive, innovative networks of small organizations are not prevalent in U.S. history, but could have been if we had taken a different path. (They were more common in Europe, where the state restricted the size and power of for-profit organizations.) Most of the economic organizations up through the Civil War were neither large firms nor part of small-firm networks; rather, the economies were local and the population rural, and although firms had the advantages of local monopolies—not conducive to social responsibility—they also had the constraints of local community pressure to minimize negative externalities. Where ample job opportunities existed, mitigating wage dependence, they at least had to be responsive to their employees.

Organizations or Capitalism

Because the role of organizations in shaping U.S. society has been neglected, I will emphasize them. Some may object that organizations per se are not so important, but rather that capitalism, in its evolving form, can explain much of what I will talk about. As one perceptive critic, Miguel Centeno, advised me, I should decide whether ours is a society of *capitalist* organizations (and therefore I am really describing capitalism), or a society of capitalist *organizations*, (wherein the organizational form that capitalists came to use was determinant). It is both, but the emphasis so far has been on capitalism; I believe an emphasis upon organizations is needed from the nineteenth century on. Capitalism predates our nation and existed without large organizations in Europe and in the United States through the early Republic. True, large bureaucratic organizations proliferated under capitalism, from its mercantile through its industrial, finance, and monopoly phases, making capitalism appear to be the independent variable (the cause). But large organizations in noncapitalist economies have most of the same organizational properties and dynamics as those in capitalist countries, and so the form has transcended the type of economy. (I can apply my view of organizations to socialist societies as well as capitalist ones; in both forms the consequences of large size, bureaucracy, absorption, externalities, and other concepts that I will use apply. But I will not discuss or analyze so-called socialist societies in this book.)

Nevertheless, I cannot always separate capitalism and organizations, because they are inextricably entwined. For example, I will explain the drive for vertical and horizontal integration (creating oligopolies and monopolies) at the end of the century as a product of the managements' and workers' need for security and predictability, but one can also attribute the integration drive to the desire of the major capitalists of the time to eliminate competition in order to hold on to their wealth and power. I would argue that the "capitalism" argument (and its associate, the "class" argument) is correct but incomplete. There is an undeniable truth in the statement that historically, capitalism created bureaucracy and bigness. But once this form was loosed upon an industrializing world, no industrializing country, whatever its political system, could function with any alternative to big bureaucracies, though the size and the democratic responsiveness of the bureaucracies could vary greatly. So, although it is both—a society of *capitalist* organizations and a society of capitalist *organizations*—it is the latter that needs more exploration and emphasis.

Noneconomic Organizations

Though I will not pay much attention to noneconomic organizations (government, nonprofits, and voluntary organizations) because they were small, relative to economic organizations in the nineteenth century, they also came to create wealth and power in the twentieth century. But noneconomic organizations centralized wealth far less; the salaries and bonuses to top management are less, there are no stock options and no shareholders. Power is centralized in noneconomic organizations much as in economic ones, in that the top managers, the "masters," control the fate of employees under them, affect the fate of the communities where they provide jobs, extract other resources, and create some externalities by virtue of being big organizations, though not as many as private organizations may. In either economic or noneconomic organizations, small size limits these powers and consequences.

Most important for government, however, is the check of democratic control on governmental masters through the electorate. The check is limited, imperfect, and subject to abuse, but there is no democratic control at all in the case of private economic organizations, on which most of us depend for our living. Only governmental regulation can attempt to control private economic organizations. Because governmental organizations are somewhat responsive to the electorate in democracies, I fear large governmental organizations less than large private ones.

European governments are large and absorb more of the economy's surplus, through heavy taxation, than the U.S. government does, but they also regulate private enterprise more closely, trying harder to limit their wealth and power and to equalize them in society. In addition, more social needs or functions (maternal and child care, health, advanced education, pensions) are provided by *democratically elected bodies*, rather than as *conditions of employment* in an organization. Less of society is contained in nondemocratic bodies (firms, most nonprofit organizations) and more social needs and functions are provided through somewhat democratically responsive governmental units, often quite decentralized ones. For this reason, the fact that government is large and strong in European democracies does not unduly dismay me. I wish that all large organizations, including government, were smaller, but a large and strong government appears to be necessary to regulate large and strong private organizations. As inefficient and cumbersome and as unresponsive as many governmental organizations are, a vigorous democracy checks the abuses of government far more effectively than the abuses of private organizations.

Power

Big organizations are not everything; a lot of power exists outside them, and I do not try to explain everything through them. My account is not intended as a monocausal theory, though the relentless search for the organizational cause will give it that tone. Other sources of power include public opinion, social movements, voters, ideologies and values, and most important the powerful cultural practices of patriarchy, sexism, and racism. Organizations are shaped by these. They cannot fully have their own way not only because of other organizations (including the state and its legal powers), but because of nonorganizational forces such as culture and public opinion. Nevertheless, organizations have the means to give effect to, and amplify, these other sources of influence or power in society, as well as to create power on their own. We will see how the New England textile mills amplified the cultural practices of ethnic discrimination, for example. Organizations deserve explicit attention in this regard.

I should note that wealth and power are not necessarily linked; an antislavery or pro-environment movement is not likely to be wealthy, but it can be powerful. The opposite — persons with great wealth who are not powerful — is not often remarked, but I assume it occasionally occurs, as with the heirs of private fortunes. But generally, wealth and power beget each other.

A word about one important way in which organizational size centralizes wealth. For economic organizations, the reimbursement structure is designed to have each employee produce a bit more value for the organization than he or she gets back in the form of salary, wages, and benefits. If it is not successful, there is no profit, and the organization is likely to lose out to more "efficient" ones, to be bought up or disappear. Many do. This "profit" on each employee (and a profit on transactions with suppliers, distributors, subcontractors, and the like) accumulates at the top of the organization.[1] The bigger the organization, the bigger the surplus is likely to be. (Though I do not have the data to demonstrate it, it is likely that the larger the organization, the greater the multiple of earnings of top officials over the lowest rank, further centralizing wealth.) If an organization buys up other firms, the profits from those employees go to the top. In addition, the larger the firm, the more market power it will have, further increasing profits, and the more political power it is likely to have because of its control of resources (jobs, capital, plants and equipment, etc.) that are vital to governments.

Culture and Other Shapers of Society

Because I want to emphasize organizations as an important force, or independent variable, I point to the cases where I would substitute organizational variables for the other variables that are generally ascribed. This strategy gives the whole project a lopsided emphasis, in that favoring organizations is only the first, remedial step; the second would be to discuss cases in which the other variables *are* the important variables and are responsible for shaping organizations as well as other things. Some early candidates for this second corrective exercise are the force of ethnic and religious identities and ties formed before organizational socialization; the retreat from business affairs of the Boston Brahmins after their textile and then railroad fortunes were secured (they chose family / class and culture over wealth and power); the Second Great

Awakening's impact on political leaders and, thence, organizations, perhaps putting brakes on exploitation; the primitive transportation system that initially limited organizational growth and thus the centralization of wealth and power; demographic changes such as death rates, age of marriage, and age of immigrants; legal structures such as primogeniture and the fellow servant rule; certainly the reform efforts of the Progressive era, which helped shape organizational structure and behaviors in ways they might not otherwise have taken; the growth "mentality" of the nineteenth century in towns and cities that functioned without significant organizational resources, but later built them—a mentality or cultural item that was furthered by the extraordinary abundance of natural resources available to an industrializing population (surely a significant independent variable that did not even need large organizations to be exploited); and the "democratic tradition" (or lack of feudal and monarchical structures) that checked some organizational excesses though it had little effect on organizational structure in the early nineteenth century.[2] In these cases organizations were significantly shaped by demographic, political, and cultural variables rather than the other way around. I will not ignore them, but their strength will not be properly assessed.

Instead, I will argue that organizations increasingly make our culture, including norms of family size and age of marriage; determine what is seen as efficient and for whom; and select our political values and direct our "will."

Organizations as the Independent Variable

The impact of large organizations on society has not been fully appreciated. The story of organizations in the United States can be found in works by historians, but quite a bit of digging is required.[3] Even in the other social sciences, organizations appear as dependent variables, created by other forces, rather than as independent variables, as actors in themselves. In many accounts of social change, wealth and power are not associated with organizations; wealth is resident in an individual, a family, or a class, and power is resident in persons or ideologies. Organizations are at best unproblematic resources for other expressions of wealth and power (W & P). This interpretation may occasionally be true, but I wish to explore the extent to which organizations may not only back up these sources of W & P, but shape them because of the characteristics of the organizations themselves, independent of persons, classes, and ideologies. To the extent that organizations are considered in discussions of W & P, they are often merely the suitcases that carry more important variables, and have no distinctive properties of their own. But I argue that organizations produce more than their marketed goods and services, and will shortly list some of these products.

The passive role of organizations in most accounts is suggested by the following familiar formulations, true but incomplete: Politicians "use" organizations; culture is "expressed" through organizations; organizations are "designed" for the efficient production of goods and services. When people do comment on particular organizational characteristics, the comments are generally limited to their imperfections as vessels, as in discussions of their best form or structure or of the leadership qualities required of their managers. But rarely do these discussions take into account any of the many characteristics of organizations that shape society. In this book, however, we shall see the effects of internal properties such as size, degree of centralization, skill requirements, and labor policies; the effect of environmental relations such as network properties, political power and the corruption of officials, and the ability to ignore social costs and pass them off to the weaker parts of society.

We hear that culture shapes our behavior, and because organizations are made up of behaving people, organizations therefore must be shaped by culture. They are shaped by culture, but they also shape culture. Or we hear that efficient forms prevail over inefficient forms, and so we think that the prevailing organizations must be reflections of this efficiency. True, in general and in a largely tautological sense, but whose efficiency is being realized; for whom is it inefficient? Organizational forms or structures may be chosen for ideological reasons by the masters and locked in by group interests; not all the stakeholders such as employees, their families, the community, and the natural environment, see their own efficiency realized by the same form that benefits the masters. Or we hear that political parties or Congress is the means of mobilizing political values or the political will, and thus politics is what we should study—this is the "independent variable." But while it is commonplace that large organizations fund the politicians, and it is noted that, for example, the sizable percentage of the U.S. senators who are millionaires a few times over have their millions invested in particular organizations, political scientists do not then turn toward the characteristics of these politics-shaping organizations. Furthermore, the political parties and Congress and the executive branch are all large organizations in themselves, with interests that are independent of any individual members and certainly the public, and thus can have a large say about which values will be offered and about the terms for mobilizing the "public will." The examination of governmental organizations has been largely limited to the inefficiency or efficiency of their services, not focusing on the way in which their properties as organizations shape our considerations of legitimate services and even hide the source of problems that require services.

What Do Organizations Do?

I am concerned with what organizations do, beyond producing goods and services. As I said, organizations are more important than most theories allow, and their importance has not been fully realized. As a device to remind us that they do a goodly number of things that we are wont to take for granted, thus missing their distinctive contribution, I will sometimes italicize these functions in the rest of this work, as we see them performed in the concrete examples of organizational behavior. I will also run through important theories that have shaped our understanding of economic activity, and I have placed a summary of each in Appendix I for easy reference.[4]

What do organizations do, beyond producing goods and services, that makes them so protean? Drawing on Karl Marx, Max Weber, and numerous modern theorists, we can be reminded of the following:

Wage Dependence. Organizations generate wage dependence — a condition where you have to work to create the surplus value that will be used by someone else as wealth, prestige, or power, or you won't survive. The condition of wage dependence at first was resisted, but it gradually changed our stratification system and centralized social and economic power in society. Dependence on a wage or salary for survival was not taken for granted in the nineteenth century, but was characterized in negative terms referring to the only two institutions that had such complete control — "wage slavery" and "the industrial army." A democratic society could not experience much centralization of wealth and power if wage dependence were not extensive; it permits the accumulation of wealth from productive activity. Thus, wage dependency *centralizes surpluses.*

Centralization of Surpluses. If you work for only yourself, accumulation is limited to your own surplus or profit, not that of all your employees. If your employees can freely choose another employer or get part of their livelihood on their own, the employees can extract a larger share of the surplus, limiting accumulation by the boss. If the organizations are large, the mounting surplus means that wealth (or prestige and power for noneconomic organizations) is increasingly centralized, and this concentration can lead to power. Those with great wealth and power can shape ideologies and values and thus shape the culture.

Socialization. Organizations socialize us to fit their needs. From working in organizations, we get organizationally friendly habits of the heart and organizationally friendly cognitive patterns of the mind, stemming from unobtrusive controls over, and extensive socialization of, personnel and even customers. Among working adults in the nineteenth century, roughly three quarters of their waking time was spent in settings that had an interest in shaping their behavior; in the twentieth century, nearly half of their waking hours were so spent. This amount of exposure to conditions controlled by the organization helps transmit the culture favored by the masters.

Divisions. Modern organizations use and shape ethnic, racial, and gender differences and divisions, acting on group identities and family structures, thus affecting much of what we call culture, and shaping the stratification system and political dynamics. They also have the power to reduce the divisions that exist in the society. In either case they are exercising power in society. We will see that in the nineteenth century large organizations used existing divisions and magnified them, reinforcing prejudices in most cases. In the twentieth century this continued, but using and creating divisions increasingly interfered with efficiency as skill levels rose and women were needed for the work force. The most striking case is that of gender divisions, as explored by Robert Max Jackson (1998), where hiring practices promoted more gender equality. Frank Dobbin and John Sutton (1998) document how human resource divisions in corporations, set up in response to federal prodding, developed justification for fair treatment that top management could accept, and thus fostered employment rights, thereby reducing divisions more than top management would have desired. Michael Burawoy (1985, 99–100) and others have noted that in modern organizations the internal divisions of seniority and skill can cut across divisions sustained outside of the organizations, such as race and gender, and thus reduce their salience; John Meyer and associates (1994) even go so far as to argue that large bureaucracies "rationalize" the world and in the process eliminate the "nonrational" divisions and distinctions that I find magnified in the nineteenth century. We know little about the circumstances that encourage the exploitation of division versus those under which organizations would ignore divisions recognized outside of the workplace. I belatedly discovered, too late for serious incorporation, the magnificent and award-winning book by Charles Tilly, *Durable Inequality* (1998), which has a great discussion of what I call "divisions," which goes far beyond my own formulation.

Structural Interests. Organizations have a "life of their own," in that maintenance and stability requirements, as well as group interests, form around their structure and activities. These two set systemic limits on elite intentions. The ususal emphasis in "neoinstitutional" theory and population-ecology theory is on the way practices become valued for their own sake and thus locked in — a cultural view. I would emphasize instead the interests served by practices, an "interests and power" view. Departments and divisions will have interests that thwart those of the masters. Organizations are tools, but only "recalcitrant tools" (Perrow 1986). (The previously cited Dobbin and Sutton work on employment rights [1998] is an example. Another is the striking examination of how engineers in a variety of industries in the late nineteenth century fought both owners and workers in order to rationalize management in their own interests [see Shenhav 1999].) I will refer to the maintenance and stability requirements, and the group interests that become vested in the structure as "structural interests." (The interests that groups can realize are small compared to those that the masters realize; masters generally get what they want. But at times groups can be quite consequential, greatly limiting theories of rationality and efficiency.) These requirements and interests are conceptually distinct from the interests of the masters; they are organizational rather than part of the elite / class / family / person interests of the masters. Of course, in practice, the interests of groups in the organization and those of the masters are most often overlapping and conflated.

The term "structural interests" hardly captures the notion of the organization as an agent, an actor with needs and preferences, but it will have to serve. The organization is structured into groups, which develop interests in survival, growth, sexism, liberalism, and so on. The expression of these interests born of the organizational structure constitutes a part of "organizational behavior." Structural interests affect the socialization, divisions, and externalities of the organization.

Externalities. Organizations shape the external environment of neighborhood, community, and government at all levels. Some of the shaping is what economists describe as "negative externalities," or an unobtrusive transfer of wealth from communities and employees to the masters of the organizations. I have in mind such obvious things as pollution, the exhaustion of natural resources, and workplace accidents, but also the externalities of urban crowding, the failure to smooth production resulting in boom-and-bust cycles and layoffs, and some of our military adventures to secure investments and markets abroad. Since these are not included in the price of the goods or services, they are borne by everyone rather than just those that purchase the goods and services.

Concentration of Wealth and Power. The things that organizations do, beyond producing goods and services, combine to produce inequalities in the distribution of wealth and power. A system with many small organizations deconcentrates wealth and power; a system with a few big ones concentrates it (Perrow 1992).[5] I am ignoring the positive externalities here. Life would be shorter, nastier, and more brutish if it were not for the enormous productivity and efficiency of organizations, some of which may necessarily be large and bureaucratic. Organizations generate wealth and power; we need them. But large organizations make it possible to centralize the wealth and power they generate. (I will pass on the possibility that by extending life, and making it more pleasant and refined for the first world, we have condemned much of the third world and, worse still, stretched a canopy over the globe that will end it for all of us. I leave these scenarios to such impressive works as Paul Kennedy's *Preparing for the Next Century* [1993].) The point, necessarily oversimplified here, is that most of the negative externalities we have experienced were not necessary; with the abundance of this continent and the skills of its conquerors, we could have made far less of a mess of it had it not been for the particular conflux of events that generated our form of organizations. But there is more to this story than the concentration of wealth and power; there are general systemic effects that manifested themselves in the middle and late twentieth century. This is a period beyond the scope of this work, so I will mention them only briefly at this point.

System Accidents. One is the systemic impact of the distinctive dynamics of social systems in which large organizations are tightly coupled to each other so that unanticipated interactions create system-wide disturbances, such as stock market crashes, interruptions of service, widespread contamination, and opportunities for fraud and corruption. (This topic preoccupied me on a much smaller scale in my essay on normal accidents [1984, 1999]).

Absorption of Society. Another systemic effect, increasingly apparent in the second half of the twentieth century, is that large organizations wittingly and unwittingly absorb the functions performed by smaller autonomous units of society such as families, kinship networks, local churches, and small governmental units and businesses, weakening those parts of society that are not governed by an employment contract, and creating a "society of organizations" (Perrow 1991, 1996). For a powerful example of corporations "absorbing" and controlling the legal system see the work of Edelman and Suchman (Edelman 1990; Edelman and Suchman 1999).

WHAT KIND OF ORGANIZATIONS?

I am primarily concerned with organizations comprising large work forces (in the early days 100 persons or more was large). Initially, there were very few of them, and thus large bureaucratic organizations played a minor role (but an important prefiguring role) in the early part of the nineteenth century, and not a major one until the second half of the twentieth century. I assert different internal and external dynamics for small and large organizations (the small foundry compared to International Harvester), and I am not concerned with most small organizations. Nevertheless, it is necessary to discuss organizations with small, even tiny, work forces that control organizations through legislative mandates (e.g., the FTC in the 1920s) or the provision of capital (e.g., investment banks), or trade associations. These controlling organizations, as they might be labeled, such as regulatory bodies or the J. P. Morgan or Jay Gould directorates, have roles to play different from most organizations; there is no adequate conceptual term for them. They need not be "peak associations"; the regulatory agency is not an "executive" organization, though a merchant bank may be; the term "controlling organizations" comes closer, but "controlling" is an awkward adjective to use with powerful government agencies that regulate rather than control.

Behavior is motivated, and I assume that wealth and power are always favored over poverty and dependence. Therefore the motivations of individuals will not explain why we created big organizations in the United States, but not to the same extent in Europe. What needs explaining is why they arose when they did in the United States, why they did not proliferate in Europe, and how their rise might insure against their decline. My explanation is that our particular history allowed less regulation of the pursuit of wealth and power, and the pursuit occurred over a socially and culturally unencumbered landscape. In Europe monarchs, nobles, and the church feared the rise of large organizations that would be beyond their control, so they limited the accumulation of capital. The United States had no such restrictions; the citizens feared a large government but took few steps to limit the size and power of private organizations. In the United States, large private organizations were allowed to grow, in spite of considerable resistance, and this growth generated inequality. The accumulation of wealth and power through large organizations is the modern device for generating inequality.

Wealth is considerably more concentrated in the United States than in most nonsocialist industrialized nations. It is hard to make comparative statements about power, but I believe that economic power is quite centralized in the United States. Social power is more fragmented and cultural in origin, and less in the hands of large organizations, but they play an increasing role here. Some other nations allow for an open contest for wealth and power (the contest is never absent) but restrict the contest considerably through structural devices that favor smaller organizations, limiting the concentration of W & P. They also distribute social services more widely or require private organizations to provide more, reducing the concentration of W & P if the political system is reasonably democratic. There are large governmental bureaucracies in Europe that, more than in the United States, mitigate the concentration of economic power and place more social activities in the hands of elected representatives rather than owners / masters, thus dispersing social power. Much of the dynamics of organizations in the late nineteenth century concerned the displacement of independent, generally proprietary organizations of small- to modest-size by large corporate forms. Unlike developments in Europe, this open field for concentrating W & P was created through deliberate nonregulation at the state and federal level. We will contrast the operation of a dispersed network of small proprietary firms with large organizations having a corporate form in the textile industry, and the modest-size firms before the 1890s with the corporate consolidation after that. Both, we should emphasize, are illustrations of the proposition that the degree of *concentration of wealth and power* depends on organizational forms and organizational regulation (the state).

Alternative Theories

My account draws on five theoretical traditions that are available to explain the success of large economic and noneconomic organizations. Technology played a big role, but I will emphasize that it was "socially constructed" — that is, particular technologies were selected and furthered by private organizations and the government. Technology is not often an independent agent acting on its own, though it sometimes is. The strategy and structure argument of the preeminent historian of business and industry, Alfred D. Chandler, is mined for its scholarship and insights, but qualified by paying attention to power and social costs, which Chandler ignored. The same power and social costs qualifications will be added to the valuable institutional economics tradition, which conceptualizes markets and industrial structures. Political scientists have given us a rich institutional argument, examining the governmental and political institutions that have tried to guide the processes of industrialization into democratic channels, but I pay more attention to organizational elites as significant actors than to presidents of governments and to party platforms. I will draw most heavily on two additional theoretical traditions, labor processes theory and neoinstitutional theory, wrought by sociologists, political theorists, and an occasional economist. But both theories, I argue, have been insufficiently attentive to strictly organizational variables. Big organizations are distinctive beasts, and their characteristics have not been fully exploited by these traditions.

Naturally, there are many alternative explanations for the events we shall be discussing. At the pertinent points of the story I will refer to them, highlighting the distinctive nature of my own interpretation. A fuller discussion of these alternative theories and their strengths and weaknesses appears in the appendix. Here I shall do little more than to list them; in the text they will appear in italics to indicate that a discussion of them is available in the appendix. Here is a list of the alternative theories:

Technology. Inventions that required large organizations drove the economy and were an independent variable; organizational size and structure, and the products produced, were dependent on the technology.

Strategy and Structure. The historical work of Alfred Chandler and the theoretical work of "contingency theorists" say that the structure of the organization is shaped by the technology and the strategy employed by leaders. This is a specification and elaboration of the pure technology argument.

Political / Administrative. Administrative theory and the theories of political and governmental organizations assume that organizations are means to political processes and shaped by them, but have little autonomous impact.

Political Power. Organizations are the means to express more basic societal processes and groups (family interests, dynasties, regional interests, etc.); organizations are not actors in their own right.

Stratification. Organizations are signals of class, or carriers of class, and the key variables are such institutions as education, ethnicity, and religion, rather than organizations per se.

Labor Process. Organizations are more central in this theory, they are the source of domination and of accumulations of wealth and power; but the efficacy of elites is overstated (because organizations are not passive tools of elite interests) and the benefits of organizations understated.

Culture / Neoinstitutional Theory. This theory emphasizes routines, imitation, unreflective responses, custom and normative practices, and convergence of organizational forms; it deemphasizes power and conflict.

Society of Organizations. My own position builds on all of these because each has some selective validity, and some of them a great deal. All are important. My own position can be summarized as the "society of organizations" view, which, by way of a brief explanation, focuses on large organizations as recalcitrant tools fashioned by particular elites. My theory involves a group interest / power model, modified by structural constraints of routine cooperative behavior. Its features include the following:

- *history* is path-dependent, accidental, only partially developmental
- *structure and environment* rather than entrepreneurship explain success / failure
- *technologies* are chosen to fit preferred structure / ideology
- *culture* shapes and is shaped by organizations; the latter is emphasized
- *labor process* is shaped in part by workers' resistance and can occasionally be a key factor, but acquiescence in dependency, and trade-offs in benefits, are more often the common lot of employees
- *bureaucracy* (formalization, standardization, centralization, hierarchy) is the best unobtrusive control device that elites ever had.

CONCLUSION

The nineteenth century is the prelude to our market society with its distinctive form of capitalism. There was nothing inevitable about the turn that the century took. It was the product, first, of the "initial conditions": a lightly populated land of great natural resources, a fear of a strong state, and a powerful industrial revolution in Europe, and second, it was shaped by the decisions of organizational leaders and a supporting cast of elected and appointed government servants. Many conditions were in place to grow a society of well-regulated and moderate-sized firms focused upon regional economic development; at various points in the century many citizens argued for this. But other conditions made a quite different society possible and it was the one we got—an economy with lightly regulated, very large firms focused upon national economic development, with all the attendant social costs that accompanied the concentration of wealth and power this allowed. My argument is that while culture, politics, technology, efficiency concerns, and entrepreneurship all played a role, the most neglected and the most significant role was played by formal organizations. Organizations are more than the shadow of the entrepreneur. Their shape affects working conditions and points of community access; their size affects their ability to control competition and control politics and regulation; the density and concentration of their employees in a community determines the degree of wage dependence, and thus power over employees and the community. And when organizations grow large enough there is the possibility of significant internal interest groups whose concern for stability and internal power deflects the direction of the organization from the path the leaders prefer.

There were very few large organizations in the United States during the first three quarters of the nineteenth century, and so culture, politics, technology, and investment capital did most of the shaping of society. But we must examine the origins of large organizations and the alternatives available. Political changes in law, contradicting some cultural themes but supporting others, and changing forms of capital accumulation, allowed for the growth of a few large organizations in the first half of the century, particularly among the textile firms. We will examine them closely because one textile area, New England, almost instantly put into place the basic features of large-firm, corporate, mass-production industry, which did not bloom as a dominant form until the last decade of the century, but which determined almost all that followed. Another textile area, Philadelphia, represented another form, that of networks of small producers, which represented a path that became less and less viable by the end of the century. Most industry was not a network of small firms, but rather, small and moderate-sized firms without mass production and significant bureaucracy. But most industry, until the 1880s or so, was closer to the Philadelphia textile model than the New England one.

After examining the legal revolution that made large private, unregulated organizations possible before they even appeared, and considering in detail the two textile models as examples of alternative possibilities, we will turn to the decisive industry of the nineteenth century, the railroads. Absolutely critical to economic development, railroads started out as public-private enterprises, but soon shed most forms of public representation and regulation in favor of privatization. But the railroads did more than privatize a public good of major consequences (and the United States was the only industrialized nation to let this happen): they

were the impetus to get (purchase, really) rulings that made organizations "persons," with many attendant privileges; that allowed firms to
own stock in, and thus control, other firms (often close competitors)
and to centralize capital in New York City; and that when they had
drunk their fill of private capital and government gifts, enabled the massive merger movement of the 1890s. Railroads also set the pattern for
labor relations, created a national rather than a regional economy, and
were the subjects of both the deadliest labor conflicts and the largest
fiscal scandal of the century. We will examine their protean impact at
length, as well as the alternative organizational forms for railroading
that appeared but were discarded.

Chapter 2

PREPARING THE GROUND

Communities, Markets, Hierarchies, and Networks

THE NINETEENTH CENTURY OPENED with an overwhelmingly agricultural base, and with local communities as the organizing principle. Gradually, industry supplanted agriculture, and markets, networks, and then hierarchies supplanted the communal organizing principle. Before we can understand the novelty of hierarchy, that is, large-scale industry, when we encounter it in the chapter on textile mills, we should briefly examine the economic and social changes that made the mills possible.

Our first conceptual tool is the fairly recent, useful, and academically popular distinction that describes two ways of organizing an economy: markets, where everything is determined by price, and hierarchy, where authority rules. Markets are made up of small, dispersed, autonomous units that bargain and trade goods and services through the medium of money. In the market, "transactions" between buyer and seller are anonymous, brief, and determined by price. No pure market economies exist, but the cities and villages of a rural nation can develop a fair bit of market behavior, and mid-nineteenth-century America was more of a market than twentieth-century America.

Hierarchies, on the other hand, characterize our present economy more than markets do. Not only can an organization produce goods and services to sell on the market, but it may extract its own raw material and make its own machinery and its supplies, and it can do its own distribution and selling. It is then fully integrated. One central authority rules over what otherwise might have been a dense market of suppliers, producers, and distributors. Many costs of the transactions among units in a market are supposedly reduced when those units are subject to a central authority, and centralization is considered a source of efficiency in this literature (dubbed "transactions cost economics"). In a hierarchy, transactions between master and servant (usually labeled the principal and "his" agent) are internal and governed by fiat or authority. There may also be scale efficiencies in hierarchies; producing many identical items in one organization can be cheaper than producing a few in each of several firms. Organizations in a market are typically small; hierarchical organizations are large. They have to be; they have bought or displaced the small ones.

It is now recognized that the "market versus hierarchy" distinction is a continuum not a dichotomy, and that the middle of the continuum swells with many mixed forms, such as holding companies, equity ownership, semi-autonomous subsidiaries, nondependent contractors, cartels, and so on, loosely conceptualized as networks by Walter Powell (1990).[6] But the football image, with its swollen middle filled with new forms, does not cover the changes in organizational forms over time, and the term "network" is still too commodious, as it has to cover all that fills the bulge. Another alternative is to emphasize the varying mix of market relations (in the form of price) and hierarchy (in the form of authority), recognizing that both exist in all organizations, and to add a third aspect of relations, trust. This is a distinctive characteristic of networks, though some trust is required in all economic relations. It is discussed in an insightful article on networks and trust by Jeffrey Bradach and Robert Eccles (1989). Drawing on these commentaries, I will make two changes in the market-to-hierarchy dichotomy, first adding "community" and then adding "networks." In figure 2.1, community is proposed as a third form that would reflect economic units and their interactions before there were either many hierarchical forms of organizations or much market-like interaction among them. The term "community" has an overwhelmingly positive image, but it will be clear that only some of its aspects are positive. Shortly I will examine the notion of networks, indicating the degree and quality of interactions among units; where these are sustained and cooperative we have a social form that is distinct from markets, hierarchies, and communities. But these three basic forms should be considered first.

Community

Consider a triangle with community at the top, market on the lower left, and hierarchy on the lower right. The three corners are extremes; in between them any point is a mixture of the attributes of the three extremes. A unit in the center would equally reflect all three. In the community of producers — subsistence farmers in the early Republic are the best example — there is little market behavior. Farms are not specialized; they produce and market only one or two products, but produce a range of goods to be consumed by the family. A minority of goods and services is produced by each farm in excess of its own consumption needs, and these are exchanged by barter or long-term nonspecific reciprocity arrangements with other farms — help in harvesting, trading pigs

COMMUNITY

Units: small, family owned.

Roles: fixed, familial, stable, low skilled.

Governance: elders, religion, custom, patriarchy.

MARKET

Units: small-medium, many, varied and changing goods, entrepreneurs.

Roles: spot contracts, high turnover, economic rationality, low to high skills.

Governance: minimal; little government, some trade and professional associations.

HIERARCHY

Units: large, routine, mass production, bureaucratic.

Roles: internal labor market, stable, low to high skills.

Governance: large and centralized corporations, government, trade and professional associations, and unions—in that order of power.

FIGURE 2.1. Three basic socioeconomic forms.

for chickens, loan of equipment, and so forth. Still other goods and services, generally few in quantity, are obtained from the village store or from the few artisans and tradesmen, often with payment in kind. There is a marketplace, as there has always been in human history, but there is little market economy. There is also only a short hierarchy: patriarchal authority in each farm, village elders, one or two officials. Productivity is low, so is the standard of living, and so is the accumulation of wealth. There is little surplus to generate power. What power exists is dispersed to each family or village, even though there it will be quite absolute, because of patriarchy.[7] This is the rural, premarket economy that resisted first the organizational initiative of the Federalist Party, then the free-market wing of the Republican party, up through the 1820s.

The community, thus, is far from both the other ends of the triangle, market behavior and hierarchy. It is far from market because the terms of exchange are rarely monetary, and because of the variety of outputs and the self-sufficiency of the primary economic units, the farms. It is far from hierarchy because of the small size of the units, but also because the interactions between the units are reciprocal. Dependency on each other is not created and dictated by a central authority, as in the hierarchy, but is locally negotiated through barter and reciprocity.

When population growth takes place and people have only limited opportunities for starting new farms and villages as the frontier land fills up or is made inaccessible because of the resistance of the indigenous owners (the Native Americans, who blocked movement to the western portions of New England), the farms or communities cannot provide for the excess numbers, and people seek livelihoods elsewhere.

This is the Charles Sellers (1991) formulation. An alternative one is that of institutional economics, which sees rising agricultural productivity creating the labor surplus and generating the economic surplus that fosters trade and investment in production (Rothenberg 1992). Both could be true for my purposes; either land shortages or increased agricultural production may generate a labor surplus, but at different times.[8] In either case, development went in three directions: toward markets, networks, or hierarchy.

The characteristics of a network are that the exchanges between units are long term, mutually adjustive, and cooperative. Trading partners share information, resources, and even personnel at times; accommodate each other's needs; rely upon trust and unwritten agreements; and share risks through reciprocity. Things that cannot easily be priced — such as quality, special orders, urgent delivery, assurance of long-term availability and long-term orders — are accessible in networks, but not necessarily in market relations.

Markets, networks, and hierarchy are not mutually exclusive pure types by any means. The new organizations that grew up in the move toward markets were more hierarchical than the family farm (though probably not as authoritarian) because they had more people in them and their roles were more stable — instead of doing all chores, people did only one or two. They were more market-oriented because they produced for monetary sale. They were even more networked because transactions with suppliers and customers took place daily, rather than intermittently. But if markets, networks, and hierarchy all differed from the community model in some respects, they differed as sharply from one another. Some economic units became starkly market-oriented, as did the home workshops (shoes, textiles, etc.); others expanded to include the functions of several small firms and businesses and became quite hierarchical; still others remained fairly focused on one product or task, and linked up with others that specialized in other products or tasks, and thus networks developed. Networks and hierarchies still deal in prices and money and spot exchanges, so there is some market activity in them. Market firms and network firms are large enough to have some hierarchy. And so on. Nevertheless, the three tendencies are distinct.

The Market Direction

Agricultural surpluses appeared and were exported, creating business for the coastal towns. The growing coastal economy required more market relations and more organizations, though they were still small.

Full-time workers required a full range of supportive economic activity, including brewers, butchers, tanners, shoemakers, tailors, and preachers, and their masters required ships, sails, wagons, plows, harnesses, and storage buildings. New immigrants and the landless sons of farmers who did not go west filled these jobs. The emerging middle class provided the clerks and judges and lawyers who were the "running dogs" of the emerging capitalists, as the old left used to say. Capitalists succeeded in transforming communal economic relations into market ones: Don't pollute our common stream, we all use it, the community said, for example, but the judges ruled that industry benefitted all of us, and it had to pollute (Horwitz 1977). Most organizations were artisanal firms, but New York and presumably other big cities had some "machineless factories" in clothing and shoes, and large printing shops (Wilentz 1984), indicating the stirring of hierarchy.

But by and large, and especially in the smaller cities, the move in the market direction produced not large factories but a system of small, autonomous firms with relatively skilled workers, with minimal local government units and small cultural institutions such as churches and schools and medical care. Society was not the communal arcadia of the period preceding 1776, if one ever existed. Anthony F. C. Wallace comes close to such a description with his "Sweet, Quiet Rockdale" (1978, chapter 1), but a close reading discloses market and hierarchical tensions. Alan Taylor, in his detailed history of Cooperstown (1995), New York, is more sensitive to market and hierarchical tensions at the turn of the eighteenth century.

Early nineteenth-century America was not an arcadia; the market was driving it and production for exchange was paramount. But neither was it a fully marketized society. True, there were probably many single-purpose units buying and selling on the basis of "spot contracts" (conducted on the spot, with no expectations of long-term obligations, no reciprocal relations beyond paying money for a good or service, and prices fluctuating with supply and demand). The "putting out" or "homework" system in its rawest form would be highly marketized; much of the dock labor and heavy construction was spot contracting and thus marketized. But it was not a heavily marketized society because there were still cultural and economic ties among the participants that moderated the contracts.

But neither was it the hierarchical society of 1890. Units were small and specialized. Except for artisans, people changed jobs frequently, worked for wages intermittently and often only part time as the situation required, and farmed or hunted or gathered on their own. Johnathan Prude's careful inventory of people and income in two tiny mill towns in central Massachusetts in the first half of the century captures the lack of wage dependence and the resistance to working in even the small but hierarchical textile mills, and something of the significant role of patriarchy before large organizations shaped gender relations more to their own liking (Prude 1983).

My favorite example of the urban community with a mixture of market and community is the "walking city," Philadelphia in the early 1800s, so beautifully described by Sam Bass Warner (1968). Michael Best's work on the Springfield armory (1991) and Philip Scranton's on the Philadelphia textile industry (1983) are excellent on networks of small firms.

We have moved only about halfway from community to market in this case. We have not gone all the way to market because many of the community features remain: long-term economic relations, reciprocity, some trade in kind, and decentralized authority in the multitude of economic units. What does move us a fair distance to the market extreme is that as exchanges are in the form of money, most things can be priced; most things are produced for exchange rather than consumed by the producer; traditional norms and ties are weakened as calculation and efficient production take over, and employees sell their labor on the basis of contract rather than status. Marc Bloch put it well: Past societies bought and sold, but not many people *lived* by buying and selling (1961, 67). I suppose the extreme of a market society would be found in those involved in the putting-out system, where there is no hierarchy (one buyer and many undifferentiated producers) and no community (producers do not interact; the market transaction is the only transaction between buyer and producer), but it was never a stable or significant form. (We shall examine a reasonably nonexploitative variant that persisted long after conventional economic theory would predict, and that perhaps even might be said to have prospered, in Philadelphia. The modern exploitative counterpart is the wholly dependent subcontractors serving U.S. shoe and clothing firms.)

A fully marketized system never appears for the whole economy; we never move to the lower left end of the triangle. But from, say, 1840 to 1870 most large industrial establishments were heavily market oriented rather than hierarchical, in that they contracted out space to small producers who fulfilled contracts for goods and services for the owners of the space, or employed "inside contractors" who used capital facilities, hired their own employees, and negotiated yearly contracts. (We do not know enough about them to be sure that a particular industry and location could be characterized as a network, but I suspect some were.) Where owners of the property and major facilities were sophisticated, there emerged innovative, highly efficient decentralized organizations, which were often the most technologically advanced, as in the case of makers of sewing machines and armaments (Hershberg 1981). (See Clawson 1980 for the essential discussion of inside contracting.) We might have remained with that form of industry, with its limited concentration of wealth and power, minimal negative externalities, and attention to broad social efficiency rather than a narrow efficiency that maximized an accelerated output of cheap goods and maximum profits. But that would have required a federal government more interested in limiting and regulating private economic power and strong enough to do so, and an independent professionalized judiciary. The United States had neither. On the other hand, the country did not take the czarist and then the Soviet Taylorizing route that destroyed all worker input, flexibility, and decentralization.

Gradually the owners bought out the contractors in order to capture their substantial profit streams, thereby increasing the possibilities of market control by ever larger organizations; and the courts sided with owners in almost all labor disputes, externalizing the social costs to workers and communities. Total control over the U.S. work force was not possible (it was possible in the USSR early in the twentieth century when the government fully embraced Taylorism and the work force had no recourse), so industry did not move that far to the right with hierarchy. Today, the quintessential market system exists in such institutions as stock trading (Abolafia 1996), home shopping networks, and the Internet. These are characterized by short-term, not necessarily repetitive interactions and by brief exchanges based on price or instant services; they are decontextualized, impersonal, without long-term memory; and trust is mostly unnecessary.[9]

Toward Hierarchy and Networks

For a minority of other workers in the first half of the nineteenth century the road from subsistence farming led toward hierarchy, instantaneously for some new immigrants, over the course of one generation for some who were born here. But the numbers were small, limited to machineless factories in shoes and apparel, most particularly in the textile mills. The embargo, the wars, and the blockades of the early nineteenth century dammed up the money made from mercantilism and relatively free trade in agricultural exports, and the rich colonial merchants were looking for other investment outlets. The blockades also dammed up the supply of textiles that usually came here from the world textile center, England. Using idle capital to build textile mills for a protected market made sense to Boston mercantilists, and later we shall detail their experience. The important point for now is that hierarchy is expensive; it requires either building fully integrated production systems from scratch — as the Boston elite did in Lowell and nearby Massachusetts communities that offered untapped waterpower — or buying up competitors to consolidate market power.

When large pools of idle capital are available, organizations go through hierarchical spurts. In Europe, substantial wealth was generated by pooling the surpluses of the landed aristocracy, and the money was lent to kings to preserve the aristocracy from foreign domination. The interest on the loans was first invested in trade, then in hierarchy of an organizational type. But the monarchs discouraged the large concentrations of private capital that might build organizations that could challenge their power. No such restrictions, however, were to survive in the nineteenth-century United States.

Only the textile mills of the Boston Associates in Lowell, Lawrence, and other New England towns seem to have moved directly from the home spinning wheels and tiny workshops with hand-powered looms to hierarchy, without passing through a significant market phase or through a network phase. The mills of Samuel Slater in Rhode Island and coastal cities took some time to establish hierarchies, but appear to have had no marked network phase (Gumus-Dawes 2000). But in Philadelphia we can see the emergence, from what might have been solely market relations, of an early network of small producers (at the turn of the century) that quickly (by 1820 or so) became a stable network of flexible producers of a large array of specialized textiles, quite different from the mass production mills of Lowell. The network prospered for the rest of the century, and in many ways may represent the experience of a majority of economic organizations in the United States up through 1875 or so. Of course, the network form had elements of markets and hierarchy in it, as well as elements of community; none of our types is exclusive. But more than the other three, it stood midway between them all, though always ready to dissolve into markets as industries became fragmented and supplanted, or to harden into hierarchies as capital infusions and government policies made consolidation possible.

In figure 2.2, I have filled in the triangle of community, market, and hierarchy with some examples of industries in the nineteenth century, and added two twentieth-century examples. In the center of the triangle, we have both "most firms" and "Philadelphia textile firms" (and "Springfield armory," which will be only briefly noted). The difference between the two is that the former are only lightly networked, whereas the small textile-firms are highly networked. Otherwise both examples partake of some of the properties of the three forms of community, markets, and hierarchy. The appearance of networks is a result of several factors. Networks are most likely to appear in connection with

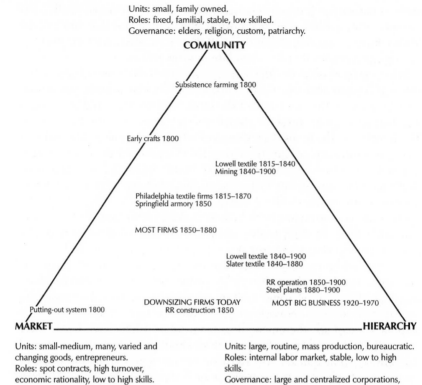

Units: small, family owned.
Roles: fixed, familial, stable, low skilled.
Governance: elders, religion, custom, patriarchy.

COMMUNITY

Subsistence farming 1800

Early crafts 1800

Lowell textile 1815–1840
Mining 1840–1900

Philadelphia textile firms 1815–1870
Springfield armory 1850

MOST FIRMS 1850–1880

Lowell textile 1840–1900
Slater textile 1840–1880

RR operation 1850–1900
Steel plants 1880–1900

Putting-out system 1800   DOWNSIZING FIRMS TODAY   MOST BIG BUSINESS 1920–1970
                             RR construction 1850

MARKET_____**HIERARCHY**

Units: small-medium, many, varied and
changing goods, entrepreneurs.
Roles: spot contracts, high turnover,
economic rationality, low to high skills.
Governance: minimal; little government,
some trade and professional associations.

Units: large, routine, mass production, bureaucratic.
Roles: internal labor market, stable, low to high
skills.
Governance: large and centralized corporations,
government, trade and professional associations,
and unions— in that order of power.

FIGURE 2.2. Basic forms with examples.

easily transported, high-quality, rapidly changing goods that requir diverse production skills, and with a regional or national market for the
goods. I expect that the Philadelphia textile industry was not the only
example of a stable and successful industrial network in the century;
historians simply have not looked carefully for other examples.

The small-firm networks of textile companies in Philadelphia are
small to medium in size, as are those in markets, and produce a variety
of rapidly changing goods, a characteristic of the market model. But
they also share the small-size characteristic of the community model,
and in contrast to markets, the trust that grows out of repeated long-
term interactions. In contrast to both community and markets, there is
at least a limited internal labor market, though not as fully developed as
in hierarchies, and a governance role for government, trade associations, and professional societies. All of these attributes of networks can

exist, however, without much networking. Most industry in the nineteenth century filled niches of local demand, rather than regional or national, and had only a limited networking of specialized producers.

I will argue that despite a fear of concentrations of private economic power, because of the social costs that such concentration entailed, a weak state was unable to prevent it. Once the legal checks on concentration were removed, and efficient transportation was available (largely the railroads), and ample capital was available, the tendency was for firms with stable products, easily produced with low-skilled labor, to move from the center of my diagram (where most industry resided until the last quarter of the century) to the hierarchy corner. More technically sophisticated firms remained in the middle, though those in new industries such as electric power or oil consolidated almost immediately into hierarchies. A move to the market corner for most industry is not favored because, in that corner, wealth is dispersed among many producers rather than concentrated.

Although the move toward hierarchy was based on the individual decisions of countless entrepreneurs and their employees, the particular forms it took and the speed with which the moves were made depended on a legal infrastructure. Markets meant money, and money meant debt. How should that be handled? Networks meant complicated transactions, and those brought about civil disputes that had to be adjudicated. Hierarchies meant dependent employees, but who was responsible for their injuries (for example, once water- and then steam-powered machinery arrived, bringing fearful injuries)? Hierarchies also could fail, so it had to be decided whether the owners should sell everything they owned to pay debts, or declare bankruptcy and keep their personal wealth. Factories polluted and diverted rivers; did they have to pay for the harm they caused? The decisions about such novel matters were to shape our economy decisively. They were made with reference to the primacy of organizational interests, whether market, network, or hierarchical. But first the very existence of privately owned and controlled organizations with limited liability and other legal artifices had to be guaranteed. That was not easy, as we shall now see.

THE LEGAL REVOLUTION THAT LAUNCHED ORGANIZATIONS

It is interesting, and rather unfortunate for functionalist theories, that the key mechanism for the *organizational concentration of wealth and power* contentiously came into existence before the arrival of the organizations that needed it. This is the legal grace for the existence of a limited liability, nonpersonal, profitmaximizing, and public-interest-minimizing corporate form. What we take for granted today was hotly debated as the eighteenth century turned into the nineteenth. Citizens and elites recognized at the time that permitting the existence of large organizations that were primarily responsive only to owners, and not to the public, was a fateful act. Arguments were amassed on either side — economic development demanded the harnessing of private gain to engines that would have nearly sovereign private authority in order to insure the output of goods; or the public good required, if not public ownership, at least public control of these engines, for the sake of communities, workers, and even the environment. (The health of the environment was a subject of debate even in the eighteenth century, as William Cronon [1983] details.) The debate was sophisticated; the shards and strands cling to public debates today, even as so much ground has been given to markets and private concentrations of wealth and power. The debate has been well analyzed, so reviewing it will not take us much time.

The review will indicate that there was no pressing need on the part of economic units for corporate status until long after it had been granted. Noncorporate forms (family-owned firms, partnerships, joint-stock companies, and the like) did well in many sectors of the economy. But the early corporations shaped the economic environment so decisively that the growth of the corporate form expanded and insured its continuance. Once the principle was established, the practice became widespread late in the century as laws gave it an advantage and the capital market established by the corporations made corporate mergers and oligopoly possible. Nothing in our tradition or culture dictated the outcome — traditions and culture were easily and freely invoked on both sides; particular interests in particular localities drove the decisions. But one cannot claim (though it would be gratifying to do so, in view of the basic argument being put forth) that large private organizations, per se, were stamping their future on the nation in the first decades of the nineteenth century. There were too few private firms and they were too small. Stamping was to come later. In the early decades the form for stamping was being cast.

If this is a case of, to paraphrase from Albert Hirschman's extraordinary book, *The Passions and the Interests* (1981), the arguments for private corporations before their arrival, we need an explanation. Several will be offered, drawing on the debates at the time. But one seems clear: the citizens had direct experience with corporate bodies from England and Europe and could envision both their ability to concentrate wealth and power, and their ability to oppress. Ambitious people and people of means were attracted by the opportunities for the concentration of wealth and power; people of average means and no reasonable ambitions of wealth and power emphasized the oppression.

First, we should note that the biggest and almost the only organizations of any consequence up through the seventeenth century were the church and the state in European nations, sometimes effectively merged. The state was threatened by the rise of large, independent organizations, and thus it dispersed limited privileges and established legal precedents that tried to ensure that the state would have no large rivals. Where large organizations were necessary, the state carefully chartered the large ones that appeared, right up to the 1800s in Europe and in the United States. The charters specified the limitations imposed on the corporations. Charters were infrequent in Europe; without a strong state intent on protecting its prerogatives, charters were more freely given in the United States, and could be given by state governments as well as the federal government (Maier 1993).

The state could discourage large organizations that might threaten its own power by making the concentration of capital difficult. "Individuals could pool their capital through legal forms as partnerships and joint-stock companies. But such forms were poorly adapted to enterprises of large scale or long duration," notes Charles Sellers in a book we shall again draw on, *The Market Revolution* (1991, 44). Indeed, as we shall see, the instability of partnerships, through death or withdrawal of the partners, gave the Philadelphia textile industry its distinctive character, in contrast to the textile industry of the Boston Associates, which enjoyed the legal privileges of the new instrument of corporate organization. A corporation, an entity of indefinite duration and with all the legal rights of an individual, was initially seen as such a powerful tool that one could be chartered only by special legislative acts. With a new class of judges and lawyers, that was to change. We shall discuss this new class later.

Fear of Corporations

American colonists feared the concentration of both wealth and power; they had seen it in England and Europe, and wanted to avoid it in America. They not only set up a federated government with the separation of powers, but they limited the powers of local governments, religious organizations, and economic organizations. They understood that the granting of privileges that would make concentrated collective action possible would lead to private power, unless that action were tied to public purposes and public review. Southern colonial assemblies only reluctantly assented to even such public corporations as parishes, cultural historian Peter Dobkin Hall tells us, and municipalities with organizational forms were even rarer in the South. No business corporations were created in the South before 1781, and then only after much debate. There was almost as much opposition in the North. Newspapers were filled with letters "protesting the danger of legislatures' chartering away the privileges and power of the state to private bodies," Hall notes in his *Organization of American Culture, 1700–1900* (1984, 300). A Connecticut newspaper in 1787 covers most of the objections vigorously, anticipating developments that would take a hundred years to come fully to fruition:

> If the legislature may mortgage, or . . . charter away portions of either the privileges or powers of the state—if they may incorporate bodies for the sole purpose of gain, with the power of making by-laws, and of enjoying the emolument of privilege, profit, influence, or power—and cannot disannul their own deed, and restore to the citizens their right of equal protection, power, privilege, and influence—the consequence is, that some foolish and wanton assembly may parcel out the commonwealth into little aristocracies, and so overturn the nature of our government without remedy (cited in Hall 1984, 301).

Note that the newspaper was not trying to rescind the laws of capitalism; it was trying only to prevent the emergence of corporate capitalism. The laws of capital were well in place in postrevolutionary America.

As an example of the laws of capitalism before the time of big organizations, take Alan Taylor's account (1995) of the attempt of William Cooper to develop the production and markets for maple sugar in the 1790s. Cooper owned and leased vast tracts of land that were rich with sugar maples. Coming from a poor background himself, he appears to have had urges to help indigent settlers streaming into the middle of New York State and northern Pennsylvania, where he leased properties. They needed a cash crop to tide them over until they could get farms established, so he promoted the tapping of the sugar maples, an immediate source of marketable product. It also, he felt sure, would curtail the brutal practices of sugar plantation owners in the Caribbean islands, using slaves from Africa and working them to death under unspeakable conditions. If maple sugar were to replace the refined white sugar from the islands, everyone would benefit, including the environment itself, because the maples would be protected instead of being burned as fuel, or burned more copiously for the ashes that could be turned into potash, in great demand at the time for smelting. Going heavily into debt, Cooper promoted maple sugar so successfully that leading Americans, including President George Washington, applauded and helped finance the operations.

Unfortunately, the spring tapping season was short and unpredictable, and Cooper had three disastrous years in a row. Furthermore, the sugar was not refined sufficiently to compete with white sugar. But most important, the laws of capitalism destroyed his project, so beneficial for the environment and the poor settlers. Deeply in debt after three unsuccessful years, he had to pay the interest on his loans. Cooper would be bankrupt "if he failed to produce an annual revenue in excess of the inexorably mounting interest on his debts," which stemmed from lending farmers the funds to buy kettles and equipment for processing and shipping the sugar. "That relentless interest expressed capitalism's demand for sustained growth; and capital imploded if it did not appreciate faster than the 7 percent annual interest" (134). To cover his debts, Cooper had to turn from being a conservationist, protecting the forests, and a humanitarian, interested in opposing slavery, to destroying the forests. He encouraged the homesteaders to burn the maples and extract the potash from the ashes, a most environmentally destructive and inefficient transformation, as was known; but there was a demand for potash, since the technology was simple and shipping was cheap. But the potash kettles were seven times as expensive as the sugar kettles, and this surge in capital investment concentrated the wealth among the homesteaders, with, for example, ninety-two settlers selling ashes to only four potash makers, who realized large profits (134). In a few years the topsoil was exhausted, the trees were gone, and the land — like Cooper and his settlers — was poorer than ever. Only small organizations were actors in this drama, but the laws of capital were strong. Writ small, we have here the paradigm of U.S. economic development, even without large organizations. The large organizations to come would speed up the concentration of wealth and power.

What Organizations Need To Be Able To Do

Cooper enlisted the state in getting a vital road improved for his project, but his capital was limited, and he relied on borrowed money. To further the "purpose of gain" that the Connecticut newspaper worried about would require much more from the state than road improvement. Gain required incorporation, which amounted to the parceling out of the commonwealth into little aristocracies. Ideally, for owners, the organization should, and eventually would:

- have full control over the selection and succession of its officers (no public representatives need be there; they might limit the organization's ability to *externalize* costs)
- continue to operate until its officers decided to dissolve it (not be limited to finite tasks, which would be a kind of "sunshine" law, but be able to take on new ones, thus favoring *structural interests*)

- be able to hold property in its own name (thus pooling and concentrating the power of the property of many, which is obviously a means of *concentrating wealth and power* in the organization) and dispose of property freely (without consulting stockholders about every transaction, thereby concentrating power within the organization)
- set and enforce restrictions on the behavior of its members (laws, rules) that might not be allowed in the community outside the organization (e.g., discharge people for voting for the wrong candidate in a public election, or for failing to attend church or a particular church, a means of *socialization*)
- allow shareholders to avoid liability for the organization's debts and any judgments against it (limit the costs of business failures, suits, and violations of the law by the business to the resources of the business, not the owners [limited liability], so that any excess liabilities cannot be recovered from the owners but are borne by the affected parties outside the organization [another example of externalization])
- operate for the private good without a requirement that it consider the public good, including externalities such as pollution, congestion, waste of natural resources, and so on.

Such an organization could be powerful indeed, and largely beyond the control of the public. These are the essential features of our modern corporations, celebrated endlessly and prescribed for all developing societies. There was widespread opposition to them, even before many large firms appeared. The large corporation violated many aspects of the culture of the new nation. How did the momentous change come about? Deliberately but contentiously. The change was deliberate in that it was driven by quite specific and local interests, all the while invoking national character, purpose, destiny, and culture. It was contested for decades, until the more populist Republican party turned Whiggish and supported industry, and the opposing farmers and artisans were defeated. Next is a bit of this colorful history that legitimated the concentration of wealth and power in the Republic.

Making Capitalism Corporate

Starting with Connecticut in 1837, states made incorporation generally available by mere registration, rather than by special charters from state legislatures. (In some states special charters were still sought because of restrictive clauses in the incorporation procedures or limitations; by the 1870s these restrictions had all disappeared. See editorial in Harvard

Law Review 1989, p. 1883.) How did this come about? Scholars differ. Most cite the functional need of organizations to remain free of, in the language of the time, "public clamor" (read "public interest") and to be able to accumulate wealth without governmental interference. Others cite American culture, with its fear of English and European despotism, favoritism, and corruption. We will arrive at an organizational interest interpretation by following the editors of the *Harvard Law Review* in their extensive and thoroughly documented (and admittedly "revisionist") interpretation, "Incorporating the Republic" (1989).

The functionalist explanation is the obvious and the most comfortable one: entrepreneurs needed to gather together scattered little piles of capital, be able to use them for ends that were in the private interest and not necessarily immediately in the public interest, and hire people who would do as they were told or be discharged, without state interference. Here was an irresistible practical demand, in the terms of the eminent legal historian J. Hurst (1970, 30), and an "overriding need," as described by the also eminent Lawrence Friedman (1973, 201).

But the surprising thing, as the editors of the *Harvard Law Review* note, is how little need there was for easy incorporation in the first third, or even first half, of the nineteenth century. Neither the market nor the technology required economies of scale that in turn would require the amassing of capital. The Lowell textile mills did have such economies and amassing of capital, but this was perhaps the only case and a charter was readily obtained. The technological developments that made economies of scale more efficient—that is, mass production—did not appear until much later in the century. Hounshell documents the slow, uneven development of mass production and shows that its successes in most of the century had little to do with amassing capital (Hounshell 1984). The true scale economies that Alfred Chandler celebrates in *The Visible Hand* (1977) came only when mass producers added mass marketing (and in many of these cases, as we shall see much later, scale economies were overwhelmed by scale inefficiencies). Virtually all the rest of the economy that became incorporated grew by adding employees and not by changing the technology to realize the scale economies of mass production.

What, then, about the capital needed to have large and scale—efficient enterprises? Accumulating it required special inducements of limited liability and centralized control in order to attract sufficient capital. As we shall see in the case of the textile mills, capital is sometimes crucial for productive efficiency. But only if there are scale economies to be had, which were rare until the 1870s. Otherwise, concentration of capital largely means market control—buying out competitors, swamping the market and preventing entry of competitors, and forestalling

technical innovations that a host of (small) competitive firms may induce. The dispersed capital of the Philadelphia textile industry
prompted innovations and varied goods; the industry required no easy
incorporation statutes. The concentrated capital of New England firms
prompted technical conservatism and standardized low-quality goods.

This account is contrary to received wisdom, which holds that small,
competitive firms will lack the "slack" or margin to invest in technological innovations. Received wisdom also argues that although monopolies may have no incentive to innovate, oligopolies — say, eight firms
with over 60 percent of the market — will have the slack to innovate and
the incentive to do so, whereas smaller ones will not. The extensive
literature on small-firm networks cited in chapter 1 disputes this claim.
For a graceful statement of the conventional case for oligopoly, see
Louis Galambos (1994). Our later contrast of Lowell to Philadelphia, a
consideration of inside contracting in the railroads, and some other case
studies will suggest limitations to this view.

Proponents of the *cultural / neoinstitutional* interpretation of easy incorporation saw a consensus emerging from disparate fragments of the
strong republican ideology of the early Republic. But even such basically functionalist and "consensus" historians as Louis Hartz (1948)
and Richard Hofstadter (1961 [1948]), both arguing that incorporation
would "liberate business," demonstrate that privatized enterprise was
not the norm before the Civil War. Why not, if it was supported by a
supposedly strong cultural ideology? Instead, these historians note, public works and mixed public-private enterprises, with public accountability, were the norm. The editors of the *Review* conclude,

> This suggests that the ideological and social conflicts surrounding the cor-
> poration during this period cannot be dismissed simply as misguided diver-
> sions from the acknowledgment of the corporate form's incontestable eco-
> nomic advantages. Instead, they formed an essential part of the process that
> redefined the character of the [R]epublic in order to justify the new oppor-
> tunities that the corporation offered for the accumulation of private wealth
> (1886–87).

The ideology of the new Republic was commodious and the defense
of incorporation subtle. On the one hand, cries were heard that the evils
of corporate forms in England and Europe should be prevented here,
where a democracy of farmers and artisans should prevail. This appears
to have been the dominant sentiment among those who expressed any
sentiments on the matter up to perhaps 1820. But those favoring easy
incorporation argued that incorporation would produce a multitude of
enterprises that would offset the centralized state and prevent the concentration of wealth in the hands of the few who would have the eco-

nomic and political clout to secure charters. Few men had large private fortunes, the advocates of easy incorporation argued, and to prevent more from appearing, the "division of capital into small shares" would equalize opportunity.

It was certainly an ingenious and not altogether unsound argument. But workers and artisans with little or no capital were not as sanguine. Property, they agreed, even if very modest, would provide independence from *wage dependence* and guarantee a commitment to the public good if dispersed.[10] But the corporation would close off opportunities to become, for example, a master in one's own shop, and permanent wage labor status would threaten shared interests in realizing a community of tradesmen and artisans that would be in the public good (Wilentz 1984, 271–76, 302–6). As an 1835 union publication put it,

> We entirely disapprove of the incorporation of Companies, for carrying on manual mechanical business, inasmuch as we believe their tendency is to eventuate in and produce monopolies, thereby crippling the energies of individual enterprise, and invading the rights of smaller capitalists (cited in *Harvard Law Review* 1989, p. 1989).

Such opposition to incorporation was intermittent in the early part of the century. Efforts to secure charters from legislatures were infrequent because the economy had not changed enough to make free incorporation a burning need of wealthy entrepreneurs. But opposition to incorporation was strong when the interests of small organized groups were threatened. For example, as early as 1801, a brother-in-law of Alexander Hamilton (who favored corporations) and prominent merchants of New York City sought to form a joint-stock company that would be capable of supplying all the bread the city would need and would hire the previously independent bakers to bake it. The bakers protested the plan as an effort to "monopolize by degrees all profitable mechanical branches," reduce wages, and annihilate "the independent spirit" *Harvard Law Review* 1989, p. 1898). It was hardly a ridiculous fear, even though a monopoly such as this would have been exceedingly rare in 1801.

The bakers' organizations were tiny, but the projected monopoly would have been an organizational force for concentrating wealth and power. In addition to this organizational point, however, note the element of interest, rather than ideology or American culture, in this protest. It appears that while there were spokesmen on both sides of the issue who spoke, as they often do, in general terms, specific interests were more telling. If organized artisanal interests were not threatened, no specific opposition to a particular endeavor such as the bread monopoly would be recorded, though generalized anti-incorporation editorials were common. The lack of opposition when organized interests are not threatened supports an interest, more than a republican ideology or a cultural, interpretation. For example, in 1811 New York passed an incorporation law intended to stimulate domestic manufacturing during the embargo against foreign trade. It was used almost exclusively by textile firms — perhaps ninety-one of them — but there was no protest by the loosely organized weavers, as it hurt only the home spinners of thread. The textile mills of the time did not create finished products (that came in 1814 with the Lowell mills) but only thread that was raw material for the weavers, whose interests were not threatened by the incorporation law (1883). Home spinners of thread, who would be hurt, were, of course, not organized. Thus interests appear to be more salient than culture.

Anti-incorporation efforts were broad-based, though, and not just tied to the specific interests of, say, bakers. They were a central plank of the various Workingmen's parties that appeared in the late 1820s (Wilentz 1984, 172–216) and the plank went down with those parties in the panic of 1837, as did much else that we will be considering. The multiplication of private corporations that required no representation of the public interest was a highly contested issue. Once their appearance was widespread and accompanied by extensive wage dependency, externalities, and concentrated wealth and power, the conditions existed that made them a necessity. Technologies were developed that required scale economies, and these economies required vast capital that could be obtained only by the guarantees for private wealth that private control could afford. Given privatization of economic activity, the continued absence of public control or even public representation became a "functional necessity."

Capitalism to Corporate Capitalism

I have promised to look at specific actors and specific organizations at the local level whenever possible, and to avoid the "state" and "the courts," where the institutionalists set their level of generality. Shortly we shall examine such details to see that the role of judges and lawyers at the state and local level was crucial. But this was possible only after deliberate constitutional changes that would give corporate lawyers the necessary tools at the national level. The legal foundations of the modern corporation had to be established at a more grand level than the daily workings of the state and local courts. Despite the importance of the daily movement of millions of citizens, the movement of a body such as the U.S. Supreme Court is vastly more important, and has the potential of ignoring the Brownian motion of the body politic. Such was the case in the Dartmouth decision, made by the Supreme Court in 1819, and just in time, because the economy was about to take off and the first large organizations and the first large investment banks were to appear. The decision made local control—that is, state, county, and city control—over corporations very limited. It concerned a private college in New Hampshire that was tax exempt and a benefactor of state indulgences. The state wished to ensure some accountability in return for the benefits it granted by placing politically appointed trustees on the Dartmouth Corporation's board and thus insuring some measure of state control. The school was, after all, very elite, and thus might not reflect the interests of the general public. Dartmouth was also rich, and it paid Daniel Webster a substantial fee to proclaim its virtues and its need for independence. Webster, "that hired gun of wealth and power," as Sellers intemperately describes him (1991, 102), argued that all chartered corporations, whether they were colleges or textile mills, should be above the state law. Private corporations—indeed, private rights in general—must be protected from the "rise and fall of popular parties and the fluctuations of political opinions" (cited on 86). Chief Justice John Marshall was presiding over the Supreme Court, and he managed the case carefully, delaying it until he had a secure majority on the court and bringing up to the court's review other cases that could help it. The Dartmouth decision—which limited public representation and ruled that corporations, like people, could have private rights—was not a mistake, an inadvertence, a happenstance in history, but a well-designed plan devised by particular interests who needed a ruling that would allow for a particular form of organization.

Nor was the new Republic any more successful at reining in the power of large organizations in the case of debts. In a word, debts were ruled harmless if the sums were large and attached to organizations such as partnerships or corporations, but a reason for imprisonment if they were small and attached to individuals. For example, a man received a six-year prison sentence for a debt of less than $50.00, and a blind Bostonian with a dependent family went to jail for a debt of $6.00. Eventually, in 1819, the Supreme Court gave in and allowed the states to abolish imprisonment for debt if they wished, but not for those already in prison. Massachusetts did not so wish, and 1,442 debtors went to jail the next year in Boston, so the number in jail for small debts in the depression year of 1819 could have been substantial. The officers of economic units (and chartered organizations of all types), however, were not threatened with jail; they merely had to surrender the assets of their organizations, and they could protect their own wealth. The reasoning is familiar to us today: entrepreneurs, if they are worth their salt, must take risks, and if they win it is in the public interest as well as their own, for the economic well-being of the economy has been improved; if they lose, society should share the risk and cancel the organization's debts. If small entrepreneurs borrowed only from big corporations, one might forgive them their poor luck, for big corporations had deep pockets; but the real object appeared to be to prevent small stockholders, vendors, and taxing authorities from imprisoning shipping or textile magnates if they could not pay the debts of their corporations.

A third major decision in 1819, in addition to the Dartmouth case limiting state regulation and the rulings liberalizing debt, found that "the states have no power, by taxation or otherwise, to retard, impede, burden, or in any manner control, the operations" of constitutional federal laws (Sellers 1991, 89).This ruling declared that the federal government acted for the people directly, and its laws would prevail over any laws of the states regarding the conduct of corporations. According to the Supreme Court, states did not represent the people when, in the case at hand, Maryland sought to levy a prohibitive tax against the Baltimore branch of the new national bank. The state was acting at the request of many farmers and artisans who opposed the national bank (89). Whatever the merits of the particular action, the ruling circumscribed state control over corporations. By implication, and soon concretely, the ruling removed local control over internal improvements such as post offices and post roads, and then railroads. Control was reserved for the federal government, but that government barely existed and chose not to exercise control over internal improvements and such matters as privatized railroads. The economy was to be unregulated. By 1819 local control over economic activity was reduced and the private corporation removed from local regulation in most areas of concern. The consequences were immense. For example, the ruling encouraged the privatization of what, for other countries, was a public good under public control, the railroads.

The states themselves were hardly paragons of nonhierarchical, nonmarket sentiments. They were scrambling to boost production and commerce, and their legislators and officers were, like those at the federal level, wealthy and interested in building big private corporations. But they were also more subject to democratic pressures to limit imprisonment for individual debt, to be suspicious of the aims of liberal national bankruptcy laws for big enterprises, to prosecute owners and managers for running unsafe workplaces, and to forbid the firing of an employee because he or she voted for the wrong candidate. The states were closer to the electorate. In such *organizational* matters, removing federal authority and strengthening state authority could have brought about a more responsive workplace, more innovative industry, and more even economic growth, as we shall see. (In many *social and cultural* matters, the advantages of a federal or state supremacy is less clear. Civil rights issues, for example, have benefitted from federal supremacy. For better or worse, the states retained much autonomy in social matters, while losing it in economic ones.)

For Sellers, the "marketization" of the United States constituted an abrupt and fundamental shift in national direction. At first, the economic liberalism of the Federalist party was defeated at the grass roots, but then it was enacted and expanded by the market wing of the Republican party, with little political difficulty (101). The dramatic reversal of republican tradition in the Republican party was widely noted and bewildered some, but for the younger party members with patrician backgrounds and especially those with concrete organizational interests, there was no need to rationalize the change.

With the Dartmouth decision and the two other historic Court decisions in 1819, the economic landscape was changed forever. The explanation, I believe, is that it represented the interests of those who saw that *wealth and power* could be concentrated through large, independent organizations. My "interest" argument is in contrast to the several alternative explanations that have been advanced to explain the emerging economy. Hardly a jot of *technology* had changed; efficiency was increased for owners but not for consumers, workers, and communities; there was no shift in culture or national values — indeed, much effort went into convincing people that the new interests were nothing other than compatible with the old republican culture of the 1780s and 1790s; *politics* certainly played an essential role, but the background of the politics and the object of the legislation was not the platforms of the Whigs, Federalists, or various wings of the Republican party; the politics and the legislation concerned organizations, specifically the liberty to function and grow with the least amount of restraint.

Lawyers: "The Shock Troops of Capitalism"

Or so writes Sellers (47). They initially came from the tiny elite of college graduates, and the initial colleges were distinctively elite schools. Between 1760 and 1840, the period of the greatest change, nearly three-fourths of the attorneys practicing in Massachusetts and Maine were from this tiny elite. And it was self-perpetuating. After 1810, over half of the attorneys were sons of lawyers and judges (47). Today we assume a college degree and then a legal degree for lawyers, but in the democracy of the turn of the century neither degree was necessary. Indeed, judges were not usually lawyers, but were respected or powerful men in the community. For example, only two out of eleven of 11 judges on the highest Massachusetts court in the fifteen years before the Revolution were lawyers; but in the next half-century all but two who served were (49). The profession boomed, and its new members were not disinterested seekers of truth and justice, but members of entrepreneurial families, looking after the family business; these were the families that could pay for their sons' education. They managed the charter bank industry, with over 200 chartered banks by 1815, offering capital to famished entrepreneurs and retaining control in return; secured charters for manufacturing enterprises from the state legislatures, who were controlled by the lawyers anyway; and elaborated sacred rights of property against the arguments of the propertyless (46–47). In quite a short time, "interests" became the dominant actors in the U.S. political scene, and interests — property owners, businessmen, manufacturers, traders — were represented by lawyers appearing before their coprofessionals, judges. Juries — unrepresented and unorganized interests — were increasingly set aside; judges gradually determined that juries could rule only on matters of fact, not on law, which the judge determined, and they could not violate the instructions of judges (49). As historian William Nelson writes, in the language of legal historians, the juries "had ceased to be an adjunct of local communities which articulated into positive law the ethical standards of those communities" (Nelson 1975, cited in Sellers 1991, 50). One can imagine how a nonmarket, communal sense of justice, concerning the flooding of your neighbor's farmland because a manufacturer builds a dam downstream, could easily be set aside by a judge whose relative has invested in the manufacturer's enterprise. In fact, a book by Mark Summers, *The Plundering Generation* (1987), is full of such examples, depicting an alarming, endless parade of corrupt businessmen, lawyers, and judges, whose boldness exceeds imagination even in our own scandalous times. The merging of corporate interests and elite judges and lawyers constituted, says Sellers, citing Horwitz's *Transformation of American Law* (1977) and Nelson's *Common Law* (1975), a legal revolution (48).

But its roots were in an *organizational* revolution. The way was being cleared for the untrammeled development of large organizations, and these could *concentrate wealth and power*. Large organizations, if they were manufacturers, had large machinery rather than the quiet tools of the artisan, thus injuries followed. The courts, in 1824 when water-powered machinery was multiplying, promptly announced the doctrine of "contributory negligence," wherein the failure to put up a guard rail was inconsequential because the employee was negligent in being too close to the machinery when attempting to clean it. If the injured or killed employee were still quite obviously not negligent, it could be held that his or her fellow worker was, and thus the employer was blameless — the "fellow servant" rule of 1842. Notes Sellers, wryly, "What the judges claimed to be protecting was the worker's freedom to enter into a contract to perform dangerous work at wages theoretically commensurate with the risk" (54). Similarly, the common-law principle of implied warranty was overridden and replaced by a free-market doctrine that held, for example, that commerce would end if everyone could seek redress for implied warranties, and the person who could not look after his own interests in entering into a contract does not deserve judicial guardianship. Not only was "buyer beware" a new watchword, but "employee beware" (54).

The new organizational interests needed laws for the expansion of the right for the state to seize private property and then turn it over to private enterprise for development, allowing, for example, the (privately owned) railroads to obtain rights-of-way on public land at almost no cost; to define public purpose so broadly that eminent domain and corporate privileges could always be justified in the name of "prosperity" and growth (53); and in general for the freedom to externalize costs. As for *externalities*, note the ruling of a judge in an 1839 Kentucky decision: a railroad will be allowed to run its locomotives into the heart of Louisville despite the noise and pollution from its smokestacks — the externality — because so necessary were the "agents of transportation in a populous and prospering country that private injury and personal damage . . . must be expected" (cited in Sellers 1991, 52) It is a trivial, but quite concrete and acknowledged externalization of the social costs of organizational activities, sanctioned by the legal system.

Before the Civil War, the United States was a rural nation, and the vast majority of organizations were small and local. The elite who sought the legal revolution were not, as yet, an organizational power. Indeed, many who occasioned the court's generous rulings were the owners of small factories, mills, and transportation companies, and would not be counted among the elite who could retain the services of Daniel Webster. But they knew where their organizational interests lay.

The change was notable because it was so rapid, rather than the slow accretion of slight changes in the individual minds of the public that supposedly make up history. It was also notable because quite different sustaining and legitimating cultural values were out there, supposedly to be realized by the gradual accommodation of the citizens' mentalities. But values were everywhere, the convenient ones to be plucked by the nearest passerby in the scramble for power and wealth; and if the values contradicted one another, let the strongest or the richest "man" win. For example, first the Federalists argued a pro-commerce destiny with a strong national state including a national bank. This was clearly a party of elite members and interests. It was opposed by the Republicans, representing agrarian, then worker, interests. But with the Federalist leadership positions sewed up by patrician members, politically ambitious men with growing commercial and industrial interests had little political outlet. They went to the less patrician Republican party. Eventually, by 1819, the ambitious entrepreneurs took over the Republican party, outdoing the Federalists in pursuit of pro-business legislation. Interests, not ideologies or values or traditions, were foremost.

So far we are talking about a few men in each party, throwing out hollow promises and honeyed words to those citizens who could vote. Only a few among the mass of citizens rose to any political influence wherein they might articulate the concerns of farmers and workers. When they succeeded in obtaining some power at the state level, the representatives of Republican farming and working-class constituencies sought to ensure that judges be elected rather than appointed by the elites of any party, sought to remove state supreme court judges for imprisoning litigants for contempt, sought to exclude those parts of the common law that were being turned against workers and farmers (such as the fellow-servant rule), and, most revealing of all, sought to require that "most cases to be adjudicated by lay magistrates and referees without the intervention of lawyers" (Sellers 1991, 61). Here was a widespread sentiment, one might even say a national value, that was to be quickly overridden by elites, who conveniently announced different supposed national values. The issues were not always distinctively organizational, but the owner of a factory or bank or construction company who relied on lawyers (from his own social class) to do battle with workers or customers, would have an organizational reason not to have cases adjudicated by lay magistrates, but by lawyers.

At the national level, interests held sway; most of our important political actors represented commercial and landed interests, since strictly organizational ones did not, in the first half of the century, offer large returns. Treasury Secretary Albert Gallatin, in 1802, "convinced Congress to allocate land revenues from the new state of Ohio for a National Road connecting it with the Potomac via southwestern Pennsylvania, where his own investments were concentrated" (62).

Henry Clay found success in organizations, however. With something of a populist start, he soon was a stockholder in, and attorney for, the Kentucky Insurance Company, which opened the Bank of Lexington, the first west of the Appalachians, and it paid 18 percent dividends (63–64). When the populist majority in the lower house of the Kentucky legislature tried to close it down, Clay threatened that he had the votes in the state senate to immediately call in all loans to farmers based on credit from the state. His threat carried the day and the bank survived (64–65).

John C. Calhoun was sent by his father, a wealthy plantation-and landowner in South Carolina, to Yale and then the Lichfield law school; he returned to claim his father's old seat in the South Carolina legislature and to marry a wealthy woman with a fortune in plantations and slaves, which was placed wholly at his disposal. He was rich in an area, the South Carolina low country, that had more great fortunes than anywhere else in the country, perhaps in the world. South Carolina planters, whom he represented, "betrayed a characteristic imperiousness, born of absolute mastery over other people, habituation to luxury, and unchallenged hegemony," says Sellers (67). Calhoun was to lead the South Carolina war party, joining Clay in pushing Madison into war with Britain over tariffs; he was the most influential in building a navy that would guarantee American trade with the rest of the world under all circumstances — e.g., when Europe was at war and European countries embargoed U.S. shipments. Land, commerce, and slave holding were the basis of his wealth, but it is interesting that he figured in the special-interest legislation that would give preference to the Lowell textile mills over their competitors (75). Class and culture and politics were still more important than big organizations before the Civil War, but organizational interests were seeking expression, and the courts provided it.

There was a legal revolution. In a few decades, the basic laws governing large organizations were remade. The national political leaders and then the lawyers in the legislatures and judgeships paved the way for untrammeled organizational growth and the accompanying centralization of wealth and power. Political values were remade, traditions were founded rapidly, and the setting was ready for our first collection of, for the times, really big organizations. We will now turn to the details of this collection, the textile mills in New England and in and around Philadelphia. They have been carefully studied. All that remains is to see them in the light of the organizational requisites.

Chapter 3

TOWARD HIERARCHY: THE MILLS OF MANAYUNK

IN THIS CHAPTER we shall examine the early history of textile production at the beginning of the nineteenth century, and the two principle examples of large mills, those of Manayunk outside of Philadelphia, and the "Lowell" mills of New England. They prefigure the dominant form of industry that materialized near the end of the century in terms of the form of production, labor management, the role of capital, the occasional evidence of state and federal government help and regulation, and the social costs of this organizational form. Chapter 4 will present the alternative path, the highly networked small textile firms of another part of Philadelphia, the Kensington area.

The best account of the emergence of large mills in Philadelphia comes from the excellent study by Cynthia Shelton (1986) of the Manayunk Mills of Roxborough township, six miles up the Schuylkill river from downtown Philadelphia.

GETTING THE FACTORY GOING: THE ROLE OF LABOR CONTROL

At the turn of the nineteenth century small spinning mills, powered by hand or treadle, and relying on "outworkers" (those who spun and wove in their houses), appeared in the Middle Atlantic and New England states. Shelton has concentrated on the township of Roxborough, in Philadelphia County, and, within the Roxborough township (which had three villages), on the mill village (and later town) of Manayunk. Other areas in the county had their own large mills by the 1820s, for example, the Globe Mill briefly described by Philip Scranton in his essential work *Proprietary Capitalism* (1983), to which we shall return again and again. But the Shelton account is the most thorough for Manayunk.

The future of the small spinning mills that dotted the area, and indeed, the East Coast, was quite insecure. Entrepreneurs were short of capital and frequently delayed wage payments or paid them with unwanted goods, and workers responded with such acts as lateness, unexcused absences, and drinking on the job. Employers explained workers' behavior as a trait of workers; workers saw the breach of employment contracts as a trait of employers. One amusing instance involves the Roxborough township entrepreneur who repeatedly paid workers with copies of books—substantial tomes of history and moral tales, some-times identical copies at various pay dates—and railed in his corre-spondence about the worker's unreliability. Presumably the workers were expected to sell the books in turn rather than eat them (Shelton 1986, 19). Employers complained of the shortage of skilled labor and its high price, but also of being besieged by the abundance of unskilled poor seeking work. The technology of the time had ample room for unskilled workers, and the abundant supply kept wages down. Whereas hand looms and spinning equipment were rather expensive, there was no difference between the equipment used in the tiny mills and that used in the homes, so the skilled labor shortage was of those willing to work in a factory rather than at home.

Even before 1820 in Manayunk, when factories such as flour or tex-tile mills or glass works might have at most a dozen employees, there was anxiety about taking labor away from the farms of the rural na-tion. Entrepreneurs were required to emphasize the social good of keep-ing women and children employed, either in the factories or at home. As one said, "It will not take one hand from the plough." They noted that there were skilled workmen, farmers who have learned to plough, and teamsters, and so there should be women who spin, thus legitimat-ing factory work. Factory labor did not come naturally or inevitably to the Republic; it was new and fearsome not just for those so employed, but for the farmers who so saw a loss of cheap hands and for the arti-sans who saw a flood of cheap goods.

The realization that *divisions* could be promoted by organizations came early. Employing women who would "work for low wages" in the factories would "prevent the rise of wages among the male manufac-turers," an advocate of manufacturing assured his correspondent (32–33). Alexander Hamilton was particularly certain that factory work would be good for women and children; Benjamin Franklin was equally certain that it would ruin the Republic, though he later changed his mind, as did everyone else who mattered.

In England, the textile center of the world, the first "manufactories" were workhouses that employed the poor. Citing Arthur Redford's 1926 study, Shelton notes that factories were considered repugnant public works and were shunned (45). But by the end of the eighteenth century, large factories employing scores of workers operating hand-powered looms and spinning mules were well established. Because the machinery and tools could be used in homes, and generally were, the advantage of putting them into a few large rooms was labor control. In comparison to what is variously called the putting-out system, outwork, or home-work, assembling workers within the factory enabled employers to con-trol quality, reduce pilfering, and, above all, maintain steady production. Employees dared not take time off for private economic activities such as wood gathering, fishing and hunting, gardening, and raising stock. All that was lacking to make the factory essential was a mechanical device that could be used not in the home or weaver's shack, but only in the factory, where it would be under the control of owners. Richard Awkwright's waterpowered frame (1769) provided that, and it "virtually eliminated the livelihood of the female hand spinner throughout Britain before the end of the century" (34). This labor-saving device spurred immigration from Britain and Ireland to the United States. The Irish were poverty stricken well before the potato famine of 1846, and families from the textile areas of Ireland had already fled to this country. In the last two decades of the eighteenth century, approximately 5000 passengers per year from the Ulster textile area came to the middle Atlantic ports, the chief of which was Philadelphia (34). The ranks of the impoverished swelled in Philadelphia County.

The First Mill—A Workhouse

But the textile business was picking up in the United States. Years of restrictions on British trade and then the war of 1812 halted the flow of British textiles and created a high demand that lasted through 1816. A Philadelphia charitable organization, The Guardians of the Poor, linked the two problems of maintaining the poor and staffing the preindustrial factories, which were hurting for hands. They established a large, tax-supported workhouse in Roxborough township; this workhouse was the largest employer of textile workers in Philadelphia before the war of 1812. Its size is impossible to tell from Shelton's 1986 account, and probably was impossible for her to determine, but it could have been as large as a hundred employees, but probably was closer to fifty, plus the numerous outworkers. I do not know of detailed material on workhouses in the United States in the first half of the century, so the little Shelton could learn is quite valuable. It gives us a rare glimpse into the resistance to factory life and the difficulty of finding and holding workers. That the largest textile establishment in the region was a workhouse suggests how little we should take the coming of the factory as natural and unremarkable.

First, the labor discipline was strict. They "strictly prescribed the daily lives of the factory boys," concludes Shelton, even though they attended schools for some period of time every other day—a positive externality that was rare in the industry (42). The Guardians of the Poor not only utilized pauper labor but employed regular workers as well, largely weavers, and also utilized outworkers. At one point, onerous new factory regulations were instituted, and several workers and paupers refused to obey the steward. The superintendent reported this to the executive committee of the Guardians and the committee ordered the refractory weavers fired and the paupers confined "in the cells" for the weekend (46, 186). We do not know what "the cells" were, but it suggests the level of discipline the workhouses could obtain.

Shelton notes, "There is evidence that Philadelphia's outdoor weavers and spinners not confined in the almshouse preferred to labor in the putting-out system and to stay out of the factory, which stigmatized them as indoor paupers and subjected them to the particular discipline of The Guardians of the Poor" (45). Scranton, in his 1983 study of the Philadelphia textile industry, makes a similar point: it would be "inappropriate to view outworkers as hapless victims. They could work at their own schedule . . . and avoid the bells and controls of factory toil." Though mill owners tried to use outworkers sparingly, mainly to absorb the disturbances of fluctuating markets and seasonal variations, the practice nonetheless "enabled thousands of weavers to stay out of the mills and stay out they did" (Scranton 1983, 87). This was evident at the Manayunk factory, where managers faced numerous personnel problems. Machines often lacked workers, and the executive committee ordered the superintendent to find them. Embezzlement of goods by outworkers was a problem, and so regular factory workers were preferred because they could be watched (Shelton 1986, 45). Still, hired weavers "frequently absented themselves from work" without leave (46), creating an ongoing need for the outworkers.

Paupers worked without wages; outworkers were paid the prevailing wage. Children who were not paupers were extensively employed along side of pauper children within the factory and in outwork. Shelton notes, "Because they had an idealized notion of how their workers should behave, grounded in the concept of the industrious poor, the management of labor was imbued with a paternalistic attempt to control and shape the values of their employees" (42). There were frequent admonitions that "virtue and industry are the well-springs of happiness" and the enterprise provided this; idleness was the devil's workshop for even the very young. Thus, from this early start, it was realized that the organization could be deliberately used as a *socializing* device.

To Mechanize or Not?

In this early period, prior to the end of prosperity in 1816, there was a shortage of skilled workers, primarily weavers for the more expensive goods, and a surplus of unskilled workers, primarily women and children, some of them inhabitants of the workhouse. Efficient spinning mills had been established in New England in the 1790s and the first efficient power looms appeared in 1814. What should the Guardians do about the new opportunity to mechanize? What, for us, should be the interaction of the new technologies and the labor supply? It is surprisingly ambiguous in the literature, but we can explore it in the case of Roxborough and its village, Manayunk, thinking in terms of three dichotomous variables: skilled and unskilled labor; mechanization through water power or not; and the availability or shortage of capital.

Significantly, the Guardians considered getting the efficient power looms during one burst of market demand, presumably in 1815–16, but relied, Shelton says, on the ample supply of impoverished workers and paupers instead. Shelton quotes with approval E. P. Thompson's observation that ample cheap labor retarded mechanization in England (49–50). But later, when discussing Manayunk, she argues the opposite: that because of the ample supply of unskilled labor in Manayunk, entrepreneurs in the 1820s invested heavily in power looms. How could this be? She also notes "a growing population of urban poor women and children provided a reserve pool of cheap unskilled labor that encouraged textile capitalists like Ripka and Borie to mechanize" (59). The social reformer Mathew Carey called for the employment of women in the factories because of their destitution, and Shelton comments, again, quite sensibly, "The Philadelphia textile capitalist understood that the city's poor women and children provided the cheap labor supply that was essential for investing capital in fixed machinery and mills" (61). But as we shall see, just the opposite is supposed to be true for the Lowell-type mills of New England: the absence of labor led to large capital investments.

I suspect that the availability of capital is a third variable that resolves the contradiction that cheap labor both retards and enables mechanization. Without capital and without skilled workers, we tend to have labor-intensive, low-mechanization production, possibly using outworkers whose tools could be used at home. This is the Poorhouse model. With capital there was no need for skilled workers: mechanization de-skilled the work, and unskilled workers could be used; and outworkers were not needed. All the tools were in the factory. This was the case in the private Manayunk mills and in Lowell, Mass. If there is little capital, but there are many skilled workers, production will be on a small scale, specialized, and producing more expensive goods. This was the case in Kensington, another village in the Philadelphia area, which I will call the Philadelphia model and discuss in detail. Thus, cheap labor may retard mechanization, but it is more probable that expensive capital will be the cause; cheap capital will probably spur mechanization;

and the presence of skilled labor fosters varied and high-quality production, without a need for cheap capital. We will see how these variables play out now in Manayunk, then Lowell, and finally in the Kensington district of Philadelphia. Together, they constitute a paradigm for the forms of industrialization that the nineteenth century was to experience. But first a note about labor militancy.

SOCIAL CONSEQUENCES

Factories and large organizations did not initiate the *concentration of wealth and power* in the United States, of course, though they increased it greatly. Roxborough township was centralizing wealth and power in its "prefactory" days. It prospered as a site for flour mills, located on a creek flowing into the Schuylkill river, and the millers competed with one another; eventually a few millers consolidated their business and power and lessened competition. Small coopers — a big industry for the time, as so much was transported in barrels — gave way to one or two large ones. The first paper-making firm in the area prospered, expanded, and had no competitors. A small mill ground drugs and condiments and made enough to establish its owner as one of the township elite. Roxborough census data from 1791 to 1822 show increasing wealth, but more particularly the increasing concentration of wealth: the wealthiest 10 percent held 52 percent of the taxable real wealth in 1791, and 58 percent of it in 1822, and the population of taxable males doubled. Though the number of taxable males was small, going from 156 to 319, the process no doubt repeated itself throughout the nation (Shelton 1986, 80). The nineteenth century was a time of steady concentration of wealth (Williamson and Lindhert 1980), and there were presumably some fully dependent wage workers among the mill hands, coopers, and paper makers, but most were skilled enough to be in demand.

The significant turning point for Roxborough was the building of a canal by a state-chartered corporation along a straight stretch of narrow flat land along the Schuylkill river, completed in 1819. Overnight — that is to say, within a year — the area was transformed. Six-story mills appeared, "manned" largely by women and children who had never before seen buildings that high, with fearsome and dangerous machinery and twelve- to thirteen-hour work days. Everything changed. The mill owners built mansions. The percent of taxable wealth held by the richest 10 percent went from the 52 percent in 1791 and 58 percent in 1822 — already two full years into the change — to 65 percent by the end of the decade (Shelton 1986, 80, 92). The change was not just due to the mill run, it was also due to the ample supply of cheap labor. Much of it, perhaps half, was Irish in origin. For example, between 1815 and 1819, long before the potato famine, Boston got nineteen ships from Irish emigrant ports, but Philadelphia received sixty-two (50).

The healthy world-wide demand for coarse cloth allowed some mills to challenge Lowell in size and output (57). By 1828, with a few large mills of over 200 employees (by 1832 one had 300), Manayunk, Shelton argues, deserved the title of the Manchester of America far more than Lowell, Massachusetts. Labor-saving devices undercut the skilled weavers, and even the power-loom operators required less skill than before. Employers rejoiced in being able to replace men with women, presumably because of the militancy of the men and because they received twice the wages of the adult women. By 1840 two-thirds to three-quarters of the employees were women and children (66). Shelton makes a strong case that Manayunk was far more exploitative than the Lowell mills of the time — just before the labor surplus changed things there.

The Manayunk mills were also quite possibly more exploitative than similar mills in Britain, contrary to most impressions today. Britain's Factory Regulation Act in 1833 cut the mill workers' day to ten hours, and was reasonably enforced; in Philadelphia it was seventy-two hours a week, or about twelve hours a day (67). The working conditions in Philadelphia were so bad that a state investigation commission in 1837 called for, but did not get, the prohibition of employing children under the age of ten completely, and a ten-hour day for those under sixteen (68). Workers were paid a daily wage, so it was a substantial temptation for the owner to add an hour to the day in a mill of 300 to 500 workers. Thus the days at one mill were thirteen hours and forty minutes long in the winter (69). Children nine years of age were on their feet for more than twelve hours. This was not about "tiny nimble fingers" intermittently tying threads. Some were doing quite heavy work. Nine-year-old children were carrying sixteen-pound boxes up four stories for twelve hours; others spent all day stooping over frames that were just two feet from the floor; they would fall asleep and be strapped to stay awake. In other areas, conditions were also worse than in England, where protective legislation was established by the 1830s. For example, ventilation was required in England because bronchial inflammations and TB of the lymphatic glands was common (70), the lack of ventilation was a repeated complaint of the Manayunk workers. Also, very few Manayunk mills guarded the gearing, but this was a common practice in England.

Wage rates in Manayunk fell below those of New England, matching those of Manchester or Glasgow. Children got from 50 to 75 cents a week, even less in some cases (71). Around 1830 children eleven years or younger made up 20 percent of the textile labor force in Roxborough (96). Families were so desperate that they went from mill to mill begging the superintendents to hire their children, for 50 cents a week (63). And although workers moved often among the mills, they stayed considerably longer than the less wage-dependent Lowell mill workers (96–97). Though employment was still quite irregular, lifetime work in the mills was becoming more common. "A textile worker could be extraordinarily mobile and still feel chained to the machines for a lifetime of drudgery" (99). Shelton contradicts the more rosy view of Anthony F. C. Wallace (1978), writing about nearby Rockdale, concerning workers' "financial ability to escape from unfavorable circumstances" and "move on to better jobs or even to homesteads in the west" (Shelton 1986, 97, 98; see also Wallace 1978, 63). Her data show little of this, indicating instead movement from mill to mill.

There was a rise in the estimated poverty rate with the coming of the mills. One estimate of the number of people in Philadelphia County, which included Roxborough and Manayunk, applying for public relief in the early 1820s was 20 percent in a city of 100,000 (80, 61). In the township, before the mills arrived, the well-named House of Industry of the Provident Society provided outwork for hundreds of "industrious poor women" (60). But soon it was not enough, and in 1833 a poorhouse had to be built (92). There is no indication that it was also a workhouse, but we would not expect one; there were now very large private mills that it would compete with.

In short, the *externalities* and the concentration of power were present in force. "Once the mills were established, the industrial townspeople of Manayunk experienced poverty, propertylessness, and the concentration of economic power to a degree unknown in the prefactory township" (99). And it was all new and sudden to the township: the many-storied buildings, the machinery, the wage dependency, the packed tenements, the new mansions, and the great wealth and its concentration.

So was the discipline, and thus the *socialization*. Uniform work rules for all mills in Philadelphia including Manayunk were established at meetings of the owners in the early 1830s. These were, as one commentator pointed out, "symbolic of the new industrial relationship. Without any change in the general character of the wage contract, the employer acquired new powers which were of great social significance" (Shelton 1986, 73, citing A. P. Usher in Sidney Pollard's important book, *Modern Management*, (1965, 184–5). There were nine central work provisions in Philadelphia. For example, being fifteen minutes late meant the loss of one-quarter of the day's wages; two days' wages were lost for each day absent without reason (Shelton 1986, 73): only one person could be outside the production room at any one time; no outsiders were allowed in the mills. Owners always held back two weeks' wages, which were forfeited if one quit without permission (74).

Prior to the mills, Roxborough had no town council, no poorhouse, no independent apparatus for repairing roads and bridges, and little in the way of political or cultural institutions. The county government of Philadelphia, such as it was, dealt with the transfer of property, assessments and taxes, civil disputes, and public works (100).

During this time, though poor and patriarchal, and certainly no arcadia, the world of the preindustrial social order was somewhat paternalistic and more intimate. The wealthy millers and commercial elites rented houses to their workforce; looked after the poor, visiting "all who were known to be in want"; donated the school building and oversaw the curriculum (101). Economic and political power were one, but were based on clientage and face-to-face interactions. It was closer to our "community" model, and far from either the full market or hierarchy model.

With the coming of the mills also came, and abruptly, we might note, more formal and institutional modes of interaction and control. A town council was established in 1824, and the mill owners dominated it from the start. The owner of the largest mill, not a native of the area or even a resident of the town, though he built a mansion nearby, was the most powerful political and institutional force (102). The issue of schooling was controversial. Cotton-mill owners announced that "it is expected that children would be educated before they are sent to work in the mills" (103). This would presumably mean only one year of schooling, as seven-year-old children were working in the factories. The mill owners wanted the children in the factories, where their wages were minuscule; but a drug-mill owner, who did not employ children, wanted them in school, and belittled the "miserable pauper system" that the textile mill owners enjoyed. There is no evidence that poor families could forego the 50 to 75 cents a week that their children brought home and send them to school instead. Had the children gone, they would have found a curriculum designed, Shelton advises us, to "inculcate discipline and morality in their factory labor force." Still, schools were quickly established, over the grumblings of the mill owners. A public education system was instituted by the state by 1836, but four years later only half of the Manayunk children between the ages of five and fifteen were in attendance. The mill owners urged their child operatives to attend Sunday schools on their one day off, and about one half did so; it was the first item on the agenda of the new town council that was dominated by the mill owners. Though the owners presumably did not control the schools completely, and reluctantly saw some potential cheap labor escape employment by attending public schools, we are still justified in asserting that the system of education was in large part dependent on organizational needs.

There is an ambiguity here, though, that needs exploring. Perhaps the paternalistic control by Manayunk elites is preferable to indifference. Philip Scranton, whose dislike of the Lowell II system (after plentiful cheap labor appeared) is apparent, believes indifference is worse than control. He sees the political and cultural role of textile elites in Manayunk and Philadelphia as duties to be performed, and not just opportunities to extend networks of domination. The Lowell elites abandoned these duties after the departure of the founding generation and the arrival in the mill towns of the mass of Irish immigrants, whereas elites in Philadelphia stayed involved (Scranton 1983, 248). He quotes with approval Patrick Joyce's comments on paternalism in England in the same period, finding it much like that in Philadelphia. In both cases, owners were involved in schools and churches and in making town improvements.

But Philadelphia was not of a piece. The location of almost all large mass-production mills was in Manayunk; the two other major textile areas in the city, Germantown and Kensington, produced specialized goods in smaller mills linked to outworkers, and this difference had its impact. Here there was the control that Scranton approves of, but, in contrast to the big Manayunk mills, it meant involvement in working and living conditions. The paternalism, or control, in the Manayunk mills concerned workers' life-styles, but not safe working conditions or decent living conditions. Had they been indifferent to the former but concerned about the latter, Scranton might have approved, and even argued as some do today that the large organization can encourage personal freedoms in life-style more easily than the small one. But the large organization should be involved in and concerned about working and living conditions. The contrast of the two types of involvement is striking in Manayunk. The large-mill owners had controlled the area's political life at least since 1840, probably well before, but after two decades of control there were miserably muddy, ungraded streets, no cheap gas from city works, no provisions for water, and little lighting. "Although manufacturers were concerned with education, temperance, and church building for their workers, their paternalistic gestures had stopped short of using the tax power to meet the health and safety requirements of that population whose labor added daily to their capital" (Scranton 1983, 254). For example, accidents in Manayunk were commonplace, but after a week in which the local paper reported five accidents, all mention of them ceased, probably because of pressure from the owners (Scranton 1983, 255).

The Kensington area of Philadelphia was very crowded, one of the densest communities in the United States, but it had good facilities such as paved streets, lighting, and gas. Accidents were less frequent too, but for a different reason: "their machines were handmade and hand-controlled, familiar rather than infernal," notes Scranton (1983, 256). Germantown textile employees were twice as likely to own real property as those in Manayunk, and the mills were less likely to have child laborers, and had many fewer orphans (259, 264, 266).

Externalities caused by organizations can vary with the type of organization, and the type shapes the community in extensive ways. Mass-production organizations in Manayunk cared little for the community; the smaller and more specialized organizations in Kensington and Germantown apparently cared more. As suggested by the references to small firm networks in chapter 1, networks of small firms may generate fewer negative externalities than large, rich organizations.

LABOR POLICIES AND STRIKES

Shelton's major concern in her book is to counter the established view that all textile workers before the Civil War were quiescent, and that labor militancy in the United States in this and later periods was singularly artisan in source and broad in ideology — and thus distinctively American. Shelton, who establishes the strong migratory link between the working classes in Britain and Ireland and the United States — a "transatlantic industrial labor force" (100) that brought European industrial experiences with it — finds that militancy was strong in Manayunk and Philadelphia County, and that it was the operatives that were most militant, rather than the artisans and skilled workers.

In our terms, we would expect that any early militancy, before the period of stable unions that can strike most effectively in times of prosperity, would come from the more *wage dependent* population of operatives in Philadelphia, who would have few employment alternatives, rather than those in the small spinning mills of New England and the early Lowell factories, both of whom had at least some employment or subsistence alternatives. We would also expect a more narrow or circumscribed interest-driven set of objectives on the part of workers rather than the broadly political concerns associated with national political parties. Shelton's data supports this. The operatives in Manayunk were concerned with (and they struck over) working conditions, particularly wages, hours, and the freedom to vote one's interests and not be fired by the mill owners for it. They were not concerned with the broader issues that preoccupied skilled workers and artisans, such as mechanics' liens and the national bank and the money supply. The workers' notions of political struggle were formed in the organizational context of the British textile industry (which included firms and plants in Ireland, where many of the workers came from), and they found a similar context in the United States. In this way, Shelton's major argument (as well as her detailed historical reconstruction) provides strong, though largely implicit, support for a basically *organizational* interpretation of protest and militancy, rather than one of a uniquely American experience involving *culture*, politics, and democratic values. Her data and analysis become increasingly important when, later, we contrast the Manayunk experience with that of other American regions, giving us a rough typology wherein our major analytical variables (wage dependence, centralized surplus, etc.) will plumb the variation.

When the labor force of Philadelphia mills, large and small, responded to wage reductions with strikes, the employers formed an alliance of mill owners led by those at the large Manayunk mills. This mobilization of owners appears natural and unremarkable today, but it should not be taken for granted at that time. Rather, we should see it as an instantly emerging institution born of the organizational imperative of controlling wage-dependent workers. The second largest mill owner in Manayunk led the movement among the owners to keep wages down despite an improving economy and a shortage of skilled workers. His actions were challenged by an economic rationality argument from another owner: raise wages and we shall have more workers. The argument in response was predictable: mill owners in other parts of the state would merely benefit the more by continuing to pay the lower wages. Furthermore, to give in now would make the possibility of future reductions of wage more difficult (Shelton 1986, 122). The organizational logic is commonplace to us today; what is striking is how quickly it popped up among the mill owners, all of whom were new to the business, as, indeed, the business itself was new. These were among the first factories in the nation.

Sociologists increasingly find such logics and justifications to be "socially constructed" rather than consciously dictated by group interests. The socially constructed viewpoint is one that sees practices and beliefs as slowly assembled, gradually shaped and spread, unwitting, taken for granted, and eventually habitual. It belongs in the realm of culture, not in the deliberate and instrumental world of "structure." I would resist the cultural interpretation in this case; the logic and justification for keeping wages down despite a labor shortage was instantly available, and served the direct interests of the owners. Wages are sticky; if they rise, they are hard to lower. Labor shortages are brief; more immigrants are on their way.

Organizational interests even overrode class interests. Though the textile-mill owners were at the top, the dominant class would have to include the owners of grain mills and drug mills, large landowners, and even some tradesmen and shopkeepers. These groups were unencumbered by the particular organizational constraints of the cotton magnates, which included the following: reliance on a supply of desperate women and children; no need to secure employee loyalty; and no interest in an infrastructure (roads, water supply, poorhouse) that might promote general business. Thus the town's elite soon split, on organizational lines, with the old elite fearing the new. "A mutual fear of the industrial social order" brought landowners and flour millers together with petty producers and tradesmen in a political alliance (Shelton 1986, 127). The split between the new manufacturing elite and the old one is a frequent theme with historians, and Shelton cites David Montgomery, Sean Wilentz, Johnathan Prude, and even Arthur Schlesinger in her footnotes. We need reminding, however, that its source is in organizations, more than class and culture.

ORGANIZATIONS AND RELIGION

Another familiar theme of historians is reinforced by Shelton's work: the conservative thrust of evangelical Christianity. "American historians . . . argued . . . evangelical Christianity was perceived by members of the emerging bourgeoisie as a means of stabilizing the social order in a volatile period of expanding capitalist relations. . . . [R]evivalism functioned to promote concord and conformity" (129). Paul Johnson's argument, in *Shopkeepers Millennium*, is typical: The rich became involved in reform politics and evangelical religion because they shared a concern about the problems of "class, legitimacy, and order generated in the early stages of manufacturing" (cited in Shelton 1986, 130.) I need not belabor the organizational connection here; maintaining order under the new conditions of wage dependency and wealth accumulation was a key concern for the organizations involved in both. It even shows up subtly in Anthony F. C. Wallace's *Rockdale* (1978). Organized religion is certainly a cultural phenomenon, and well before the coming of large bureaucratic organizations it led a flourishing existence. And the Great Awakening was not as "organizational" as subsequent religious movements. But it is important to note the evidence that it was consciously used, even organized, by the masters of organizations to promote organizational interests. For example, Barbara M. Tucker documents the efforts by foremen of a Fall River mill company, acting as Sunday school teachers, to socialize the child workers by preaching about obedience to foremen, discipline, and timeliness (Tucker 1984). It would be even more important to see if the reverse took place, that is, that the form and content of organized religion were shaped by these organizational interests. Although I suspect this is true, and implied as much in my introduction, at the present I will have to be content with the established link between religion and the problem of order that the new organizational forms had precipitated.

The best point that Shelton makes is speculative: In the long run the revivals may have done more to organize and politicize the workers than quiet them. Brought together in formal ceremonies, enjoined to establish groups to proselytize, raise funds, and plan events, I suspect the cotton-mill hands would have had perhaps their first experience with self-organization, given their seventy-two-hour work week and scant resources. Another source of tactics would be the immigrants from Manchester and the northern textile districts of England, where labor unrest was prompting organization and strikes at the same time (Shelton 1986, 134–35). Isaac Cohen notes the effort of labor unions in the Lancashire area to finance organizers who were blacklisted in Lancashire for emigration to Fall River and Philadelphia, to organize textile mill workers (1990). As Shelton notes, as soon as the revivals faded in the spring of 1833, there came two years of organizing and striking unprecedented in the nation's short history (133). It is tempting to argue that the revivals briefly suppressed or channeled discontent, which later broke out in strikes and which could have built on the rudimentary organizational experience provided by the revival meetings.

FROM WORKING CLASSES TO A WORKING CLASS

This period in Philadelphia, from 1833 until 1837 when the Panic shut down much of manufacturing and produced an immiseration of the working class that Marx could have marveled at, highlights the salient organizational variable we have been concerned with. Drawing explicitly on their own experience with and knowledge of similar labor troubles in England, the factory operatives acknowledged their permanent status as a working class in an industrial society, and rarely conjured up visions of a harmonious prefactory past and or produced rhetoric of an industrial "community." This is striking. Upon one of the first appearances of widespread *wage dependence* and factory organization in the nation, the workers instantly rejected a notion that was to characterize much of the writing about our subsequent labor history — the notion that there is no "working class," but only "working classes" that included managers, the skilled trades, artisans, shopkeepers and so on, as well as common workmen. In this convenient view, common among historians, these classes could work together, and prevent the appearance of a two-class society. The position of those at the bottom of the working classes, the factory operatives, would in no way be a permanent one. But the factory operatives knew better. The search for a preindustrial harmony and equality of classes would still be a remarkable part of the rhetoric of the Knights of Labor at the very end of the nineteenth century. Yet here it was rejected a mere decade after the six-story mills first appeared. The strikers, writes Shelton, "measured the workplace conditions and system of exploitation, which were as harsh and transparent as any in industrializing America, as mobile and permanent wage-laborers, not as expectant mechanics" (1986, 145).

Their analysis of industry was, as Shelton notes, a proto-Marxist one using a labor theory of value wherein the owner captures all the difference between the value of the workers' output and the wages paid; none of that difference is converted to higher wages. They were not only doomed to permanent wage dependence; the 20 percent reduction in wages demanded by the Manayunk textile mill owners in 1833 threatened to reduce them to the condition of slaves, the only model in their experience to which they could sink. Furthermore, women were very active in the strikes, as they were in Britain, leading some demonstrations and particularly drawing the ire of representatives of the owners. They were, after all, a majority of the workforce.

The Politics of Class

The political and economic conflicts from 1833 to the Panic of 1837, which we will now briefly examine, impressively lay out the major issues of the new mill town, and the deepening divisions. In 1833 and 1834 the Manayunk workers unsuccessfully struck over 20 percent wage reductions, occasioned by a 50 percent increase in the price of cotton that the owners felt they could not pass on to garment maker and dry goods outlets: the vituperations exchanged by each side (e.g., vermins, vicious, ignorant, aristo-rats) did not bode well for a productive dialogue, but the economic arguments traded in the local newspaper were surprisingly sophisticated and informed. I suspect that owners had amassed great surplus profits in the previous periods of prosperity, and also could have passed on the rise in raw material costs to customers. But their competitors in New England had greater market power, sunk costs, and capital reserves, so perhaps the wage cuts were necessary. And these competitors could undersell Manayunk because they owned total communities, as we shall see.

In 1834 the workers turned to politics to seek their goals and thus expanded the working-class base of the Jacksonian Party, increasing the conflict. With this threat the old-line business class and the new factory owners suppressed their conflicts and combined in the new Whig Party. The Whigs won the presidential election overwhelmingly. The next year, 1835, saw the rise of the temperance movement, perhaps an attempt by owners to drain off worker energies and direct their grievances elsewhere, or perhaps an attempt by the poor, workers and others, to handle their grief. More important, 1835 also saw the outbreak of the first general strike in the nation's history, largely initiated by Manayunk mill workers. It was successful for the trades and artisans — 20,000 in Philadelphia walked off the job — but not for the textile workers.

The fall of 1835 and the spring of 1836 saw both the Jacksonian and Whig parties break up in factions, and again the division between mill workers and owners increased. Both became more isolated from their allies, representing the extremes of an elongated continuum and a declining middle. A bifurcation of wealth would represent the future of the nation as factories and wage-dependent unskilled labor increased. Both sides lost a fair bit when, in 1837, the economy went to ground as a result of federal fiscal policies. By then, barely seventeen years after the big mill-owners first appeared, as Shelton notes, "all social groups in Roxborough came to recognize the industrial mill owners as a capitalist class whose attitudes and interests were in opposition to their own" (134). The owners appear to have recognized it themselves. Prior to the crash the owners had been discharging workers whom they knew to vote against Whigs, and easily passed a resolution at a Whig party meeting on the eve of the Panic that the owners had "a better right to discharge any man from their employment for differences of opinion on political questions than either the President of the United States or Governor of the State" (169). These bold and pugnacious words announced that they were not only in full control of the political life of their workers, but were also not responsible to the highest governmental offices in the land.

Several of the mills closed in the six years of depression that followed. Some never recovered, resulting in more economic concentration among the remaining. The work force scattered, and we have no way of knowing about *its* recovery.

CONCLUSION

A year or two before these events the ever-prescient Alexis de Tocqueville visited the eastern seaboard and commented on the coercive power of the new industrial capitalists. Shelton's quotes from his *Democracy in America* are apt: "[T]he the manufacturing aristocracy which is growing up under our eyes is one of the harshest which ever existed in the world. . . . The friends of democracy should keep their eyes anxiously in this direction; for if ever a permanent inequality of conditions and aristocracy again penetrate into the world, it may be predicted that this is the gate by which they will enter" (134). In Manayunk, the new aristocrats were self-made men, some immigrants, all new to large organizations and six-story mills, which had 500 or more workers, largely women and children. The organizations, the gate to increased inequality, were new to the country, and were to shape it and its culture profoundly.

We will return to Philadelphia later, even to Manayunk, but first we will examine what was for twenty-five years or so a quite different industrial model, the celebrated "Lowell" mills, run by a group of investors that came to be called the Boston Associates. For a time it was a quite humane alternative to the mass-production mills of Manayunk, justly celebrated for its wise industrial labor policy. We will refer to the first twenty-five years of the complex of mills and associated activities in several cities of Massachusetts as "Lowell I," and for the period from about 1846 to the end of the century as "Lowell II." Lowell II resembles Manayunk in its labor policies, but Lowell I and II are corporate structures, rather than proprietary ones, and that difference will be quite important.

More important still is finding in two geographical areas of the country, in the early part of the century, the emergence of big organizations that could control communities and buffer themselves from local, state, and federal regulation. It was still a rural nation, and though large for the time, these were small organizations. But they constituted a prelude of what large organizations would be able to do and were to do in great number by the end of the century.

Chapter 4

TOWARD HIERARCHY AND NETWORKS

Lowell and the Boston Associates

Wage Dependence and Labor Control

As noted earlier, the embargo, wars, and blockades of the early nineteenth century dammed up the money made from mercantilism and relatively free trade in agricultural exports, and the rich colonial merchants, concentrated in Boston, were looking for other investment outlets. (This is the conventional account and will serve us adequately; a much more sophisticated and complicated account can be found in Zerha Gumus-Dawes's dissertation [2000], which also presents a thorough and novel interpretation of the Slater mills that is consistent with the views I am putting forth but that is much more striking.) The blockades also dammed up the supply of textiles that usually came here from the world textile center, England. Using idle capital to build textile mills for a protected market made sense to Boston mercantilists, but first the technology had to be purloined. England forbade the export of skilled workers or machinery plans. But a mechanic named Samuel Slater managed to escape with knowledge of spinning mills, and set up the first efficient one in 1790. By 1810 there were almost 250 little cotton mills in the United States. But they were small, financially precarious, with limited markets, and they depended on outworkers weaving the yarn they produced into cloth in their own homes. They were as insignificant in social terms as they were in organizational terms: "manorial paternalism" is how historian John Coolidge described these little clusters of houses. With a company store and a church, next to the mill and waterfall, they were "an extension of the recognized scheme of things, rather than the first step in the creation of a new order" (Coolidge 1942, 12).

The first step in what proved to be a new order came with new *technology*, the waterpowered loom. It is customary to see the power loom as having been invented in order to speed up weaving, and it certainly did that. That would make it, in terms that social scientists find useful, a "dependent variable," an invention developed to solve a specific problem and used primarily for that purpose. (The purpose, fast weaving, is the independent variable, the outcome; the loom, "depends" on it.) But as we shall see it was not that simple; production speed was probably a side benefit. In terms of technology, an "independent variable" is an invention whose appearance causes usages that are independent of the original purpose. Nuclear fission was not discovered and developed as a power source for utilities, but as a weapon; the technology turned out to have an unintended use, nuclear power generation, and thus can be considered an independent variable. Steam engines were mere curiosities for some time, searching for a use, and thus independent variables, as we shall see later on.

Sorting out independent and dependent variables relies on when you enter and exit history; context is everything. The power loom transformed the textile industry and gives us our first look at the rush toward hierarchy. It appears to have been invented not only to improve the output of weavers, though that would always be a factor, but also to centralize production so that workers came to work, and came every day for twelve to thirteen hours, rather than coming to the spinning mill to get work to take home to their own looms, where they might farm or fish or drink part of the day. It has been increasingly recognized that the motivation of employers for establishing factories was labor control, not as a convenient place to keep machinery too large to be housed in private dwellings. The first factories in a wide range of industries involved no change in work methods or machinery (Braverman 1974, Clawson 1980; Pollard 1965; Ure 1836). Once large numbers of workers were conveniently gathered in one place, an investment in large, stationary, waterpowered machinery could be justified, and inventors went to work.

The problem was not to make something more efficient than hand looms; there were plenty of hand looms about and plenty of women and children who could work them. The problem was that the putting-out or homework system used a type of machinery, hand looms, that could be used at home. This system was unreliable not just because of quality control problems that would be helped by supervision, but more important, because the workers were not fully *wage dependent* — they would neither quickly nor automatically starve if they didn't work at their looms, because they might raise some of their own food, work as farm laborers, fish and hunt, and so on. They had some independence. The value of the power loom was that not every cottage could have one; one needed a fast running stream and a central building with a water wheel and belts. If workers came to the mill to work twelve hours instead of coming there to pick up yarn to weave at home, output would be steady, thievery reduced, and the continuous labor of a hundred souls in one room guaranteed under the eyes of the overseer (note the name) his assistant, and their two runners. In one room, four people — two managers and two clerks — could control a hundred workers. That the loom greatly increased production per worker/hour was obviously also important, but the looms — the technology — would be useless without a fully wage-dependent work force. The first factories were set up without any change in technologies, in contrast to the *technological* argument and much of the *strategy and structure* argument; they were established for reasons of labor control, a *labor process* argument.

The control features of factories, rather than their technology and machinery, is still not familiar to many readers, so some examples are useful. Harry Braverman's extraordinary work *Labor and Monopoly Capital: The Degradation of Work in the Twentieth Century* (1974), gives some of the details. He quotes from Sidney Pollard's *The Genesis of Modern Management: A Study of the Industrial Revolution in Great Britain* (1965), who in turn is quoting from an early work, N.S.B. Gras's *Industrial Evolution* (1930), which describes the reason for the factory:

> It was purely for purposes of discipline, so that the workers could be effectively controlled under the supervision of foreman. Under one roof, or within a narrow compass, they could be started to work at sunrise and kept going till sunset, barring periods for rest and refreshment. And under penalty of loss of all employment they could be kept going almost all throughout the year (Pollard 1965, 11–12).

Pollard gives a striking example of an English firm circa 1725–1750 — very early in the history of large bureaucratic organizations with wage dependency — that produced and fabricated iron, employing more than 1,000 workers. A Book of Laws has survived that anticipates the *society of organizations* of the twentieth Century: The firm provided a doctor, a clergyman, three schoolmasters, and a poor relief, pension, and funeral plan, and by his instructions and exhortations, the clergyman Crowley attempted to dominate the spiritual life of his flock, and to make them into willing and obedient cogs in his machine. It was his express intention that their whole life, including even their sparse spare time (the normal working week being eighty hours) should revolve around the task of making the works profitable (Pollard 1965, 56). Where would one find the personnel to man such enterprises? Pollard, speaking of Britain in the late eighteenth Century, answers: "There were few areas of the country in which modern industries, particularly the textiles, if carried on in large buildings, were not associated with prisons, workhouses, and orphanages. This connection is usually underrated, particularly by those historians who assume that the new works recruited free labour only" (163).[11]

Lowell I: The Benign Phase

But first the power loom had to be acquired. Francis Cabot Lowell memorized the designs on a visit to Lancashire while pretending to be a customer, and with a skilled New England mechanic, built some looms that were operating by 1814. But significantly, as Gumus-Dawes (2000) points out, he also brought back a novel organizational form. Lowell spent most of his two years abroad in Scotland. While he visited England and got the designs, it was probably more important that he received notions of financial management from Scotland. Scotland was the only part of the British Empire that allowed a corporate form to exist, which permitted unlimited accumulation of capital, in contrast to the partnership form, in the rest of the Empire, which was much more restrictive. He brought the corporate form to the United States, and without a monarch to forbid or check it, the form took hold quickly. (Recall that New Englanders were seeking court rulings and laws that would make large organizations legal before there were hardly any of them. The weak federal government was indifferent to the possibilities of the private accumulation of wealth and power, whereas the British crown was quite alert to the danger this activity posed to its own power.) Gumus-Dawes speculates that had Lowell spent the two years in Manchester, England, rather than Edinborough, Scotland, textile production in Massachusetts might have consisted of many small organizations, following the English textile model (178).

Once a working model was completed, which took a year or two, a site was sought for an operating plant. It had to be built near large falls or rapids where power could be generated. There were semi-urban locations that would serve, but Lowell and his associates wanted one where a great deal of surrounding land could be obtained as well as full control over the river and the canals that would provide controlled flow. This required a largely unpopulated area, but that meant there was no labor on site. A "family labor system" (where the principle workers would be low-paid children from age seven or nine up) might be obtained by advertising and providing housing, but was not practical because the equipment required the strength of young adults, though that was to change. Importing workers had been tried earlier in Beverly, Massachusetts, but the aversion to the new factories was strong and workers would not stay put. But there was an available labor force nearby that would stay put: youthful Yankee maidens from the surrounding farms (Gitelman 1967, 230–31). To attract these women, and house and provision and church them, company towns were built, the first one in Waltham. They recruited farmers' daughters, willing to escape the "idiocy of rural life" for as much as three to five years, working the customary twelve-hour day at tedious but not hard labor, and saving money for dowries, their families' needs, and bonnets. These were not in any serious way *wage-dependent* workers, as they could return home, and were not supporting a spouse and children; and in any case they made more money than women could in most other positions available to them. They were secondary earners in a labor market that was not competitive with male labor markets (Gitelman 1967, 233). It is important to note that if all labor were as independent as these women we would have much less to fear from large organizations. The basic condition of labor exploitation is the absence of other means of survival than wage work (these options declined with urbanization) and the absence of competition among employers for workers, because competition improves wages and working conditions. The good fortune for the Lowell I workers was short-lived, as we shall see.

Profits and Market Control

The Lowell system was even more fortunate for the owners and stockholders, remarkably so until the Civil War, but substantially so for the rest of the century. Indeed, the property of the Boston Associates, as they came to be called, would still have been a goldmine if they had doubled the wages, especially prior to the Civil War (a case of centralizing the surplus value, in my list of variables). The Locks and Canal Company, the Associates' holding company, had phenomenal profits — 24 percent per year during the twenty years of its existence — based on their natural monopoly, and this far surpassed the returns from the mills themselves. When the company was liquidated and reorganized in 1845, it realized nearly a half million dollars, and it had originally cost $50,000 (Scranton 1983, 13).

In many respects the Boston Associates are the first large and sustained example of entrepreneurial force in our economy. Indeed, as Gumus-Dawes points out, and is first to do so, they were less interested in producing textiles per se than in owning and controlling whole communities, profiting from every economic activity therein. (That their profits came from company town investments as well as production and distribution does not make this case less accommodating of an *organizational* interpretation. Without their large organizations, Boston Associates could not have had these sources of capital.) They bought up all the good water sites in New England and built towns around the textile mills and other industrial activities, sometimes having to let other merchants in to raise the capital (Gumus-Dawes 2000). But we need to know why the entrepreneurial spirit, present in many other textile owners up and down the East Coast, succeeded so well here. We might turn to Alfred Chandler's model — throughput coordination and integration forward to the market — this was, after all, one of the first integrated mass-production systems in the new nation. (The mills of Manayunk were another.) But I would argue that their good fortune was due to market control and its twin, available capital, rather than efficient technology.

Competition from England was blocked for some time, giving all textile firms a big advantage; the Boston Associates went further and secured from Congress a prohibitive tariff on textiles from India that competed with their Waltham product, but defeated a prohibitive tariff on the goods produced by other textile mills, such as those in Philadelphia (Dalzell 1987, 36). They owned the basic textile distribution system for rough goods and thus did not have to share profits with primary distributors. With the profits of each mill they bought up other promising waterpower sites and expanded, thus limiting competition. They secured high economic rents from anyone doing business in the towns and denied waterpower to potential competitors in such trades as spinning, weaving, machine building, and lumbering. There was ample raw material; cotton was plentiful from the South. And the market grew with the rapid growth of the country. These are all very important market control variables. But probably the single most important advantage Boston Associates had over their competitors, historian Robert Dalzell notes, was the size of their initial capitalization and the size of their initial property (1987, 70). The amount of capital has mattered ever since in our economy.[12]

Profits were not as high as those of some counterparts in England, but the dividends were very high, with returns of a minimum of 10 percent to up to 25 percent on invested capital, continuing for decades, though there were ups and downs. As Gumus-Dawes points out, the success of the Boston Associates came from both their organizations and their financial speculations; they had exceptionally high dividends because of their speculative investment in their textile-mill stocks. These were traded privately, but still yielded enormous returns through extensive insider trading. The high dividends led observers to think that the companies were efficient and highly profitable (Gumus-Dawes 2000), though in fact they did little innovation, and some of the mills had to be bailed out.

Lowell II: The Exploitive Phase

But something overwhelmed the *social* system of the factory: the supply of farmers' daughters declined, but more important, the supply of cheap labor increased, first the starving Irish fleeing the potato famine and then the influx of the hungry French Canadians. No longer concerned with attracting a labor supply, labor policies changed and exploitation grew. Wages were cut in times of exemplary profits, the blacklist was intensified, there were steady speedups, and the boarding houses deteriorated. When other industries were moving toward the ten-hour day, the mills did not. After 1850 or so, the workers at the Lowell mills made up a fully *wage-dependent* population, and along with workers at the large Slater mills, which I will come to, they were the first concentration of such a population of any substantial size in our history. The workers were powerless, in any practical sense of the term. Even though there were many strikes, prized by *labor process* theorists (a historian of the system, H. M. Gitelman, briskly notes that these were "demonstrations" and should not be confused with trade union activity [1967, 237]), they appear to have had only brief and trivial impacts on the masters and the organizational form.[13]

I am arguing that when cheap labor arrived and the technology allowed the employment of children, the *structural interests* of the organization took precedence over the interests that the owners might have had in creating a viable community. Others disagree. Most notably, the graceful account of Robert Dalzell, *Enterprising Elite* (1987), emphasizes the effort that Lowell and Nathan Appleton, the most active partners, made to avoid the degradation seen in the English mill towns. There is no reason to doubt these sentiments; Lowell and Appleton were honorable men, as were most of the Boston financiers of the time, and if graceful profits could be made, they would try to make them.

STRUCTURAL FACTORS

What interests the organizational theorist, however, is how the sentiments of the masters might be constrained by the organizational factors they put in place: an inflexible production system built around unskilled labor and mass marketing. No doubt Samuel Slater would have gladly employed a nondependent workforce like the Lowell ladies if the combination of resources, technology, and product had allowed it. It didn't, so he used children and their parents. The test, in the case of the Boston Associates, is what happened when the highly profitable enterprises found a cheaper source of labor. How does Dalzell interpret this test?

The degradation at Lowell, he says, was not, as so many historians have argued, due to the "utilitarian, business-oriented" character of the venture, but actually the reverse. They tried too hard. There was "too strenuous a determination to counteract the economic logic inherent in the situation. With their horror of crowded urban industrial settings, the Lowell promoters had gone to great lengths not to create one." He reasons that they could hardly have anticipated that this was to be impractical, and that more space was needed than was available for the thousands of people drawn to Lowell, and for the provisions of utilities, transportation facilities, and commercial arrangements. He would have us believe that they simply misjudged how successful their effort would be, and this success created overcrowded conditions.

Gumus-Dawes has a different view. When the Associates' business interests clashed with the most basic needs of the communities that they created, the former won. Here is but one of her examples: "to protect the volume of water flow for the operation of their textile mills, for years they collectively blocked the construction of a municipal water distribution network that could have prevented the frequent cholera epidemics that claimed the lives of many" (Gumus-Dawes 2000, 8). Dalzell does make one or two unfavorable comments on social costs in his book. In 1845, he grants, it was "a moderately cramped and inconvenient place, complete with areas *that candor would have labeled slums*" (Dalzell 1987, 69, emphasis added). We are not offered any more candor on the matter until the end of the book when Dalzell does succinctly acknowledge the degeneration of the company towns and the exploitation of mill workers: "the steady growth of a permanent labor force, largely propertyless and openly exploited; urban crowding, squalor, and disease" (226).

I would argue that if it were possible to avoid these conditions easily and cheaply, they would have. But consider these structural factors. They built large facilities utilizing the machinery of mass production that could use unskilled labor. There were no "structural interests" in the organization promoting a production system that utilized skilled labor and thus paid higher wages, or flexible production that would promote innovation and the use of higher skills. The mills were geared to unskilled labor and mass production. Even the distributors, whom the Boston Associates also controlled, were geared to cheap goods and high volume. With this "organizational logic," a location with a secure and ample source of waterpower was required, and the only available ones were in remote farm areas, requiring the organization to build company towns. Now a capitalist logic enters, but only through the organizational door, which is prior. Wealth is being concentrated. Maintaining high dividends is demanded by the owners, and it is easily obtained by lowering wages, sweating labor, and allowing the community infrastructure to decay. Starting from a quite different organizational base, the small-firm networks of Philadelphia found it in their interests to promote skills and build a strong community infrastructure. Their "capitalist logic," as we shall see, dispersed wealth and owners were satisfied with a reasonable "competency" (enough wealth for security and to support noneconomic activities after early retirement).

If we need to explain the Boston Associates through entrepreneurial motives, as Dalzell does, we must ask, as they were already fabulously wealthy, what could be behind the further extraction of profits from exploitation? It is not a question Dalzell explores in anything other than pious and self-serving quotations from their letters, except once. At the end of his book Dalzell touches briefly on the question of motives, or agency, one last time, and he sounds a quite new theme: in the final analysis the Boston Associates had achieved their goal, which was, for themselves and their descendants, "a secure and remarkably durable position at the top of the social order" (Dalzell 1987, 227). A labor-process theorist, however, would mumble "class counts." The return on their investment secured their ambition for a place at the top of the Boston social order. Here a "class analysis" adds to, but has to build on, the organizational explanation.

EXPLOITING DIVISIONS

Finally, on the labor question, we can see the organizational role in reinforcing social *divisions* in society, and again we have to give class interests primacy, because their organizations are tools for those interests. The Irish may have been discriminated against by society in general from the start, and discriminated against outside of the employment context; thus the employing organizations might be said to have just "reflected" the "norms" of the community. Perhaps. But once under the employment contract, under conditions of wage dependence, contractors reinforced the discrimination and thus probably perpetuated it for longer than it might have otherwise obtained. Furthermore, they had an economic incentive *not* to do so. Discrimination is inefficient, as economists tell us, and thus should disappear of its own nonrational accord. One of the reasons it may have been so exceedingly durable, though, is that owners and managers, the "masters," have strong class interests in maintaining an elite identity, and use ethnic, racial, and sexual distinctions to distinguish themselves from others. Their organizations are a means of helping this interest along, one that is more important than extracting a bit more surplus value from their work force.

But this may seem to presume too much regarding their motivations. Let us explore the contrast of Lowell I and Lowell II in more detail to see the interaction of societal divisions and organizations, which is intimate. A remarkably careful study of the Lowell mills by Thomas Dublin, *Women at Work* (1979) reinforces the rather pleasant (for the times) aspect of the boarding house period, before the coming of the Irish. The female employees came to Lowell knowing others who were or had been there, thus as members of larger supportive groups. "Mill employment had not recast women within a completely individualistic mold" he says (48). They married later—seven out of ten married a mechanic rather than a farmer—and, in the words of a contemporary journal article, chose not to follow in the footsteps of their worn-out mothers (52–53, 55). Still, women did not become supervisors, no matter how long they worked nor how skillful they were, though it would appear to have been a rational, self-interested move on the part of the masters to utilize the experience and skills of the women. An important pattern of male hegemony from nonorganizational society was thus reinforced—what we have called a "Division." But it hardly needed much reinforcing, and one doubts that the admitted mobility gains, even without promotion to supervisory status, of the farmers' daughters were much of a threat to the masters' likely notions of social structure. Marrying mechanics rather than farmers would fit into their social scheme.

But the Irish were something else. They were Catholic, very very poor, and uprooted from a miserable land where the English treated them almost as slaves. One imagines that their advancement would not fit into the social scheme of the masters. Dublin, in his careful analysis, makes it clear that the productivity of the Irish immigrants was as high as that of the Yankees, but they were kept in the lowest paid positions, and indeed, in virtually segregated rooms. Gitelman notes that rather than promote Irish males to supervisory positions, for which they would be qualified, and which had high turnover rates, Yankees in their early twenties were brought in from outside (1967, 252). Discrimination against the Irish occurred despite the Boston Associates' discovery that "the Irish for their part turned out to be surprisingly tractable factory workers" (Dalzell 1987, 163). Thus there is economic evidence for the irrationality of the discrimination that existed. Discrimination exists independently of large organizations of course, perhaps even mostly so, but this appears to be a case of using organizational power to reinforce it, a case of divisions.

One final suggestion of the power of organizational masters to at least reproduce, and perhaps further, the prejudices of society, concerns the interaction of prejudice toward the Irish and child labor in the mills. Child labor was extensive in the family labor mills in the coastal towns from the start, but uncommon, except for a few bobbin boys, in the Lowell mills. But technology changed in the Lowell mills sufficiently to make it possible for children to tend the increasingly automatic machines, and they could be paid a pittance. Unaccountably, Gitelman suggests that the Irish parents were responsible for the exploitation of children, as if they could have gotten work but sent their kids instead. He uses italics to stress that the Irish responded to wage cuts "*by sending their children into the mill*," to keep busy their idle hands and increase the family income (1967, 244–45). But he also notes, and we might stress it instead of stressing the voluntary behavior of the Irish parents, that the company sought technologies that would cut labor rates on some jobs by 50 to 90 percent if children could be used, and reduced other rates to induce families to put their twelve year old daughters to work for ten to eleven hours a day, six days a week. He also notes that the shift to child labor in Lowell, Waltham, and other towns went unremarked by the newspapers, the company, or the city fathers. By 1865, 45 percent of the males and 47 percent of the females employed by the Boston Manufacturing Company were children, something that might have been commented on, but which, over the course of twenty years, had become an organizational commonplace.

Meanwhile, in the family labor mills on the coast there is some suggestion that by the end of the Civil War the technology had changed enough to make children less efficient. If so, this might account for the "surprising" move (Gitelman 1967) of the state legislature in Massachusetts restricting the conditions under which children could be employed, in 1865 and 1866. "It did so mainly on the basis of evidence of abusive child labor in southern Massachusetts where the family labor system prevailed and where many of the operatives were English, not Irish, in origin." Note carefully Gitelman's next sentence: "Irish children working under the Waltham system, of whom no one took cognizance, undoubtedly benefitted from this windfall legislation" (246). The point of all this is not to demonstrate the existence of the exploitation of the children, but the easier exploitation of Irish children, a division in society that large organizations with wage-dependent employees could exploit.

Explaining the First Modern Business

The most important legacy of the mills of the Boston Associates was not their company-town aspects, though this was repeated in a far less humane way throughout the century in most of the extractive and timber industries that needed to import labor.[14] These mills constituted the first modern business in that they had a fully integrated production and distribution system, with raw cotton hauled up to the top floor and crude sheeting coming out four or five floors below, and in that its profits went straight to a distant corporate office, rather than to a partnership or family. It was also a major creator of a fully wage-dependent proletariat, on a larger scale than the Mills of Manayunk.[15]

Within the triangle of community, market and hierarchy (figure 2.1), the Lowell mills did not move strongly in the market direction of spot contracts, nor even all that far in the hierarchy direction, because elements of community remained (long-term employment was possible, most wages were payments in kind of a sorts, and patriarchal authority existed over leisure time and religious observances). It was hierarchal because of its division of labor and gradation of skills, the separation of ownership and control, fully integrated production and distribution, and because something of an internal labor market existed.

For those who would favor a *cultural* or a *neoinstitutional* interpretation that would see the mills emerging from our culture, it is well to return to the evidence, presented in chapter 2, that the Hamiltonian ideal of markets and manufacturing was rather repugnant to the Republic. On the defensive, Alexander Hamilton had to "point to the unused labor of women and children as proof that factories would not draw away much needed workers from the fields" as Carolyn Ware documents from Hamilton's American State Papers. There was a "strong prejudice against manufactures" (Ware 1931, 7). Ware reports that most people believed it would not add to the nation's wealth. But more telling than reported "beliefs," which contribute to a culture argument, are the strong statements of the commercial interests. This is where the wealth lay, and they portrayed manufacturers as dangerous competitors in supplying the domestic market (an interest, which thus supports a *society of organizations* argument). One example is an 1820 report of a merchants committee on the tariff, warning against manufacturing. Others include the frequent statements of the beloved Thomas Jefferson, for example, portraying artisans, no less, as "the panders of vice and the instruments by which the liberties of a country are generally overturned" (cited from his collected papers in Ware 1931, 8). As late as 1845 — just before the influx of the Irish changed a labor shortage into a surplus — a book on factories took pains to reassure readers that manufacturers would not degenerate their laborers, reduce their happiness, or detract from the wealth of the country (Ware 1931, 8). The population that was forced to work in the factories resented factories for the rest of the century, but those who came to own them and the middle class that consumed their cheap, gargantuan outputs, found them to be very American, even culturally adept, in the booming spirit of American Enterprise.

In this latter sense there was a cultural change in the "ethos" or "spirit" or "institutional logic" of the country, in that great efforts were made to legitimate all sorts of manufacturing using dependent labor. It was just that the change was propelled by specific economic and class interests, creating, so to speak, a convenient new ethos. The war of 1812 shut off the commerce, and the dominant party, the Republicans, seeing the returns from commerce evaporate, now extolled self-sufficient manufacturing rather than redoubtable yeomen. Commerce did not revive after the war of 1812. So, in 1816, a Republican Congress passed a tariff that was to continue, in various forms, throughout the century, protecting a new "cultural" idiom of self sufficiency. As we saw in chapter 2, restrictions on corporations were relaxed and those on labor tightened by the courts, but at the bidding of nascent industrialists, and on the principle of various freedoms.

Structural Constraints

The lack of innovation in the Lowell mills is explained in organizational terms. The *technology* of mass production on the looms was refined and the looms enlarged and speeded up, resulting in both bigger profits and, to society's benefit, lower-cost goods (though the high tariff the owners received from Congress may have been more important to profit and lower consumer costs). Mass-production technology separated ownership and control, creating tensions between the two that interfered with adaptive responses to labor and new technologies. The profits were used to finance more facilities and thus the owners gained market control, and market control was increased by investing in the primary distribution system. (Owners were not primarily interested in profits from production per se but in the larger ones from real estate developments [Gumus-Dawes 2000], and profits from real estate necessitated vertically integrated production facilities). Prices for the goods fell, to society's benefit, because of technological improvements, scale economies, and declining labor costs. But labor and the mill towns did not share in the high profits from the high volume and greater effort, and this was a substantial externality for that part of society. Organizational *structure* and technology barely changed in the textile industry from 1840 to the end of the century, perhaps the only substantial industry of which this can be said.[16]

Why were the mills owned by the Boston Associates in the several towns of New England not adaptive? Why did they let Philadelphia prosper in the woolen and fine goods market, allowing the New England mills eventually to lose out, beginning in the 1900s, to southern mills? And why was their profitability maintained by "sweating labor," as almost all historians agree, rather than innovation? We could argue from a cultural, technological, entrepreneurial, or even labor process theory. But the organizational one is the most telling, and the best teller of this tale is the excellent work of historian Philip Scranton, in *Proprietary Capitalism* (1983).

Prefiguring the "flexible production" tradition established by Michael Piore and Charles Sabel a year later (1984),[17] Scranton points out that the organizational form established for mass production and market control—a quintessential Chandlerian *strategy and structure* form, we might add—precluded continuous innovation and adaptation to the changing environment. The Boston Associates drew large profits from monopolizing the power from the rivers (and later, from steam), but this did not allow small, flexible, and inventive businesses to set up in the vicinity, businesses that could have offered continuous improvement as metallurgy, engineering, and power usage improved. New equipment was introduced in major, discontinuous steps, much as Henry Ford introduced new models by shutting down the plant and tearing out the machinery and starting up a year later. If small businesses had been tolerated, more varieties of goods could have been produced. But the organization was structured for continuous mass production, and marketing was geared to that. This is what I have defined as the *structure of group interests* argument. Flexibility would have trampled on the interests of all those groups in the organization, including the marketing apparatus, that were configured around, and loyal to, the mass-production structure. (A *labor process* theory of an exploiting capitalist class might explain the lack of innovation, but then it could not account for capitalist innovation in Philadelphia, whereas an organizational explanation can.)

Structured interests also eventually proved costly for the mills with respect to their attempts to control the environment. Much as it happened in Manayunk, Lowell's owners set up the town governments. The first one proved recalcitrant, and began to concern itself with the externalities born by the dependent work force. The owners threw it out and installed a new structure that fitted their organizational demands, once again closing off sources of adaptation and change (Scranton 1983, 21–22).[18] As in Manayunk, their hostility extended to education. When a minister managed to lead the city officials to erect two grammar schools, which the corporation largely had to finance as the chief taxpayer, the head of the mill never entered the minister's church again (Coolidge 1942, 205, n.4).

Structural adaptation to changing conditions was imperiled by the needs of the organization; any technological innovations had to fit into the firm's structure, and the structure could not easily accommodate new products. When cotton was no longer available during the Civil War, the New England cotton mills could not shift to woolen goods. The mills were not surrounded by sources of innovation; changes in techniques had to come from within, where group interests might be reluctant to support even these. In contrast, the more flexible Philadelphia mills changed their structure to fit the new technologies that came along; drew on small artisan shops for innovations; had a more skilled labor force that could accommodate changes; and, being smaller, were less likely to have large groups with vested interests and the power to protect them. In these senses — the firm creating its own environment out of its structural characteristics (e.g., the presence or absence of a surrounding technological community), acting out its structural interests, creating negative *externalities*, making technological change largely a dependent variable, and *concentrating wealth and control* — we can argue that an organizational interpretation is the superior one for understanding social change. Capitalists were operating in both New England and Philadelphia, but they set up different types of organizations, and it was the organizational structure that allowed the adoption of one type of technology or another.

THE SLATER MODEL

We know far less about the "family" model pioneered by Samuel Slater, once his mills grew large and multiplied along the New England coast.[19] But the family model offers a more direct route to the industry that developed in the latter half of the nineteenth century, because it had few of the community-oriented paternalistic aspects of Lowell (although it retained severe partiarchical control) from 1814 to about 1846, before abundant labor allowed exploitation. These were the large integrated mills established in the declining coastal towns of Rhode Island.

Samuel Slater, a textile worker in England, evaded the ban on migration of skilled workers and in 1779 brought his skills to the United States, where he was hired by the commercial firm of Almy and Brown to explore opportunities in textiles. (Brown University was named after one of the partners, who included slave trading in his portfolio.) The first mill spinning cotton (tended by nine children) was set up in 1791 near Providence. Cotton was first "picked over" (to clean it) at home by "children too small to work in the factory" notes Ware (1931). They must have been very small indeed, because by 1801 the factory "employed over one hundred between the ages of four and ten." This was a very large establishment for 1801, and appears to be an exception. The work was so simple, historian Carolyn Ware notes, that children could do it, though an adult had to be present to oversee these four-to-ten-year-old factory workers (1931). (Up through the middle of the nineteenth century, it was customary for children to work, but these children were unusually young, and the hours long. Think of a four-year-old that you have known, working twelve hours a day, six days a week.) The industry grew slowly; marketing the unfamiliar cotton yarn was difficult, and the Embargo Act of December 1807 caused great hardship.

Slater and his imitators set up small yarn-spinning mills in coastal towns, especially in Rhode Island. He farmed the yarn out to cottage workers to weave on their looms. He did not have the financial ties of Mr. Lowell, so his establishments were not huge, nor did he integrate forward into marketing, as the Lowell mills did. Market control was not established and this left him vulnerable to competition from the Boston Associates and the mass-production Manayunk mills. Although his mills were profitable, he did not leave a fortune when he died, but ended up poor because of unwise investments.

The family model did not expand into large mills until the railroads brought down the price of coal after the Civil War. There were steam-operated mills before that, but they were small (Coolidge 1942). So were the villages clustered about a spinning mill. But when coal-fired steam engines could compete with waterpower, the mill could locate where there was already a wage-dependent population. For the new factories, "the favorite locations were in the decaying commercial centers like Newburyport and New Bedford, for they offered a double advantage. On the one hand, the steam mills benefitted from cheap, waterborne transportation; on the other, impoverished sailors and fishermen provided a large supply of helpless and exploitable labor" (Coolidge 1942, 106).[20] The family mills went right to child labor, where possible locking the families in through indebtedness to the company store and through the blacklist, and left them to find their own housing and recreation in the grim slums.

There is a remnant, in the Slater and other textile firms, of a perverse aspect of community that should be mentioned. Communities, like prisons, are not voluntary, and the Lowell II and Slater models did much to imprison their workers. They owned them, in a real sense, by blacklisting those who attempted to leave—it is well-documented by Ware (1931) and especially Gersuny (1976). Leaving the company could mean imprisonment, too. By forcing them to buy necessities, at inflated prices, at the company store, communities kept workers in debt, and thus exposed them to the possibility of imprisonment if they left the company and could not pay their debt. There was no shortage of unskilled and semi-skilled labor, but such techniques increased workers dependency on a particular organization, and made collective action more difficult. Also, many textile and other workers in the early years were simply indentured workers, paying off their passage to the United States. Thus the Lowell II and Slater models still retained some of the absolute patriarchal authority of the community, without any shred of community paternalism to soften it.

These practices existed in other industries, especially the extractive ones, even without labor shortages. But the most important legacy of Lowell II, the Slater firms, and the large Manayunk mills was the development of an organizational format for the mass-production industries that did not appear in great numbers until the last two decades of the century. Most of industry remained decentralized, craft and job-shop oriented; it was composed of an accretion of work groups, with unit production rather than mass production, with some connection between the small firms and the community. What the Lowell II and the Slater models represented was the first large-scale experiment with mass production using "contingent" workers (semi-skilled at best, subject to immediate layoff with no benefits) in ample supply, thus with low labor turnover costs, and no responsibilities by the owners for the environment in which employees spent their nonwork hours (housing, education, religion, transportation, etc.). The transition was slow during most of the century, but sudden in the last two decades of the century, which witnessed with the consolidation of markets and production in the brief, intense, merger movement—a movement that eliminated the small shops and artisanal labor that had existed within the large firm.

But until massive capital shifts could favor hierarchy, most firms in the United States followed the third textile model—the Philadelphia textile industry, to which we shall now turn.

Toward Networks with the Philadelphia Model

By the 1950s we were accustomed to thinking of the large, mass-producing, corporately organized firm as the epitome of advanced capitalism and the source of our worldwide hegemony, and as an invention of supreme importance for productivity and prosperity. The nineteenth Century would then constitute, and was generally regarded as, an uneven but basically steady movement toward this form. The mills of the Boston Associates represent a prime nineteenth-century realization of corporate capitalism, lacking only widely diversified ownership. But there was an alternative to this corporate model that was more typical of the century, up to the 1880s or so, and we shall explore it in this section, drawing on Philip Scranton's *Proprietary Capitalism* (1983).

Though the "network" system of Philadelphia appears as an exception to either the emerging market system of most of the economy, or the hierarchical system of Lowell I and II, it was indeed the most traditional of the three. Mass production at Lowell is the exception that only became the rule at the end of the century. The Philadelphia system came pretty much straight from the English Lancashire cotton and Yorkshire woolen industries, a noncorporate, flexible production system providing a variety of specialized goods from the start. It was the norm, and corporate Lowell the novelty.

The Philadelphia form was a prosperous and serious alternative, though hardly noticed in the history of industrial firms until Scranton's brilliant work. In 1880, before its decline set in, textile manufacturers in Philadelphia had 849 firms. Scranton declares that this was "the single greatest assemblage of textile mills in the nation, without recourse to the device of corporate ownership that keyed the development of New England's heavily capitalized mass-production mills. By the 1880s, they and their 55,000 workers had erected a manufacturing system that stood as a fully realized alternative to the corporate industrial model" (Scranton 1983, 3).[21] It represented an alternative and successful path to profit and capital accumulation from that followed by Lowell I and II. Many historical factors contributed to the difference between the hierarchical form of Lowell and the network form realized in Philadelphia, including the initial labor supply, immigration patterns, and the early adaptation of the power loom in Lowell. But the key variable is probably the abundance of capital in Boston for the industry and its scarcity in Philadelphia. This itself requires some brief explanation because both Boston and Philadelphia were large and wealthy cities.

When Capital Counts

When the financiers of the Lowell system were incorporating and quietly buying up farmland near falls and rapids, Philadelphia already had a vigorous textile industry, characterized by flexibility, product quality, and innovations. The organizational form was that of partnerships or single owners, with only small capital needs. The firms were so small that the practice of renting rooms with power was common, and as the industry grew, machinery could be rented along with room and power (Scranton 1983, 91). (The Boston Associates' mill towns were vertically integrated; every room for every specialized function was owned by the firm.) Mill expansion was piecemeal and factories, or parts of them, were often sublet. Philadelphia's textile history, as Scranton nicely puts it, is one of buildings far more than firms, as new firms started in the rooms that old ones left as they expanded, failed, or sold out. Textile buildings "regularly housed a number of tenants (sometimes including the owner) who shared a common power supply" (106). Notes Scranton, "How different this is from Lowell, where the leasing of space to fledgling firms was unknown and the sale of a mill unthinkable, where enormous capital funds and easy access to further borrowing made vast construction the first order of business" (50).

Gumus-Dawes argues that state government in Pennsylvania regulated the banks heavily and insured that the banks favored direct investments to public infrastructure ventures such as canals and railroads to promote development. The unregulated financial scene in Massachusetts left more opportunities for very large investments in private manufacturing enterprises (Gumus-Dawes 2000). The culture of the two cities certainly differed, as Digby Baltzell demonstrates in his *Puritan Boston and Quaker Philadelphia* (1979), but a *cultural* argument does not explain why the Philadelphia elite invested in New England textile mills, not Philadelphia ones, and were quite willing to invest heavily in railroads, mines, ironworks, and basic manufacturing. (Scranton 1983, 133). Why did they not invest in local textiles?

The suggested answer to this puzzle is historical and organizational. Both areas had large mass-production mills by 1820, at Waltham in Massachusetts, the Globe mill in Kensington township of Philadelphia, and two in the Manayunk township. But the consortium that was to be called the Boston Associates had an immense amount of capital (for the time) from mercantile operations that had fewer and fewer mercantile outlets. The Philadelphia elite did not lack for capital, but were more diversified in their sources of capital and had more diverse outlets in mining, canals, railroads, and heavy manufacturing. Additionally, the state governments took quite different routes to development and relied on different sources of income, dispersing the capital opportunities of the Philadelphia rich to state infrastructure needs and allowing the concentration in Massachusetts that then financed consumer goods such as textiles (Gumus-Dawes 2000). After the initial success of Waltham, the Boston Associates could move immediately to even larger establishments at Lowell and nearby waterpower sites. The necessary capital was concentrated in their hands (they allowed few additional investors in, though outsiders clamored to come aboard), and their projects were vast. Furthermore, they did not have to attend daily to the business; its mass-production character allowed distant, intermittent oversight from corporate headquarters in Boston.

The large Philadelphia mills were not financed by a consortium of wealthy individuals, but by individual entrepreneurs. Only the family that founded the Globe mill (300 employees in 1820) had connections to Philadelphia's wealthy elite (Scranton 1983, 83, 93). Possibly the early success and market control of the Boston Associates discouraged Philadelphia investors from making local investments, as Scranton suggests (133). But I think it was the scale of investment that made the difference. If Pennsylvania left banks unregulated and Massachusetts regulated them, there could have been a Philadelphia Associates and no Boston Associates, and the former could have been the dominant mass producers in the nation. For a new venture such as large textile mills, the initial conditions might be highly determinant. (By 1830 or so, the advantage of more waterpower sites in New England might have been decisive, but initially it probably was not a major factor, and, in any case, when the railroads could move coal cheaply, steam power prevailed.) The Philadelphia mill owners operated on the fringes of elite society, without access to idle capital, and none formed major corporations. In 1850, with work forces of nearly identical size, Philadelphia firms had one-third the capital investment of Lowell (137).

Philadelphia's Large Mills

Philadelphia did have its Lowell-type mass-production mills with 500 or so employees, but such mills were very few, and by 1850 all had ceased. In some cases, the owners had made as much money as they needed to retire gracefully with a "competency" and engage in cultural or political activities, and the mill buildings were sold to specialized producers. Some failed because of fires that plagued the Philadelphia mills in their crowded locations. (The Boston Associates' mills were initially located in newly planned rural areas and they designed the new facilities with an awareness of the fire hazards, and had twenty-four-hour watchmen.) And some failed because of competition with New England products.

One that we met in our discussion of Manayunk, the mill of immigrant Joseph Ripka, is instructive. Initially, in 1820, he produced cheap staples. But by 1831 he was following the flexible production model. Although the Lowell corporations were perfecting the staples that would be the backbone of their output for a half a century, "Ripka was busily introducing a series of new and sophisticated fabrics as one element in a more complex production strategy" (Scranton 1983, 149). But by 1850 it had changed. "Ripka had evidently abandoned the manufacturing of the specialty goods," according to Scranton (157), and was producing a single staple, "pantaloon stuffs," with more than 1000 hands in his scattered works. Reputedly he was the largest cotton cloth manufacturer in the United States in 1850 (156). He was ruined by the Civil War because the bulk of his markets were in the South. (He was already over seventy years old and died at age seventy-five.) His children were spread about other occupations or mills, and his mills were reopened by another immigrant entrepreneur and continued on (159).

There was an inflexibility about the Ripka mills that, although resembling the Lowell ones in terms of labor and production matters (integrated mass-production of cheap goods), differed in others. Family-owned, the Ripka mills did not bring in outside management and new ideas. This would not have been a problem for smaller firms in a flexible production system, because one or another of the small firms would have been likely to make the necessary innovation; if the innovative firm had replaced the outdated firm, it would not have meant a significant loss of capital or hardship to employees, because it was small, and because the building and equipment and the employees would have been absorbed by another small firm. But for a mass production unit that was not a part of a corporate complex, unable either to exercise market control or to absorb losses and rebuild the facility, this *structural interest* in keeping family control was fatal. Ripka utilized direct marketing and twice had to absorb significant losses when his customers (e.g. the southern market in the Civil War) defaulted, whereas the Boston Associates had the buffer of massive capital invested in multiple sites producing different products, which diversified risks (Scranton 1983, 172). Ripka achieved scale economies by focusing his few facilities on one market. When the war closed that market, he was especially vulnerable. So were the cotton mills of the Boston Associates when the supply of cotton ceased, but they had some woolen mills that were not affected. The smaller flexible mills of Kensington were able to shift from cotton to wool.

After the Civil War, some large firms reappeared in the Kensington area, but they were an early form of "flexible mass production." Scranton (1983) quotes from a history of manufactures in the United States, published in 1868, reporting on a large mill in Kensington: the mills were run to supply different demands of customers in the South, Middle States, the West, and New England, and these demands were "temporary." In the words of the 1868 historian, the mill differs "from the large mills of New England, which are generally provided with machinery for making only one class of goods—and consequently when demand for these ceases, they must suspend operations or accumulate stock." But in the Kensington mill changing the fabric according to the changes in season was the rule, not the exception (52). The historian emphasizes the variety of output: cottonades in all grades (and only of fast colors), pantaloonery ginghams, striped and plaid osnaburghs, and so forth. (53).

The distinctiveness of the Philadelphia textile industry, what northern manufactures and later historians dubbed as its "peculiar" character (317), persisted through the 1880s, even though there were similarities to the Lowell model at the bulk-production end. But even Philadelphia's bulk producers did not have the extreme form of integrated production that the Northern mills had. In 1869, with another crisis of overproduction, the national trade association of the wool manufacturers met for the first time in Philadelphia, now the largest area for wool manufacturing in the country. The Philadelphia owners gloated over their business success and their power in the association. They joined their northern competitors in calling for tariffs and the like, but it was the first time many had even joined the association. Writes Scranton (rather densely I fear), "To some degree at least, the structure of textile production in Philadelphia made lateral cooperation within the region a matter of considerable moment and of tangibly more interest than activism within a national organization that was defined along sectoral lines and dominated by integrated mills whose problems and interests differed markedly from theirs" (317).

The secretary of the association and editor of its quarterly bulletin, who represented northern manufacturers, commented on the important changes in the industry, and one in particular that well demonstrates Scranton's thesis: He spoke of the "greater specialization in our industry of distinct branches of the same general manufacture, such as wool-scouring, spinning, weaving, finishing, as separate branches of industry — a system insuring greater perfection of work, and permitting the embarking in manufacture of workmen with moderate capital and whose success is nowhere in this country so well illustrated as in Philadelphia" (318). Smaller firms with dispersed capital investments attended by more skilled workers and higher quality production apparently could overcome the supposedly fearful transaction costs that vertical integration was supposed to avoid. The notion that cooperative networks are indeed possible and efficient gets some support from this contemporary account.

Size and Technology

The lack of concentrated and available capital meant more small-scale textile operations in the Philadelphia area. Small-scale operations can survive only by diversified and flexible production (quick changes of materials, styles and types of product), where there are few economies of scale for the single firm. (Economies of scale arrive with well-developed networks of small producers.) Small-scale operations can reduce the role of large, powerful *structural interests*. These will favor permanent and fixed operations and stable business practices. If a firm dominates a stable market, this is efficient. Small amounts of capital, spread among people with diverse cultural backgrounds and skills, will allow for more trial and error and for innovation that draws on a wider range of experience (Scranton 1983, 133). This pushes capital-short systems toward innovation and change, though of course the capital short-age also makes them vulnerable to extinction or to a dependent sub-contractor role.

Small-scale operations that are flexible require a higher proportion of skilled workers than do mass-production facilities. (The immigrants who came to Philadelphia were more likely to have had textile experi-ence in England and Ireland than the Irish farmers who fled the country during the potato famine.) The immigrants to Philadelphia, familiar with spinning and weaving could not only "man" the mills (or more accurately, "child" the mills), but be outworkers who could absorb the fluctuations of specialized production.

Flexibility was enhanced by the use of outworkers spinning or weav-ing in their homes. (Recall that this was not necessarily a sign of exploi-tation, but preferred by most people over factory work.) As with the English system "the spinner, the dyer, the weaver, the printer and fin-isher were for the most part independent manufactures, serving the cloth merchants" (95). Finally, flexibility required larger numbers of skilled labor, despite, or perhaps because of, the lower levels of mecha-nization. Scranton emphasizes the high skill level required of the silk, woolen, and worsted workers, and many of the workers in Philadelphia had migrated from England (93–94), and most likely had the needed skill.

Small, specialized production also requires dense interfirm linkages, with each speciality complementing the other. The compactness of the textile production areas—confined, essentially, to three townships—made interfirm linkages easier. This was also another capital-saving de-vice; small interlinked firms could use the savings of many families. The savings were small, but so were the capital requirements. And because of the interlinkages, the savings could be responsive to rapid changes in demand and technology—people knew where small bits of money were and trusted one another because of the experience of linkages.

In a flexible production network, the role of *technology* as a causal agent is very problematic. Scranton observes that "steam power did not march in and replace handwork, rolling like some technical juggernaut. It was, rather, one element in a larger complex of options, to be consid-ered alongside the potential for changing output mix, modifying out-work relations, seeking government contracts, or opening direct sales outlets" (171). Hundreds of home knitters running foot-powered knit-ting machines, chiefly for stockings, were still plying their trade in 1880, an enormous knitting industry having grown up around them, but not displacing them. Indeed, outwork persisted into the eighties, still a po-tent component of the Philadelphia industry (171). "[T]here was no sudden plantations of giant hosiery mills at Germantown," Scranton writes. "Instead there were cautious, individual experiments, with the capitalism of 'more' and 'bigger' contained within the context of family legacies and punctuated by occasional quiet statements of 'Enough!' as men like Conyers Smith withdrew from manufacture entirely" (236). Smith had obtained what he considered to be an adequate "competency" or degree of wealth, and turned to politics and culture. This would have been unthinkable for the Boston Associates, who, despite their cultural entrepreneurship after acquiring immense fortunes, stayed with the business of accumulation to the end. Scranton could not have put this very important point better: "It is only with the acceptance of the notion of endless accumulation that the survival of a firm in a capitalist society seems natural and its disappearance evidence of catastrophe" (131–32). The demands of the structure of their organizations shapes the cultural view of wealth accumulation.

NETWORKS OF FIRMS

Flexible production for the Philadelphia mills depended not just on "renting rooms" and on greater numbers of skilled workers. It required a complex network of exchanges. This is not like the small-firm networks of Northern Italy, some Northern European countries, and some Japanese networks today (Perrow 1992), where no large organization dominates. This was probably a moderate- to small-firm network, with a handful of firms employing a hundred or so workers, and many ten to twenty. There were two components of this network's success.

First, around the moderate-sized firm there needs to be a cluster of subcontractors. We cannot say for sure that these were nondependent subcontractors, as with the small-firm networks of the present day, having more than one large firm as customer, getting technical help from the large firm but also convincing it to modify its procedures or products to enhance the efficiency of the subcontractor, and so on. But we do know that outworkers and small contractors were quite capable of organizing and bargaining with the bigger firms (e.g., Scranton 1983, 122–27).

Second, for a moderate- to small-firm network to exist, there must be durable ties among the moderate firms indicating reciprocity and trust. The firms should have cooperative as well as competitive relations with each other. The evidence for this is unfortunately only inferential, rather than direct. (Given the scant historical material, we are lucky to have evidence of any structural details from the period, let alone evidence of cooperation and reciprocity!) It is to be found in the extensive histories Scranton provides, and would require reporting here the minute surrounding details to support the inferences. (See, for example, the section "Sevill Schofield and the Networks of Family Capitalism," 1983, 57–71.).

One small bit of evidence from a contemporary historian whom Scranton quotes and some remarks about the trade associations will have to suffice. The historian, describing the Campbell mill, notes that when demand for colored cotton goods, known as "Philadelphia goods," exceeded Campbell's capacity, "they call[ed] into service the machinery of other manufactures" (55). How frequent this was can only be guessed, but it was clearly a tight-knit community of owners, and the exchange of personnel with the changing fortunes and specialties of the firm was high. We know that the division of labor among firms was extensive, separate processes were performed by separate firms, and the sheer movement of materials at various stages of processing must have been bewildering, though the distances were small. With this complexity we can posit three possible outcomes: (1) collapse because of complexity, (2) sustained operations because of exploitation, or (3) success because of cooperation.

1. The complexity could bring down the system because of the "transaction costs" (in today's economic terms), which would be enormous with so many self-interested parties bargaining and trading and cheating (Oliver Williamson 1975, 1985). The system would have to be replaced by a Lowell-style hierarchy to reduce the chances for opportunism and cheating. Clearly, this was not the case; the "network," if we are correct in assuming that, prospered and grew from the beginning of the century until the 1890s, when the whole industry, New England as well as the Middle Atlantic states, began its long decline in the face of foreign competition and domestic mismanagement.

2. If the system were not to flounder, the transactions would be so one-sided that it really resembled an implicit hierarchy or even feudal system. Here there would be fully dependent subcontractors, existing only at the sufferance of the big firm that gave them business, and big firms that had no need for cooperative relations with each other, but were in fierce competition. This is a possibility, but the vitality of the small contractors, and the evidence (see later in this chapter) on wealth holding, does not suggest fully dependent subcontracting. The relations among the big firms remains quite obscure to historians today, but Scranton's account does not turn up evidence of intense competitiveness unalloyed by cooperative relations.

3. That suggests the transactions were not costly because of trust and cooperation, and this is why the system prospered. As noted, the Philadelphia textile industry was vigorous and successful until the

1890s, and it was the fully integrated mass-production firms that suffered the most during various economic crises.

Labor Conflict

We would expect a network form of economic activity to include provisions for managing conflict between owners and labor, and between owners themselves. Unfortunately, until after the Civil War, there is very little indication of this in the historical record Scranton (1983) gives us. There were crises aplenty, as well as strikes, and ephemeral organizations of both workers and owners, but nothing on which to make any confident assertions about how the cost of owner-owner and owner-labor conflicts were contained. After the Civil War there were more strikes, and more employers' associations, and Scranton details these at length. The general conclusion is that in the more specialized and skilled ends of the industry, there were few permanent wage cuts and few strikes. These involved wool and worsted fabrics, knit goods of all kinds, silks, and the related independent dyeing and spinning operations. They were flexible and faced few risks of overproduction. Wage cuts were accepted because the wages were restored with prosperity. According to Scranton, "This was not the labor peace of magnates and benumbed operatives but a fairly durable expression of the mutual competence of workers and proprietors, each of whose obligations the other understood" (356). In these sectors, associations of owners appeared, concerned with technical advances, lobbying, and in time, encouraging technical education. On the other hand, in cotton and carpets, where there was bulk production, the risk of overproduction, and more intense national competition, the associations were defensive, cutting wage rates or trying to cut output, and provoking hundreds of strikes (355–56).

Externalities

What of the *externalities* of this flexible production system? On balance they appear to be fewer than Lowell II or the family mills of Rhode Island, but it was still a grim life for well over half of the workers — half of whom were children. Scranton (1983) notes that "though the Lowell Mills ultimately engaged thousands of young women to spin and weave, they were not notorious abusers of child labor, whereas the Philadelphian manufacturers were so charged time and again in the '20s and '30s" (100). (Lowell II, however, was to reap charges of exploiting child labor.) One moderate-sized mill employed five men, six women, and seventy children, for a total of eighty-one. Few had such a high ratio of children, but in many cases the children outnumbered the adults substantially, especially in the larger mills (98). We have already noted how the big mill operators, such as Ripka, met and established harsh rules for their factories governing lateness, absenteeism, and even eating at work (150). The workers replied with the familiar cry, in New England as well as Philadelphia, "shall we be slaves?" (151). The labor relations of the workshops were only somewhat better than the big mills; they "were linked fundamentally with the exploitative measures of their factory cousins, the one welcoming handloom immigrants, the other introducing the factory system to women and children whose labor was keyed to the pace of machinery and the skills of veteran male workers" (129).

Still, there were other factors that limited the externalities, factors not present in the hierarchical model. Many employed in the industry were outworkers, and for them there was some independence. "Hand loom weavers spoke in terms of a 'price' for loom work, continuing the eighteenth-century custom of separating themselves from factory operatives who received wages. From this period through the 1870s, hand weavers in Philadelphia demanded, negotiated, and struck for the price of work, submitted price lists to shopmasters, and resisted all attempts to treat them as, or classify them with, 'wage earners'" (112). Scranton quotes a contemporary historian who makes a striking observation regarding the attitudes of the outworkers: "The distinctive feature of the business is its hand-looms and domesticity. Full one-half of the persons engaged in the production have no concern with the ten-hour system, or the factory system, or even the solar system. They work at such hours as they choose, and their industry is mainly regulated by the state of their larder" (166).

The more flexible production firms responded to the high price of cotton, Scranton demonstrates, not by cutting wages but by importing new, improved machinery that would produce goods competitive with their biggest competitors, the British (56), and strikes were few in this sector. Even the mill workers showed some degree of firm loyalty and appreciation. When, in three cases, employers kept the mills running despite the slack economy just before the Civil War, the workers arranged for ceremonies, presenting the owners with huge flags in gratitude (250). Producing for stock to avoid layoffs is a "positive" externality.

Most significant, however, is the contrasting response to the Civil War of the Philadelphia and the New England branches of the industry. When the Civil War came and the supply of cotton was shut off, instead of taking the year's supply to continue to produce in the mills, the directors of the Merrimack Manufacturing Company, for example, cut production then suspended it entirely and sold bales of cotton on the bull market as the price of raw cotton soared, reaping windfall profits without manufacturing a yard of cloth. This shut down their mills. They expected a short war, and when they didn't get it their "grave miscalculation fractured the system of manufacturing that had frozen in place over the previous four decades" (23). The unemployed went into the army, possibly the only alternative. City records imply that single men and women emigrated whereas family men enlisted (24). In five years the city population dropped from 36,827 to 30,190 (24). The woolen mills kept going, but the mills that tried to convert to woolens failed—a measure of the inflexibility of the system. Scranton estimates that more than 9,000 workers were laid off in the first year—in a city of only 37,000 (25).

In contrast, several Philadelphia mills formed militia from the men in the mills, who went out to fight in the Civil War. The company paid the men their regular wages (69–71). Scranton notes that "the contribution of wages to the families of workers who volunteered for military service seems to be an extension of the same compound of mutualism and hierarchy evident in the [previously described] flag incidents" (25). Forming militia units from employees that would have otherwise been laid off, and paying the families their wages, is a striking case of a "positive" externality, and is quite possibly related to the network character of the Philadelphia industry. What we might want to ascribe to differences in local cultures (Philadelphia vs. New England) might better be ascribed to differences in the predominant organizational forms that shaped the local cultures.

The Decline of Textile Firms

Lest we quickly and easily embrace flexible production as a solution to industrial problems, Scranton documents and interprets, with bewildering complexity, the *decline* of the Philadelphia model and textiles in general from the late nineteenth century to the present, in *Figured Tapestry* (1989), a sequel to his *Proprietary Capitalism*. The decline of textiles in the United States was not primarily a case of large New England mills saddled with high labor costs moving south for low labor costs, but then not investing in modern technology as foreign competitors did. That is only one part of the story. The flexible production firms of Philadelphia and elsewhere also died out, and it does not seem to be a case of over-priced labor, but rather, a thousand blows, including mismanagement and more creative foreign production. Detailing the "thousand blows" in *Figured Tapestry*, Scranton produces an account that, in his own words, is "more cinematic than architectural, jump-cutting from close-ups to aerial views" (13). No grand theory, including one that extols flexible over mass production, appears to sort out the complex story.

One thing to note is that some big firms did develop a form of flexible mass production, so that flexibility need not be coterminous with small to moderate size, though it usually seems to be. This is a conclusion of one of the two who first identified and analyzed the nature of flexible production, Charles Sabel (see his "Moebius-Strip Organizations and Open Labor Markets: Some Consequences of the Reintegration of Conception and Execution in a Volatile Economy" [1991]).

The decline had much to do with the emerging power of mass outlets and the firms' customers, whose buying power overwhelmed the community of producers, driving them into ruinous price-cutting and labor exploitation, much as global textile and shoe firms do today. The power of mass buying for retail outlets is a neglected topic among organizational analysts even today. Perhaps small-firm networks are only viable on a long-term basis of several decades if the product remains technologically advanced, complex and customized; in the late nineteenth century, this was less true of textiles. Finally, Scranton details quite nonoptimal and perhaps destructive behavior on the part of flexible producers, organized labor, and certainly heavy-handed and shortsighted government. It is a depressing and frustrating account. He is not optimistic about drafting flexible specialization programs "for renewal that would redress the self-blocking weaknesses flexible producers displayed historically" (505). But the fact that flexible specialization reemerged so dramatically (on a small scale, of course) in the late twentieth century, a phenomenon he does not examine in-depth, may make his pessimism premature.

Figured Tapestry, which extends well beyond the period we are concerned with, is an encyclopedic, and nearly indigestible, answer to our initial question "what do organizations do?" It is a sobering reminder that much of organizational life and behavior is simply beyond the generalizing powers of analysts at this time. But this does not gainsay the enlightenment we receive from Scranton's contrast of Lowell II and the Kensington district of small-firm networks in *Proprietary Capitalism*. These two dramatically different organizational models existed, prospered and competed side-by-side for much of the century. Both could be contained in the commodious realm of American *culture*. Indeed, each elaborated on quite different aspects of that culture, and could be said to create culture at least as much as each model responded to it. The mass-production model had powerful negative *externalities* that would not only be characteristic of the surge of mergers and the corporate form at the end of the century, but legitimated the cultural drive for ever more accumulation of wealth and its celebration; whereas the flexible-production model had far more benign consequences for the local community and society in general, reinforcing artisanal cultural values and the satisfactions of moderate wealth. This flexible production model was a form that the rise of lightly regulated, heavily subsidized, and thoroughly privatized railroads did much to violate. The railroads centralized capital, nationalized industry and its development, gave labor a self-seeking, defensive role, and established a compliant judiciary that extended the power and freedom of the corporate form for the century to follow.

SUMMARY

The large, mass-production Lowell-type mills scattered over New England were the first big business in the United States. The owners were stockholders, living in Boston rather than in one or more of the mill towns. A charter gave the enterprise a corporate form, allowing larger concentrations of capital than the partnership or joint-stockholder forms would allow. The large amounts of capital allowed big firms to be built and a large marketing firm to sell the output. The firms owned by the Boston Associates, as they were informally called, captured most of the market for inexpensive textiles. The Boston Associates lobbied for high tariffs to protect their products, and for low tariffs for the products of their competitors, and were successful.

The Boston Associates were somewhat different from future mass-production firms in that they formed a powerful bank to service their interests, and operated company towns, owning everything and profiting from everything. But only in these respects did they exceed the standard industrial model that was to blossom at the end of the nineteenth century.

The firms' internal structure was simple, as was the manufacturing process. But it was a well-realized bureaucracy with an agent of the corporation at the site, a small staff for rudimentary accounting and financial matters, a superintendent of production, department foremen and assistant foremen, and a rudimentary hierarchy within the hourly employees. A separate marketing organization, and a headquarters staff in Boston, completed the system. The principles of the internal structure were easily copied from European textile firms, especially those of the British.

What interests us the most is the movement from a non-wage-dependent wage-labor force to a wage dependent one (characterized as Lowell I and Lowell II). In Lowell I, the women from the local farms worked for three or four years before marriage or return to the farms, and thus were not fully dependent upon wage labor. The firms, thus, were required to treat them decently. Once the Irish immigrants arrived (along with some French Canadians), a wage-dependent population was available; more children were employed; wages, working conditions, and community infrastructure declined; and high profits were secure. The structure of the Lowell II organizations hindered technological change and innovation for the rest of the century, as a result of *structural interests*, and promoted *divisions* inimical to a democratic society. Variations on these themes were played out in the Slater family-control model.

A distinctive alternative to the corporate control model was to move not toward hierarchy but toward networks, as in the Kensington model of Philadelphia textile firms. Lacking concentrated capital, the firms were small, innovative, and had more positive externalities for workers and for the community. Renting "rooms with power," the buildings housed small firms that cooperated with, as much as competed against, each other, and successfully dominated the high-end market for sixty years, adapting to new technologies and market shifts. They were not corporations but partnerships and joint-stock ownerships, and thus made less use of the favorable legal rulings that the Lowell firms enjoyed.

These two models—the large, centralized, bureaucratic, mass-production and mass-distribution firm, and the small networked firms with flexible production—bracket our industrial experience in the nineteenth century, except for the railroads. In between was most of industry: modest-sized batch production, relatively skilled in many industries and with "driving labor" in others (shoe-making is a good example of the progression from skill intensive to labor intensive), serving largely local and regional markets. We are not going to examine these intermediate firms in this book. The middle way gave substantial ground to the mass-production model at the end of the century, and the network model seems to have disappeared. The main reason for this was the organizational innovations of the second big business, the railroads.

Chapter 5

RAILROADS, THE SECOND BIG BUSINESS

WE WILL HAVE A substantial journey through railroad territory, and it will begin rather gently. Our first conductor is
Wolfgang Schivelbusch, whose delightful *The Railway Journey* (1986) offers unusual insights and intellectual entertainment. After
that short trip, the real work begins when we consider alternative explanations for the privatization of U.S. railroads when other countries were
moving toward state regulation, or outright ownership. The alternatives
are two economic and two institutional theories, and, of course, organizations and interest groups. But first, some Schivelbuschian technology.

It's hard to believe that something as momentous as the steam engine,
which brought us railways and factories and electricity, could have had
its beginning in such a distant problem as deforestation in Europe. For
one of our key theoretical concepts, *technology*, it is a case of technological *in*determinism — an invention that cast about for a justification
and utility. The shortage of wood in eighteenth-century Europe accelerated the development of coal production; the mining of coal was im-
peded in soggy England by the flooding of the mines; this lead to a
search for a powerful pump, accounting for the first commercially used
steam engine, the Newcomen steam engine, in the mid-eighteenth century. The coal fields were soon saturated with the Newcomen pump
engines, which were huge and very crude, capable of only a back-and-
forth motion. That was the start; then other applications for this new
wonder were sought. What could the engine manufacturers do with the
beast, as the market became so saturated? The firm of Watt and Boulton
urged James Watt to develop the engine for the newly emerging manufacturing industries. Watt's new engine was capable of a rotary motion,
rather than just a back-and-forth motion, but still used low pressure
and thus was not very efficient. By the turn of the century, a more efficient high-pressure engine had been developed, and it was small enough
to use on a wagon, as a local source of movement, a "loco-motive"
(Schivelbusch 1986, chapt. 1). James Vance points out that inefficient
engines were just fine for Britain because there was a long history of
rail-way and plate-way development — whereby wagons on rails or
plates were pulled by horses, and even men. (The term "railroad" came
into use after the railway was more established.) This resulted in very
gradual grades and very wide turns. The problem with turns was that

the inner and outer wheels moved at different speeds and tensions; the wagons tended to jump the track on sharp turns (Vance 1995, 6–7, 35–36).

But there was still no great demand for putting a steam engine on a wagon; horsepower was cheaper than steam power, and coal trains were pulled by horses. The locomotive was more of a curiosity than anything else. But the coal fields were far from the source of provender, the grain needed to feed the horses that pulled the coal trains, and the price of provender for the horses that pulled the coal trains began to mount. Then, in a nice case of historical contingency, through an act of parliament, the grain price jumped. By the time the steam engine had been perfected sufficiently that its size could be greatly reduced and put on a wagon, the price of horse food had gone so high as to make horse-power expensive. Schivelbusch (1986) notes:

[F]rom 1815 on, coal became cheaper to use than provender in all of England and that year, parliament, dominated by agricultural interests, passed a corn law which, by imposing steep taxes on imported grain, forced grain prices to rise. Obviously, the artificially high level of grain prices helped replace horse power by mechanical power in much the same way as the shortage of wood in eighteenth century Europe had accelerated the development of coal production (4).

As one contemporary noted in 1834, the "landed capitalists of Britain" had more than doubled the price of animal labor, "whether of man or horses." Thus the "monied capitalists," he went on, spent their capital to develop engines that could replace both kinds of animal power — horses and humans. The high cost of grain was a recurrent and standard argument for pushing on with steam, and, according to Schivelbusch, Adam Smith calculated that feeding a horse cost as much as feeding eight laborers, thus the savings on every horse would have provided additional food for eight laborers (Schivelbusch 1986, 5). Of course, only the artificially high cost of grain made the results of such a calculation possible, and the "path development" of contingent history a necessity.

The new British entrepreneurs held forth about the enormous expense of the beautiful, symbolic animals, the continual renewal of the stock that was necessary, and the expense of their keep, and argued that the railways could solve the problem of expensive (though beautiful) horses. England had coal aplenty to feed the "iron horse." France on the other hand, without artificial grain prices and with much less coal, which was scattered about the country in small deposits, pointed to the obvious advantage of horses over coal. One engineer in France noted, in an argument that would get full play only 150 years later, that the natural deposits of coal were not inexhaustible, whereas horses draw upon products of the soil that are renewable and thus can go on forever. The British replied that it was the increasing demands for speed that brought about the destruction of animal power, but added a cultural fillip, that this was a destruction "no one can contemplate with feelings except of the most painful nature." On a steam railway, an average rate of fifteen miles per hour was kept up with the greatest of ease, they pointed out (8). Furthermore, the animal was inescapably irregular in its movements, whereas the steam engine is "wholly unimpeded by the speed of its own motions" — a commanding image — and moves smoothly along the smooth tracks (9).

Still we did not leap precipitously and inevitably from the portable engine to the full-blown railway. It took quite some time for engineers to believe that a smooth wheel would have traction on a smooth rail; for a time, cog wheels were used instead, and there were other devices. Schivelbusch found plans for one cumbersome device that used steam power to move stilts in order to walk much as a horse would. (This would be called linear thinking today.) But the engines performed well, hauling the coal the short distance from the coal pits to the canals and waterways, and soon began hauling goods between the villages and over longer distances. The form of the stagecoach was replicated, and put it on a flatbed for people to ride in. More striking, it was assumed that rails should be open to all users just as highways and canals were. As late as 1838, there were private vehicles using the Liverpool-Manchester line (27). In fact, it wasn't until 1840 that a committee of parliament decided that, "from the nature of their business," the "railway companies using locomotive power possessed a practical monopoly for the conveyance of passengers" (28). Previously, elaborate plans had been made to solve the problem of private vehicles using common rails, based on visions of double-decker railroad beds that were four abreast and mixed horse-drawn carriages, freight trains, and private trains with carriages. (Steam carriages, resembling private buses a hundred years later, were designed for the United States.)

But as resistant to monopoly as these attempts to plan common carriers were, monopoly was built into the *technology*, a convincing, if uncommon, instance of technological determinism. There was simply too much danger of vehicles colliding; additionally, there was the lack of technically necessary facilities along the line, principally supplies of coal and water; and there was the disregard by private users of any technical regulations. Free markets would not work here. Whoever owned the railway, whether private or public, would have to control it completely, and this characteristic of the system brought about the development of organizations that were larger and more powerful than any seen in any other form of transport, and in the United States, larger and more powerful than any organizations heretofore seen.

But monopoly was not to solve one *externality*—the problem of safety. It would take public regulation to solve that in England. Trains simply ran into each other either head on or by overtaking one another. But a technology was ready at hand—the telegraph system. This had already been technically perfected before the railroad came along but, as Schivelbusch puts it, "it did not, at first, find any practical application, as there was no particular need for it" (29), another case of indeterminism. On the early railroad journeys, every train required one, two, and even three persons whose sole task was to scan the line ahead for obstacles, such as cattle or approaching trains. Tunnels, which were used much more in Europe than in the United States, proved to be the toughest problem and provided the telegraph with its first practical application. The line was divided into separate blocks and each one had a telegraph transmitter signaling to the block ahead when the line was clear. The engine driver then received an optical signal that told him when to go ahead. Ever attentive to the subtleties of the new technology in railroading, Schivelbusch notes that "because a train runs on a predetermined line, an engine driver can never aspire to the social role of a 'captain on dry land'; the electric telegraph confirms his true status, that of an industrial worker, an operator of a machine" (30).

The railway system was grafted on to the industrialized class system immediately, he notes.

> Travel by rail, being pulled by the power of steam, is experienced as participation in an industrial process. For the lower classes this experience is quite immediate: in England they are transported in open boxcars on freight trains, up to the 1840s. They are not regarded as recipients of passenger service but as freight goods. The Gladstone Act of 1844 requires the carriages of the 3rd and 4th class to be covered, they still look more like covered boxcars than passenger cars. The traveling situation of the more privileged classes is entirely different: their carriages look like coaches mounted on rails (72).

In passing, we should particularly note the existence of the Gladstone Act; England regulated its railroads, even though they were owned by private citizens, to a much greater degree than did the United States.

In America the industrial revolution began with agriculture and transportation, in England with manufacturing. The English revolution in transportation was due to the development of industrial production, first and foremost, the textile industry. This industry needed transportation between Liverpool, the main port where the cotton came in, and

Manchester, the textile center of Lancashire. In the United States water transport already linked cities of any size—otherwise they could not have been built—and the railroad did not so much link cities as it reached out to make them. As Schivelbusch puts it, the railroad system in Europe facilitated existing traffic; in the United States it created traffic (90).Vance points out that English railroads created no new towns more significant than the rather insignificant Crewe, Swindon, and Middlesbrough, but the United States quickly saw Atlanta, Charlotte, Omaha, and Albuquerque emerge as significant cities only because of the railroad (Vance 1995, 25).

At the dawn of the nineteenth century, when steam power was first introduced, America was characterized by enormous and practically worthless natural resources and a chronic labor shortage outside of the main urban areas. Later we shall reflect on the process of exploiting labor in order to exploit the enormous but otherwise worthless natural resources; it will be an *organizational* and an *interest* argument. But with Schivelbusch we have an unusually attractive *cultural* argument that I cannot resist. Though railroads were decried in some quarters— by those holding interests in canals, citizens who lived near the soot of downtown terminals, and perhaps by some critics of technological juggernauts—the railroads clearly supported an ideology of conquest and growth through mechanization. Schivelbusch offers an immensely perceptive summary of the American viewpoint: "As it does not cause any unemployment, every form of mechanization is experienced as creative. The mechanization of transport is not seen, as in Europe, as a destruction of a traditional culture, but as a means to gaining a new civilization from the hitherto worthless (because inaccessible) wilderness" (1986, 91). Building railroads appeared productive to a degree unimaginable to Europeans, and this belief found its expression in the American policy of generous land grants from the state and federal governments. "The mechanized transportation system becomes, as it were, a producer of territories in the same way that mechanized agriculture becomes a producer of goods" (92). It is also the guarantor of national unity in an aggressive effort to unify a continent. The cultural argument has no better champion than this.

But structure and interests give us the crucial details. The United States was blessed with many inland water routes, far more than Europe, and these required the least capital to utilize, so early transportation in the nation was based almost exclusively on natural waterways, and then canals.[22] Vance provides a dramatic map of the navigable waters and canals in 1830, showing both the great extent of water transport and the essential need for a route across the Alleghenies (Vance

1995, 17). The railroad did not offer economies for decades on established water routes between cities, and so was used to extend transport into inaccessible regions. So dominant was our water transport that today we continue to use the verb "to ship" for all forms of transport. The river steamboat was the basis for the design of railroad carriages, which looked like steamboat cabins; and for the layout of the railroad lines themselves, which followed the easiest route, they flowed like a river around hills, avoiding the construction of tunnels and bridges. In England a line was built as straight as possible, partly because of railroad technology but also for economic reasons: labor was cheap and land expensive. In the United States labor was expensive and land practically worthless. According to Schivelbush,

> An article published in 1858 in the *Atlantic Monthly* observes that the English railroad engineer "defies all opposition from river and mountain, maintains his line straight and level, fights Nature at every point, cares neither for height nor depth, rock nor torrent. . . . On the other hand, the American engineer, always respectful (though none the less determined) in the presence of natural obstacles to his progress, bows politely to the opposing mountain-range" The American engineer proceeds in this manner not so much out of respect for nature as out of the wish to build the line as cheaply as possible (96).

It was estimated that the cost of building lines in the United States was only a third of that in England.

The dual-axle chassis developed in America in the 1830s was "an elegant example of the thesis that a technological innovation becomes a historically significant one only when there is an actual economic demand for it" (99). It had been invented twenty years earlier in England, but wasn't needed because there the tracks were straight. In the United States, however, such a chassis allowed tracks to be curved despite the length of the car. As a consequence, the long car without compartments became standard in America from 1840 on, in contrast to the stagecoach mounted on a flat bed, as developed in Britain, the influence of which can still be seen in European railway compartments (100). The railway journey was longer in the United States, and so the car was filled with all kinds of amenities; the model for this car was the coastal steamer and riverboat, equipped with lounges and a kitchen. The trains even published their own newspapers. The Pullman cars appeared in 1859, and were named "palace cars" after the "floating palace" steamboat. They also introduced a "first class" into a system that had until then been classless in its treatment of cargo (110).

RAILROADS IN FRANCE, BRITAIN, AND THE UNITED STATES: THE ORGANIZATIONAL LOGIC

That is the background for our railroad journey; the United States needed to open up territories with long routes and new cities, snake around obstacles to enable cheap construction, amass immense, unimagined amounts of capital, and compete with the public investment in canals and turnpikes. But who was to finance the railroads, manage them, and, as they were common carriers, regulate them? The answer to these questions has little to do with technology, and a great deal to do with *politics*, which in turn depends upon *organizations*. To see the novelty of the U.S. answer to these questions, we will compare the United States with France and Britain. I will draw upon Frank Dobbin's excellent comparative study of the railroads in these countries, *Forging Industrial Policy* (1994). When Dobbin's analysis is used to highlight the importance of organizations, rather than what he calls "institutional ethos," we will see the organizational source of ideology and politics. This will also prompt our first serious consideration of the role of the state in our story; it hardly existed in the United States but was moderately strong in Britain and very strong in France.

My thesis is simple: France had a state organization, the Bureau of Roads and Bridges, at the start of the railway age. It dictated railroad development in its own interests, ran the railroads, and allowed only a passive role to private capital. Britain had a strong parliament, warring with the crown, and it regulated private interests. Because of the restrictions the crown placed upon finance capital, requiring partnerships rather than allowing limited liability corporations, large railroad companies did not emerge. So parliament allowed cartels to get the necessary national integration of lines, but it regulated them. The United States had no such capital restrictions, and so private corporations could become large national monopolies, and there was no Bureau of Bridges and Roads — that is, no state organization — to prevent monopolies or compete with them. The initial railroads were joint public and private investments, and local governments attempted some regulation. But the local governments were no match for the private interests — the railroad entrepreneurs, railroad firms, and interested business concerns. The legislatures and judiciary at all levels — federal, state and local — deferred to private interests and soon the railroad companies were more powerful than even the states or the federal government.

Thus the development of the U.S. railroads, a common carrier, was privatized without significant governmental control. All three countries built tracks between geographical points, but the French emphasized national efficiency through one firm, the British, through cartels that protected dozens of firms; whereas the United States, emphasized private gain by a few giant firms. We should not mistake the novelty of this view. A much more obvious view is that of the economic historians Lance Davis and Nobel prize-winner Douglass North: "The choice between levels of institutions (individual, voluntary cooperative, or governmental) is dictated by the costs and revenues associated with each alternative" (1971, 25). Economic rationality, in their view, should determine which level shall organize the system: private, public and private, or public. In contrast, I will argue that the national context (largely the state) determined the system, whether it be private organizations, as in the United States, state-managed cartels, as in Britain; or a state monopoly, as in France. Costs and revenues (that is, efficiency) had little to do with it. (In terms of narrow economic efficiency, France won.)

It was the different forms of the state, especially their attitudes toward the role of private capital, that determined the alternative routes that the new railroads took. Initially, before the rise of large, powerful private organizations, the state was the important independent variable. It set the context in which the massive investment in a common good would take place in all three countries. It was strong and centralized in France, and remained so through the industrial revolution, limiting the ability of private organizations to shape society. It was divided in Britain, allowing moderate power for large organizations. And it was weak in the United States, allowing the growth of a "society of organizations." In France, the strong state fostered a national elite, an upper class of birth and breeding, that remains, to this day, more cohesive in its control of business and industry than in the other two countries. France is thus less of a "society of organizations" than the other two, and more of a society of inherited positions, strong elite culture, and organizationally independent communities. Because the organizational absorption of society is now worldwide, France is not greatly different from Britain and the United States, but it is still noticeable. Britain limited the power of private business and industry to some extent and retained something of a national upper class, but business success has increasingly been a route to elite status, and employment status is increasingly the source of citizen rights. As such, Britain takes on more of the characteristics of a society of organizations. The United States, with a weak state initially and strong private economic organizations, has had to build a state to manage a nation of such immense size and complexity, but the state has been built along bureaucratic organizational principles and partisan politics rather than birth and privilege, or professionalism. The state is vital to our history of organizations in the

United States, but because of its initial weakness, in contrast to that of France and Britain; this weakness allowed the logic of private organizations to rule to a greater degree than in the other countries.

France

France is the best place to start in our railroad comparison. The state was powerful from the start, and had to be if a nation were to coalesce and protect itself from hostile states on three of its sides. In fact, inferring from Dobbin's account, we could say that the French state, as an organization with its own interests, was more important than *politics* and ideology. These came and went, but the centralized state endured. "During the infancy of the railroad industry" Dobbin writes, "France was in one moment a monarchy, in the next a republic, and in the next an empire" (Dobbin 1994, 95). Despite these dramatic political shifts in the age of Bonaparte, the French state, drawing upon the resources and structure of the ancien régime, was steadfast in its professionalism and centralization. Politics was not only a dependent variable, depending upon the organizational structure of the state, but also nearly irrelevant in explaining the behavior of the central organizational organs of the state. Whether France was politically and ideologically a monarchy, republic, or empire, the state was steadfast.

It was steadfast, I would assert, because it succeeded as a centralized bureaucracy, and bureaucracies have *structural interests* in maintaining their power. It sent its minions, called "intendants" to all the provinces and cantons and made sure that no local strongholds emerged, just as a centralized industrialized bureaucracy would make sure that all major functions — such as sales, production, and R & D, and all branch plants and operations — could not develop their independent powers. Throughout the history of the growth of coherent, centralized states in Europe, the state was chary of other organizations; potential competitors were not allowed, or were closely circumscribed as chartered organizations. Even today, in Japan the many powerful ministries closely control the activities of independent organizations that wish to operate in the ministry's sector, or forbid them entirely. Thus, independent nonprofit organizations concerned with, for example, the plight of the aged, can not raise money the way nonprofit organizations do in the United States. The issue is not ideological, but organizational.

Nor is it a peculiarity of "political" organizations; private corporations behave similarly. In France, as Tocqueville noted (quoted in Dobbin), the kings chose men of humble origins, posted them to alien regions, and rotated them regularly, to ensure their loyalty to headquarters. Business corporations do the same. Just as professional managers in business corporations would be little without their employment, so were the agents of the French state. Venality could pervade the practices that the state used to allocate positions among its citizens, but once in the position, no independent stronghold could emerge. Every effort was made in the French state to prevent the formation of independent interests outside of the state, such as labor, agriculture, manufacturing, and commercial organizations, all of which might mediate between the citizen and the state. Similarly, in industrial organizations, every attempt is made to prevent independent internal interest groups from forming around political, religious, or labor interests. The composition of the people at the top of this bureaucratic pyramid might change: just as the king was replaced by a premier and then the premier was replaced by an emperor and so on, family dynasties came and went in the large industrial corporations, where takeovers and mergers roiled the small pot at the top, but all without great effect upon "the organization."

Since the eighteenth century, economic power has flowed not so much from the barrel of a weapon as from the bowels of an efficient organization. One can even strike the term "efficient" because shear numbers of employees can overwhelm smaller organizations. They have more political and economic clout, regardless of efficiencies and productivity. But an efficient organization is all the more superior. To achieve efficiency requires trained personnel, especially at the middle and upper managerial levels. The local, state, and federal governments in the United States had little of this talent. Because of strong Republican traditions, anyone could be a senator or governor or mayor. Democratic forms ensured that there would be turnover in these positions, as one party lost and another took over. Perhaps fear of a large state prevented the growth of a large well-trained bureaucracy that could stay as officials came and went (the usual explanation); but it is just as likely that the party organizations and business organizations recognized permanent civil servants as a threat to their influence, and prevented them.

France was quite different. "French monarchs," notes Dobbin, "developed a modern civil service that was unparalleled elsewhere in Europe" (99). This included the public engineering corps and the écoles, which date back to 1697, during the reign of Louis XIV. They were responsible for building bridges and highways on an independent basis from 1716 on, and came to be known as the Corps des Ponts et Chaussées (Corps of Bridges and Roads). The Corps started receiving the best graduates of the newly formed Ecole Polytechnique after 1795. By the time the locomotives and their tracks arrived, the Corps had over a hundred years' experience overseeing a vast system of roads, canals, and waterways. While the U.S. military had its engineers, who were put to use in the building of the railroads, nothing like the Ecole Polytechnique or the Corps des Ponts et Chaussées existed in the United States.

The French state had the finances to do the engineering studies and plan the roads, and then it put them up for bid for private capital to build. No railroads could be built, even on private land, without the authorization of the state. Though over half of the financing was private, this is misleading; the state guaranteed a good return on the loans and bore the risks, thus it was effectively a form of state borrowing. Private firms had little say over the location of the lines, the construction priorities, the standards for the track and engines, safety devices, and fares. The French state did not own the railways, as did the states in Belgium or Germany, and railroad financing was "privatized," but not in the sense in which we use the term today. (France was not a socialist state, it was preeminently a capitalist one; the state sat "above society in order to transcend the interests of particular groups of capitalists in the pursuit of the long-term vitality of capitalism as a whole" [Dobbin 1994, 103].) No duplicate and competing tracks were allowed. Safety measures were quickly established and inventions quickly adopted, such as automatic decoupling (so that workmen were not constantly being crushed) and air brakes (invented in the United States but not adopted there for decades). Apparently, the French never considered the British, much less the U.S., alternatives to state management. Dobbin rightly points out that the differences in the three systems would not be predicted, or explained, by *technological, economic,* or even the new *institutional economics* arguments.

There was never any doubt in France that this was the way to plan a rational and coherent network of railway lines. No other solution, Dobbin notes, was put forth. Nor was there any question that the private interests building the firm were to be completely controlled by the state. Dobbin summarizes the argument made by Minister of Commerce and Public Works, Adolphe Thiers, and others: "if capitalists were left to their own devices, France would find itself with a mess of disjointed, poorly constructed stretches of track that would ill serve the nation . . . and squander the nation's resources on local projects without a view to constructing a national network" (109). It was as if they were describing just what had happened with railroads in the United States.

There were some costs to central planning, of course. The engineers insisted that the shortest possible line between two points be followed, rejecting digressions that could serve important market towns, or even refusing to have a key line veer sufficiently from its straight route to service the royal palace at Versailles. One commentator at the time said that the ministry's lines meant "a little too much as the crow flies" and ignored the potential for increased traffic that could have been obtained by deviating from a straight line enough to touch at intermediate cities (110). Having a huge investment in canals and roads already, the engineers were reluctant to approve some lines when the value and efficiency of the railroads was still in some dispute. Dobbin quotes from a history of the railroads regarding a response to an application for a line from Roanne to Dijon: "where there is already a national road, when there will shortly be a second artificial water route. . . . It is impossible to recognize . . . the public utility of a third rival route" (110). Finally, a thoroughly centralized system preferred the "hub and spoke" layout of lines, with every region linked to the hub, but not to adjacent regions. The link between Bordeaux and Marseilles, or Strasbourg and Lyons, would be through Paris. The layout of the lines, Dobbin notes, bore a striking parallel to the structure of political authority in France, where Paris was supreme and the lines of political authority ran directly from there to the provinces. "French political centralization had spawned a plan for the most centralized rail network in the world" (113). True enough, but it was also the organizational interests of the Bureau of Bridges and Roads to see such a plan, independent of political centralization. The cost was born by the regions, and one might also argue that a more decentralized, regional system might have provided more experimentation and innovation and more variations adapted to local needs and terrains. Such an argument, we shall see, was put forth in the United States, in opposition to an emerging system of national railroads with just four major terminals for a nation much larger than the French one.

One final point that will be important later regarding Dobbin's contrast of France and the United States is the matter of "agency" — who or what did whatever was done. When Dobbin speaks of the American situation, the key agent is "Americans," or "the public," or "public opinion." In the absence of a strong state, there are only citizens, the carriers of the "institutional ethos." When he speaks of the French, the key actor is the state; only occasionally is it the Bureau of Roads and Bridges . He has depopulated the United States of organizations; the railroad firms are not significant actors or sources of "agency." For France, the source of agency is the centralized state, or "French political centralization," another abstraction; references to "the French" or public opinion are absent, presumably indicating that citizens did not matter. It is true that the United States was more turbulently democratic than France, and citizens had more of a say and the state less of one. But dropping down from that abstraction, and getting at the concrete mechanisms of railroad affairs in the two nations, we clearly find from his detailed account of France that the agent is the Bureau. His account of the United States, unfortunately, has little to say about railroad firms as agents. My account will try to rectify that.

Britain

In contrast to France, Britain did not have a strong state; power was dispersed among members of parliament and the crown. The crown, with a history of fear of large independent organizational interests, made it difficult to amass large pools of capital, and only reluctantly agreed to partnership arrangements. Industry and the railroads thus were made up of units smaller than in the United States or France. But the state was more centralized than that of the United States, though not as centralized and strong as in France. As Dobbin puts it, in the United States, decision authority was dispersed across three levels of government — federal, state, and local — and across three branches at each level — legislative, executive, and judiciary.

In Britain, financing for the railroads came from established pools of agricultural or industrial wealth; in contrast to France and the United States there was never any thought of public financing. Dobbin explains this in terms of the "institutional ethos" of the country — a "taken for granted" view of how things should be, a view that is grounded in the culture of the nation. But I would emphasize more specific configurations of interests and the capital for the new venture. The established agricultural interests of the gentry and the new manufacturing interests of the new middle class that would benefit from cheap transportation had the capital or access to it. Britain was already industrialized when the railroad came along; the investment in the railroads just linked established enterprises and agricultural and natural resources areas. The United States, however, was not industrialized, and not even that well developed. The railroads enabled American industrialization; capital had to come from elsewhere in the nation. But capital was scarce, and in the hands of Boston and New York merchants and ocean traders, who had less need for railroads. Indeed, initially they found them to be competitors for their traditional trade in raw materials and the importation of finished goods from England.

The English gentry and new manufacturing class would own and manage the railroads, and parliament, where most of these wealthy interests were seated, kept the crown out and even limited parliament's own overseeing of the investments of its members. The railroads would be "privatized," as we would say today (private ownership), but it was not a "free market." Realizing that unrestricted competition could lead to oligopoly, parliament allowed the formation of cartels to control competition. The cartels were made up of many small companies, but many were represented in parliament by their owners or stockholders. ("Free markets," as the United States has learned, can lead to consolidations and oligopoly, imprisoning rather than freeing the market, if there is no significant legislative oversight to prevent the accumulation of wealth and power.) With many small railroad lines, a great deal of integration and standardization was needed, but the British cartels achieved it; long lines with unmixed freight — supposedly the only efficient form according to railroad interests and the judiciary in the United States — were not used. Instead, regional, rather than national development was promoted, and local and regional towns were able to prosper. Land was both expensive and occupied, so they did not have the waste found in the United States, where Americans built parallel lines as a form of competition, or zig zag lines, as a way to get every little town to contribute capital. The British cartels fostered the cooperation that made extended runs possible without changing equipment, regulated track size, standardized equipment, and coordinated schedules from the start. (It took several decades to achieve this in the United States.) The last remaining problem, safety and comfort standards (putting roofs over the flat cars that the common folk used, for example), was established by parliamentary acts. The result was private capital, ownership, and management, which was coordinated by cartels and regulated by state agencies set up by parliament, and which was flexible and promoted regional development.

Operating under the laissez-faire principles that were soon to be formulated by Adam Smith (though not applied by him to public goods such as railroads), nonintervention by the state in business and commerce was a basic principle in both Britain and the United States. But the British, in contrast to the United States, protected the vitality and independence of individual firms as a source of industrial efficiency. "The logic of British policy was that rationality ensued when scores of small entrepreneurs competed freely without interference from politics or from larger, dominant, firms" (Dobbin 1994, 160). Thus Britain fostered cartels as a way to protect small firms from the predatory practices of big firms. In legal matters, the British believed that the law would enforce itself because self-interested individuals would use grand juries and common informers to protect their rights, and the best that government might do is to provide inspectors who would provide the grounds for private legal action. Britain did not even have the system of public prosecutors that the United States had. Government posts were staffed by parliamentary and local governments; although locally run, as in the United States, the railroads were subject to policies that emanated directly from parliament.

Colleen A. Dunlavy's account of railroads in Prussia describes yet another pattern: the railroads were thoroughly private enterprises, and during the 1830–50 period they received little state support. After that, the state took control (Dunlavy 1992). The state appears to have remained on the sidelines initially because it did not have the money, but it did have a well-developed highway and canal system that it ran and from which it profited. Prussia was not pressed, as was the United States, with development of virgin lands — railroads ran between established towns, alongside the state canals and highways, rather than to new areas where towns could be built. Dunlavy describes the U.S. railroads in this early period as heavily regulated by the individual states, but as we shall see, that regulation soon disappeared, if it was ever particularly heavy. Individual states imposed tariffs to protect their canal investments, as we shall see, but these were marginal by 1850.

As in most historical accounts, we are told nothing about the Prussian private railroad companies — their ties to the Prussian elite, their power as organizations, the corruption issue, and their source of capital. But it is clear that the Prussian state, once it moved into railroad transportation after the revolution of 1848 was defeated, was able to raise capital and begin an aggressive program of state building and bought out some private lines and established controls over the others, imposing heavy regulations on the railroads, as the national government did in Belgium (state-owned from the beginning), France, and Britain.

Dunlavy's account is in the tradition of "new economic institutionalism," which gives more weight to political factors than traditional historical or economic institutionalism. As such, there are no national "logics" or cultural attributions; the structure of the state and its politics is what counts most. In the case of the railroads, the dispersed powers of U.S. federalism could not cope with the capital intensive and interstate rail systems, and they went unregulated until a federal state finally gained some power in the 1880s. In Prussia, politics was centralized at the national level, but initially it had little economic power. After 1848 it achieved centralized economic power and established a bureaucracy that took over the control of the railroad industry, and the power of railroad companies counted for little. This interpretation is not inconsistent with the thesis advanced in this work: organizations matter. In France and Prussia they were state organizations, in the United States, with its weak state, they were private.

Thus, the key organization in France (and quickly in Prussia) was the state, with the railroad companies being very dependent; in the United States, the railroad companies were the key, with the state being dependent; in Britain, organization meant parliamentary supervision of private companies. State bureaucracy in France, independent and unregulated private interests in the United States, and legislative regulators of private interests in Britain, are three distinct expressions of an "organizational logic" that became institutionalized.

The Importance of the Railroads

It is obvious that the railroads were decisive in American industrialization; it is almost impossible to over estimate their importance. But it is useful to have a brief refresher regarding what historian Alfred Chandler dubbed "the nation's first big business" (1965). In the mid-1840s Chandler notes that "natural waterways still carry the lion's share of American commerce and sail remain the primary mover of goods and passengers over any extended distances, as they had been since the days of Greece and Rome." After 1846, the standard method of transportation, as well as that of communication (telegraph), changed "almost overnight" (3). During the late 1850s more canals were abandoned than built, and by 1860 the basic network of the railroads east of the Mississippi had been completed. The critical part of this mileage was completed in just five years, between 1849 and 1854. The length of a trip from New York to Chicago went from three weeks to less than three days, and this could be made during the winter when canals and rivers were frozen. The steam engine drove ships, too. The time for transatlantic travel went from an average of thirty-five days to under fourteen, and the tonnage of goods and passengers expanded greatly. The Western prairie was opened to settlement, and its basic crop, wheat, and its processed product, flour, could be moved to the urban markets of the East by rail and to Europe by steamships.

Here was *technology's* determinant moment: "The new volume and regularity of transportation made possible the swift rise of the factory in the United States. Prior to the mid-forties the modern factory, employing regularly as many as two hundred hands, existed only in the textile or closely related industries." In the 1850s, manufacturers had for the first time the transport to allow mass (factory) production. "In that decade, shoes, clothing, clocks, watches, sewing machines, agricultural implements, machine tools, and small arms for the civilian market as well as such basic materials as iron and brass all began to be mass produced" (8–9).

I have argued that the mass-production firms of the textile industry (the Lowell II model), predating the railroads, laid down the social pattern of industry. The mass-production firms institutionalized *wage dependency*, fostered the *concentration of wealth and power*, encouraged market control rather than innovation, and generated labor and community *externalities*. (This is why I consider the railroad as the second big business; these characteristics are more important than Chandler's criteria of the separation of ownership and control.) Chandler is correct to emphasize the overwhelming importance of the railroads. He points to their speed, efficiency, organizational innovation, and how they fostered mass-production industries. His "master narrative" (Somers 1992) is that the drive for efficiency created organizational forms that would determine the economic structure of the nation for the twentieth century. Here is the argument in brief for the importance of the railroads in terms of a sociological narrative.

Steam-powered iron horses and steam-powered iron ships radiated into the economy and the social structure of the United States much more than the textile factories could ever do. The steamships provided the export market that surged ahead of the goods and foodstuffs that the nation required, and created significant sources of wealth and global power. The railroad itself by the 1850s "was the largest single market for iron and a major market for coal, wood, machinery, felt, glass, rubber, and brass" (Chandler 1965, 9). What Chandler and other economic historians do not note is that this is the natural basis for exercising monopsony power — the power of a single or few buyers over many suppliers. The railroads used a small number of suppliers in the case of big items such as steel (consuming 80 percent of all Bessemer steel until 1880), locomotives and freight cars, and this concentrated these industries immediately (Roy 1997, 112–14). For leather and wood they dictated prices and conditions by playing off a large number of small firms against each other and keeping the industries disorganized. The men and families that headed the leading firms in concentrated industries became a part of the capitalist class, sharing a preference — along with the railroad leaders and the finance capitalists — for large organizations, because of their power, and for national rather than regional markets, because they concentrate power. The federal judiciary and much of the Congress supported the argument that big meant efficient. Thus in the United States (but not in Europe), the railroads concentrated wealth and power more rapidly and permanently than all other industries combined in that great gulp from 1850 to 1890. They transformed the weak national state and the somewhat stronger federal states through patronage, corruption, and many forms of subsidy, keeping the central political and regulatory power weak, and placed the concentration of wealth in private, rather than community, hands. This became the basis for the organizational revolution.

In the hands of most economic historians, including Chandler, the imprinting by the railroads of "the modern ways of finance, management, labor relations, competition, and government regulations" was a

matter of sheer necessity (9). To quote Chandler again, "[R]ailroad promoters and managers pioneered in all these areas not because they were
a particularly intelligent or perceptive breed of entrepreneurs, but *because they had to*" (9, emphasis added). As we have seen, they did not
have to do it this way in Europe, and they didn't; and the alternative
ways were efficient for those nations. And as we shall see, when we turn
to the scholarship of William Roy (1997) later on, the system of private
control and private financing with government subsidies that "made
possible the swift rise of the factory" did so in a way not apprehended
by Chandler and other economic historians. The factory was rising not
primarily for efficiency reasons, but because big factories meant market
control, and were made possible by the wealth concentrated by the railroads. Thus we must be wary of the economic historians' account, and
question at each point the necessity of the system that evolved. By the
1990s the notion that the economy is "socially embedded," to use Mark
Granovetter's felicitous phrase, is fairly well established in sociology, to
some extent in political science, and even a bit in economics. But the
embeddedness thesis as applied to the development of the railroads still
remains at a very general level—culture, "national logics," and public
opinion. We will dig deeper into that "bed" in which we all toss and
turn today.

WHY WERE THE RAILROADS UNREGULATED AND PRIVATIZED?

What has to be established in this section is why we arrived at the
private, barely regulated (but competitive) form that lasted from 1830
to about 1880, followed by a lightly regulated oligopoly, rather than the
British version (private, cartelized, but well regulated) or the French
version (nominally private, in terms of capital, but a state-run, single
system). This involves establishing four key points:

1. Neither the pure efficiency argument of economic historians,
nor the more nuanced organizational efficiency argument of Alfred
Chandler, will explain the development. I will label both of them the
"efficiency argument"; it is the dominant one in the literature.

2. The logics argument is that institutional norms rejected state
ownership and regulations that interfered with private liberties. I will
argue that there was no general, public agreement that railroads
should be privatized and barely regulated; the form that emerged was
not taken for granted, an "institutional logic" asserting itself, as neo-
institutionalists would have it. It was contested, and emerged victo-
rious because specific interests sought it. There is a weaker form of
the institutionalist argument that invokes public opinion and booster-

ism, without claiming a national ethos, that we shall review more favorably.

3. Cultural symbols were invoked to justify the arguments of the various sides at the time, but culture is always rather vague and commodious, and the culture of the United States at this time was sufficiently diverse and contradictory to allow support for four alternative tracks: state ownership and control, state ownership with private operation, private ownership and operation with state regulation, and private ownership with little state regulation. If our culture had arguments for all four, it is hard to see culture as decisive. (The cultural argument is a part of the neoinstitutionalist view, but worth considering on its own.)

4. The corruption argument takes into account the widespread corruption that existed in connection with the financing, construction, and operation of the railroads, but rather than being just a form of regrettable waste, corruption was an "agent" of the process. It enabled large centers of capital to shape the system in their interests and made the possibilities of regulation in the public interest quite remote. It was recognized as corruption by the criteria of the times. Thus, corruption was not incidental, but a key force; it was as integral to the system as were the factors of land, labor, and capital. Some corruption would be inevitable, but if it had been controlled, the system would have been quite different. I will focus upon the agents of corruption, the corrupters, not the recipients. It was not that legislators and government officials were, either by nature or because of the low standards of the time, corrupt, but that organizations were so successful in corrupting them. The very scale of corruption indicates its source was organizational, not individual.

The lack of regulation and enforcement by government authorities meant substantial inefficiencies. Communities poured money into schemes that never produced (trains never ran, ties were untreated and rotted, wooden rather than iron tracks were laid and useless within a year, bridges collapsed). There was overbuilding to destroy rivals and gain market control, or for sheer fraud. Innovations that would promote safety were resisted. Without regulation, competing lines chose different track sizes, resulting in gross inefficiencies. There was wasteful duplication of lines for speculative and monopoly purposes, routes zigzagged as towns put up capital, and then the lines were abandoned. Families were imported from Europe through deceitful advertisements and then dumped on inhospitable prairies and saddled with debts (Brown 1977), and exorbitant rates were set for local hauls, starving productive communities.

Only in a few respects was there much to praise about our first great industrial venture on a regional and national scale. Chandler is correct to argue that initially the greatest importance of the railroads was not so much their speed but their all-weather reliability (just as the value of the steam engine was its all-season reliability). For reliable operation, as well as high speeds, they needed precise scheduling and above all, few collisions. The organizational structure that developed (strong head-quarters with a divisional structure) was well suited to this and one other distinctive problem—fare setting, which was complicated, and fare collection, which offered opportunities for individual fraud. In all but scheduling and fare setting and collection, U.S. railroads were far behind European ones in their first fifty years. Compared to Europe they were poorly built, overbuilt, inefficient, dangerous, and slow to adopt innovations. (After the first fifty years, their oligopolistic and pro-tected market shielded them from the new competition from trucks and airlines and pipelines.) The costs to society can be assumed to have been enormous. The costs are rarely enumerated, however, because, in the view of most historians, whatever the costs, the railroad was *the* key to industrialization, an invention so tremendously important that by this logic all wastes seem trivial in comparison. But the importance of an undertaking should not shield us from inquiry into its wastefulness and its unfortunate legacies. (The railroad revolution is said to have brought about the second industrial revolution; it was followed by three more "revolutions": electric power, at the end of the century; the substitution of oil for coal from about 1930 to the present; and the current transis-tor and computer revolution.)

The Efficiency Argument

The economic explanations assume an efficient rational process that should prevail in any country. As noted, Davis and North (1971) argue in the standard economist logic that market considerations—cost of production and expected revenues—dictate whether the enterprise will be privately owned, quasi-governmental (that is, with strong govern-mental regulation), or fully governmental. Seavoy (1982) and Mercer (1982) make similar arguments. But the logic that makes private owner-ship of a nation's railroads efficient (the market capitalism logic) did not apply to France, Britain, and Prussia. If the economists' argument were correct, the nearly identical technology applied to quite similar tasks should have resulted in privatization in these countries as well, unless we are to believe that only the U.S. railroads were efficient. That is clearly not the case; despite some evidence of corruption and some unfortunate route setting, the French railroads were clearly more efficient than the U.S. ones.

According to Davis and North, the first U.S. railroads were largely owned by the states because only they had the capital. When demand for railroad services increased, future profits became more certain, and so the railroads relied less on public capital and, "naturally," became fully privatized ventures (1971, 140–43). This account requires some heroic assumptions of rationality that are puzzling in view of the tumultuous ups and downs, failures and bonanzas, overbuilding, contingencies, and corruption seen in the historical record. Omniscient economic actors in this account make nearly impossible calculations of the "discount rate," or opportunity cost, of capital invested in railways, while admittedly miscalculating wildly by not anticipating the unexpected windfall of Mid-Western economic growth, unforeseen even by the early proponents of New York's Erie Canal.

The level of corruption was unprecedented for the nation, but while acknowledged, is treated as irrelevant to the rational economic account. There were phony investment schemes, financial heists, planned bankruptcies, and absconding with public capital. The climate of careless overspeculation was partly responsible for the Panic of 1837 and the ensuing depression. While the financial collapse of the late 1830s prompted many state legislatures to get out of the railroad business, thus hastening privatization, cities and towns continued to fuel the investment boom in railroad construction through the 1870s. This suggests that investment in the railroad industry was motivated more by short-term profits (on the part of developers) and overoptimistic projections of future earnings (on the part of municipal investors, who contributed to the widely noted "boosterism" of pre–Civil War America) than by the rational calculations of costs and long-term profits, as economists assume. These notably "irrational" actions (their term) seemed to have stimulated the growth of American railroads nonetheless, evidence that there was much more at work here than well-reasoned calculations and conventional business acumen.

At one point in their account, Davis and North make a short sideline excursion that fits poorly with the logic they lay out: an "attempt to explain the location of railroads in Jay Gould's western empire would turn any economist's hair grey if his or her only analytical tool were distance minimization, traffic generative abilities, or any other twentieth-century criterion. Instead, the location of those roads, twisting and turning across the plains like a terrified snake, can only be explained in terms of the bribes certain towns and counties were willing to pay" (Davis and North 1971, 155). Duly noted, the real world is then ignored and the rationalist account speeds down the tracks. As we shall see later, even corruption is formulated as a sin of the public official; that the railroad companies offered the bribes is conveniently ignored.

Alfred Chandler's explanation for the privatization of U.S. railroads is alarmingly simple: "Because they operated common carriers, railroads, unlike the major canal systems, became privately rather than publicly owned enterprises" (Chandler 1977, 82). That is, the railroad companies built and owned the tracks, the rights-of-way, and also operated the trains that ran on them — (this is what is meant by "operating the common carriers"), and these actions necessitated private ownership. (Why other countries did not find private ownership a necessity is not addressed.) The state built canals, but allowed anyone to put boats in them; they did not operate the common carrier. Private ownership of the railroads, according to Chandler, is required because trains can't easily pass one another as barges can in a canal. The railroads, when they were horse-drawn and slow, allowed others to use their rails and experimented with hauling cars owned by local merchants and freight companies. But the coordination problems were immense, and once the steam locomotive speeded everything up, coordination and safety considerations dictated that the railroad companies operate all the trains, and thus we have the privatization of the system. It is, at least, an organizational explanation. But the coordination problem could be solved by state ownership, and was in Europe; it does not require privatization. For a more complex and interesting explanation of privatization in the United States than the efficiency arguments, we must turn to historians and then the neoinstitutionalist account of Frank Dobbin.

Historical Institutionalism

First we will consider the traditional historian's natural institutionalism, which is less heroic and self-conscious than that of the social scientist. Carter Goodrich (1960) is one of the most eloquent supporters of this view, but Louis Hartz (1948) is not far behind. Both recognize the factors we shall be emphasizing: railroad interests and corruption, cultural ambiguities, and contingencies; and I will use their works to document these factors. But these are not out front; they are behind two more important forces: "boosterism" and decentralized political power. The United States was a rich, virtually unpopulated and undeveloped country, pushed ever westward by waves of immigrants and high natural population growth. Major cities such as Philadelphia, Baltimore, New York, and Boston attempted to control the trade as the railroads first conquered the barriers to Pittsburgh, Albany, St. Louis, and so forth. Citizens demanded railroad transportation, at whatever cost. This demand would suggest that the federal government could easily have been the agent, as it was generally in Europe. Not so, says Goodrich, but not because of antistatist or cultural concerns, but because of the clash of interests.

> The rejection of the federal government as the principal agency of the program is partly to be explained by constitutional scruples and the doctrine of states' rights and perhaps even more, as has been suggested, by the inability of rival local and regional interests to agree on a common national program. Yet the selection of the alternative agencies is also to be understood as reflecting the fact that the individual states and ambitious commercial cities were themselves object of political and civil loyalties that were often more intense, and much more easily lined with specific economic interest, than the more general sentiment of national patriotism (Goodrich 1960, 288).

That is to say, there were qualms about the constitutional legality, but at basis it was the rivalry of the local areas and indifference to the national good. He does not cite, as we shall see that Dobbin does, either an enduring culture or hostility to federal ownership or control.

The systems were initially local — short lines — and the interests were local; local governments had the authority over the lines and "were willing to incur such heavy charges for them." Government at all levels was utilized, of course, but there was a strong "preference" (on the part of the railroad companies and merchants) for governmental aid to private corporations rather than for public construction and public ownership. Public construction and ownership appears to have been the last resort, and the towns would have been happy if private firms had bought out the public ones. Regarding regulations, "there was a general tendency to leave initiative and the responsibility of management mainly to the private elements in the combination, even in cases in which the greater part of the funds came from public sources" (289). Whence this tendency to turn public funds over to private corporations without control? It could have been cultural or due to efficiency reasons, or it could have been the product of lobbies and bribes. Goodrich gives us ample evidence of lobbies and bribes, but refrains from giving these as the cause.

He notes that "private investors" (i.e., the railroad companies) did not like government directors to take an "independent attitude," and that the president of the Baltimore & Ohio line "waged a long campaign to rid his company of its majority of state and city directors." In many cases the legislatures simply forbade public directors — there by law, because as much as 80 percent of the funds were public — from voting (289–90). Goodrich accepts the justifications put forth by the railroads and their government allies: private enterprise is efficient, government is not. It is assumed to have been too obvious for him to document.

But some of the public's representatives seem not to have agreed. When ample evidence of corruption appeared, the legislators and commissions tried again to exercise the public interest with different forms of support or different agencies of overview. Communities were desperate to have train service. Goodrich knows that there is an organizational pressure and railroad corruption explanation, but discounts it in favor of boosterism and the political culture. "There were also, as we have seen, cases in which protestations of public purpose were no more than a cover for cynical raids on the public treasury. Yet it would be quite impossible to read the history of American improvements without realizing that they were commonly regarded as a 'great cause' appealing to the enthusiasm and 'zeal' as well as to the economic interest of subscriber and citizen" (292–93). Thus we have "a set of characteristics long familiar to students of American history. Among them are a decentralized structure of government, a distrust of centralized national plans, and a pragmatic attitude in the choice of means" (294).

As convincing as this last quote might sound, it can be questioned. The United States certainly had a decentralized government structure; but regulation would not have been inconsistent with decentralization — only federal ownership of the lines would have been. And there is much evidence that regulation was attempted, but failed. Why it failed is the key question. (Dobbin has an extensive discussion of the quite sensible attempts to control the railroads [1994, 19–34].) That private interests would be more efficient — even from their private-interest point of view — if left unregulated is certainly disputable. Indeed, we could easily argue just the opposite, given the problems with overbuilding, price wars that led to abandonments, the use of different gauges, resistance to safety devices, and so on. These inefficiencies harmed the public more than the railroad companies and the bankers, but the latter lost money from them nevertheless. States were at times quite effective in regulation and the operation of railroads. Massachusetts imposed rate regulation and it worked, and the state of Georgia ran an efficient, profitable line for decades (Phillips 1906), and the city of Cincinnati did so into the 1920s (Persons 1934, 53). Historian Persons says that the "repudiation" of state railroad investments was "mainly confined to the Southern states" (76–77). Federally operated plans for a centralized national system were put forth, but it is clear that they had little chance.

A STATE OWNED AND RUN RAILROAD

The story of the Georgia railroad is instructive in the details that contradict the economic explanation and even the softer one by historians such as Goodrich and Hartz. Could the state of Georgia, or any state, run an efficient railroad? Would it not need a strong, reasonably incorruptible state government, the likes of which would not be easily found anywhere in the New World, and certainly not in the South? Ulrich B. Phillips, a renowned turn-of-the-century historian, describes one that did work, the Western and Atlantic Railroad in Georgia, which operated from 1836 to 1870. He called it the most important example in our history of government ownership and operation of a railroad. (Phillips's staunch Southern conservatism and defense of slavery hopefully has not influenced his account.) All the reasons cited by subsequent historians and social theorists as to why such an enterprise was against the American "spirit" are contravened. The railroad paid revenues to the state and had only one (fatal) episode of corruption, whereas few private ones were without corruption; and it was apparently supported by libertarians in the state. The railroad successfully negotiated the presumably intractable problems of sectionalism and even got along with privately owned spur lines that fed its track. While small by later standards, its 138 miles were over twisting and steep mountains.

Initially the railroad was based upon the needs of cotton growers in the Piedmont region to get their goods to the Atlantic coast, and shortly thereafter, as a route to the West to bring in cheap foodstuffs. The first proposal was in 1826 by a gentleman who would soon become the governor of Georgia. As steam engines were unheard of in 1826, teams of mules would pull the wagons over the wooden rails. Ten years later, in 1836, when steam power was becoming available and some private steam lines were built (they would later become spurs of the main line), business leaders and politicians met to consider the original mule route proposal. It was an urgent matter, for South Carolina threatened to build a competing line to the West, and Georgia's cotton was threatened by the booming cotton fields in the Alabama and Mississippi bottoms. But private capital was not to be risked. If the planters had any surplus capital at all, says Phillips, they "were so eager to buy additional land and slaves" that they had little left for corporate investment (1906, 260). The profits on both land and slaves was high and rising; the profits on railroads seemed insecure in comparison. It was decided that the state should own and build and run a steam railroad, and lend money to those who would build branch lines. So far, a typical story. Most of the nation's railroads started out with substantial or full public financing.

But then the "tremendous crash of 1839" hit the state. Those who found themselves in debt called for the state to make loans to private corporations. But the state, for unexplained reasons, continued to support the state-owned railroad. It was almost abandoned and contractors suspended work in 1842, but none of the private feeder lines were being built either. Work soon resumed, and the line reached Chattanooga in

1851, using profits on its completed sections to reduce the drain on state finances. A town at the southern end of the road was initially called Terminus; with increased traffic, it became Marthasville, and finally Atlanta (278).

During the whole period from the 1839 panic to completion, the possibility of selling the railroad to private interests was vigorously debated. The arguments are familiar — on the one hand, the sunk costs were so large, the state should continue; on the other, don't send good money after bad, and furthermore, private ownership was more efficient. Even abandoning it was proposed, and one argument for this in particular illustrates the economic sophistication of the commentators. Tapping the West would ruin the splendid isolation of Georgia, bringing in cheap foodstuffs and increasing the state's dependence upon cotton, which in turn would lead to overproduction and ruin the market. Diversified agriculture would be better for the whole South; driving the farmers out of cereal and live stock production would permanently injure the wealth of the community. (It seems that they were right!)

Philips, like all historians and social scientists, reverts to "the people" arguments at times, but here "the people" made an unusual choice — for state ownership.

> The people were anxious lest the road and its money should become the instrument of political tyranny and corruption, but feared, on the other hand, that a still greater power would be established for possible evil if the road were sold or leased to a private corporation (279).

Note the ease with which we may invoke the "public" when x happens, but also when non-x happens, without requiring that we provide hard evidence about "the public." Perhaps the public didn't know or even care much about the issue, and the decision was based upon the organizational interests of the well-established government agency that had not been corrupted by outside interests or corrupted by its own structural interests. Perhaps they were responding to colorful, but hardly implausible, arguments such as the following editorial concerning private interests:

> A large corporation, like a mighty colossus, with one foot at Savannah and the other at Chattanooga, will bestride the state, whilst its iron fingers will be felt in every election and will direct the future legislation of the State. No matter what guards and checks this legislature may throw around such a corporation, when they once get control of such immense resources they will elect a legislature to suite themselves and will break all these bands like cobwebs. We are willing to entrust the management of the road to the people, whether the Whigs or Democrats are in power, for we believe that the large

majority of both parties are honest men and their agents are always responsi-ble to the people for their conduct, but a gigantic corporation has neither soul nor conscience and owes no responsibility to any tribunal whether in heaven or on earth. The influence of corporations is already felt in every fibre of our legislation; it can be seen in every vote that is taken on this subject, and if ever these corporations get control of the State road, they will govern the State (cited on 274–75).

The construction of the railroad by the state was not without its "un-questionable extravagances" and some shoddy construction, but it was graded for two tracks from the start and was inspected by bipartisan committees of the legislature a few times and found to be free of cor-ruption. It did not pay as much as the private feeder lines, but it was argued that by following the mule team route, the state railroad faced the high cost of maintaining tracks on continuous curves, and it did not, in the end, have the precious freight of large cotton traffic with its high tariffs to defray the expense. But it still paid good dividends with net earnings of four- to five-hundred thousand a year before the Civil War and Sherman's destructive march through Georgia. After the war, the railroad returned large profits while spending large sums on rebuilding. But in 1870 the governor appointed a new administrator and suddenly there was "wholesale mismanagement, extravagance, and plundering, shared in by numerous politicians" (281). Disclosure brought pressure to sell or at least lease the road. Companies were quickly formed to buy or lease it, offering bargain prices. The decision was to lease, and the successful bidder was headed by an ex-governor, accompanied by rail-road presidents, politicians, "Democrats and Carpet-Baggers." The terms were generous for the private interests that leased it.

We might conclude that even a less-than-pristine state was able to run a successful railroad without corruption for thirty-four years, bringing in good revenues, until a corrupt governor privatized it. Successful pub-lic ownership, anti-big-government cultural sentiments notwithstanding, was possible. Public ownership of a common good, when possible, would seem to be preferable to private ownership.

Historical Institutionalism Assessed

Rather than citing an "ethos" or culture of "public distrust" toward a strong central government, I will argue that a federal system was quite unlikely with the absence of a federal organizational interest compara-ble to the Bureau of Bridges and Roads, with the local nature of the lines up until the 1850s, and with the role of the railroads in creating new sectional economic opportunities (rather than linking existing eco-nomic centers, as occurred in both Britain and France). Local communities clamored for service, and if private capital could do the job, they accepted privatization, since there was no national plan and few state plans for state-owned lines. Many of these initial local lines, public and private, failed. There were not many privately owned lines that were large enough to lobby at more than the local level, and large enough to attract private capital and also public funds. But when they did emerge in the late 1830s they opposed government ownership (while seeking public funds if no regulatory strings were attached) and lobbied at the local and state level for friendly laws. There was not so much distrust of a federal railroad transportation system by citizens (one can find statements on both sides of the issue), as a lack of examples of federal railroads. By the time a national railroad system could be conceived, say in the 1860s, government at all levels, and especially at the judicial branch, had made it impossible, and government was responding to the direct and specific interests of the emerging railroad barons more than it was responding to "public distrust."

Dobbin joins Goodrich on the issue of expanded public controls with a dubious generalization: "Americans believed that the only cure for corruption—expanded public controls—was worse than the disease" (Dobbin 1994, 58). He seems to contradict himself by also saying "graft soon put an end to federal, state, and local activism" (24). In point of fact, neither assertion bears much weight, neither the urgency to build at any cost (if the urgency was so great, why did state after state pass "anti-investment" laws that would presumably hamper railroad expansion?), nor the notion that public controls were worse than private corruption (if so, why the widespread reaction to corruption and the extensive pubic control devices to thwart it?). Indeed, to be convincing, the institutional argument from the historians would have to demonstrate that (1) government was inept, even where private interests did not attempt to corrupt it, (2) that even if the corruption facilitated privatization without regulation, privatization would have happened even without corruption, and (3) that restricting state funds would somehow promote the expansion that should come at any price. A far simpler explanation is that railroad organizations and the commercial and banking organizations behind them prevented efficient regulation, and they sought state funds without controls, but not when controls were attached. For the railroads, the cure for capital shortage—public controls—was worse than the disease.

The Neoinstitutionalist Account

The neoinstitutionalist view, put forward elegantly and forcefully by Frank Dobbin, is a more muscular, theoretical, and conceptually sophisticated version of the historian's institutional view. It holds that large chunks of social life are not subject to continuous rational inquiry in terms of costs and benefits, as economists might think, but simply taken for granted. Most of our activity is of this sort; it is the supreme social efficiency to live by stereotypes, "common sense," routines, standard operating procedures, and so forth. We often speak of these chunks as "culture," or norms or values or national character. They tell us how to evaluate, what to expect, what to do. Thus, it was unthinkable that the Bureau of Bridges and Roads would allow private interests to operate the railroads in France, or that government money should be used to finance construction in Britain, or that the U.S. government should own and operate the railroads in the United States. These chunks are described as "logics," that is, a cluster of practices that make sense and appear logical; they are "institutional" logics because the word "institutions" connotes an enduring and valued structure of behavior.

As such, a sociologist can have no quarrel with the notion of institutional logics; we do take things for granted, value some of these — and enough practices are associated with these things to justify a grand term like "institutions." But one may have some reservations with Dobbin's use of the notion. First, in his terms it marginalizes not just the rational economic interpretations it is primarily directed against, but also the interest group interpretations that he also criticizes. I will argue that *interests* are the source of many logics — e.g., the organizational interests of the French Bureau of Bridges and Roads in controlling the new railroad technology contributed to the "logic" of government control of common carriers and other public goods. Second, I will argue that contrary to Dobbin's view, and indeed most such cultural views, competing logics often exist, and the one dominant in one decade can be replaced by a quite different one in the next if either large organizational interests put their mind to it, or if exogenous historical shocks (e.g., the Panic of 1837 or the embargoes of the early 1800s) appear. This gives a greater role to organizational interests, but also to contingencies or happenstance in a path-dependent view of history. (As an example of the latter, the timing of the appearance of the railroads meant that large state investments in canals were unexpectedly devalued, contributing to public support for privatization. Interests could seize on this opportunity, but they did not create it.)

Dobbin's war is primarily with economists, and their insistence upon rationality and universal economic laws. We have already joined him there. Secondarily his war in his book on the railroads is with those who see behavior as driven by interests, group interests, and, by extension, organizational interests, and there we cannot follow him. (Much of his later work, however, emphasizes power and interests, e.g., the

discussion of early Massachusetts railroads in Dobbin and Dowd 2000.)
He is opposed to the "pervasive interest-group thinking in the social
sciences" (1994, 129). As evidence, he finds that "strong" interests
groups "lose political battles all the time," making one wonder how
they could be strong if this were true. Why do they lose? "[I]t is often
because political culture offers their opponents [other interest groups,
presumably] compelling arguments and offers them little in the way of
rebuttal" (129). This is hardly compelling, because strong rebuttals met
every compelling argument at the time. Strong interests not only lose all
the time, in his view, but are not independent variables anyway; he argues that they are simply manifestations of cultural "logics" or ways of
seeing things and ways of thinking. Interests are dependent variables,
logics are the independent ones. (I will argue that in addition to being
quite mutable, logics are often the product of interests, not the other
way around.) Once we understand the logic, Dobbin argues, we can
understand the policies that will flow from public opinion and from
interest groups. Once a nation has a "logic," a way of thinking, an
ideology, "one need only to grasp the logic underlying current policies
to guess what future policies will look like, because policies in different
countries follow fundamentally different logics." In the United States
they are "organized around a logic of natural selection," a survival of
the fittest, that follows from a hands-off policy on the part of the federal government. If the federal government is limited in its scope, this
will allow the competition of private interests to select winners and
losers. Furthermore, "these logics are palpable and enduring," not
vague and transient (11). (Today's reemergence of natural selection and
privatization arguments after about sixty years of welfare state growth
suggest that the enduring logic went to ground for an awfully long
time.)

A brief note about *culture* is appropriate here. Historians use the
term casually and find it neither compelling nor problematic. Sociologists and political scientists, however, have a large stake in it. The logics
are a cultural product; but, it seems, everything is a cultural product.
Dobbin has a totalizing cultural approach; culture is not to be contrasted with "structure" or "instrumentality," it includes them. It includes instrumental means, "such as government, markets, firms, and
science." He does not limited it to symbolic systems "such as the arts,
religion, fashion, and education" (13) because to do so would impov-
erish cultural studies, and would remove "instrumentally rational institutions from the purview of cultural analysis" (14). Instrumental institutions are not to be contrasted to cultural ones, because they represent
"means and ends in the world, and as such they are necessarily cultural." Because everything has a cultural aspect, no distinction is made

between what is often referred to as "the culture of industry," (the norms, values, and practices of industry), and the structural and instrumental aspects such as investments, technology, forms of power, organizational structure, concentration, and so on. The term "industrial culture" is the one used, rather than the culture of industry, and industrial culture is everything—the "practices and associated meanings" (18). Dobbin simply does not tell us what is *not cultural*. Instruments and means are culture. So are "rationalized organizational policies" because they are "social constructs," socially constructed policies. That which is not culture, then, is presumably that which is not socially constructed. But for a sociologist such as myself, it is obvious that everything is socially constructed—our perceptions of "economic laws," our interests, our power, our technologies, and so on. The only distinction he allows, and it is not explicit, is between interests (a not very important agent in history) and all else (that is, culture).

Dobbin's account (and that of most historians as well) is that the institutional ethos of free market competition and natural selection forbade either a federally owned system or a closely regulated private system; public opinion, not organizational interests, determined the shape of our first big business and the shape of our subsequent national industrial policy. He sums up our early history in an important, if uncharacteristically ponderous sentence:

> In short, the social practices associated with community self-rule were constitutive of order in the United States' institutionalized political culture, and social practices associated with the concentration of authority in the central state or in private hands were destructive of order (35).

What this says is that people preferred local community power over centralized federal power or the power of private corporations. No doubt. We would all agree with that even today, and as an "institutional ethos" it cannot be denied. But did the American people prefer a virtually unregulated set of private interests running the transportation system that was to bind us as a nation? There is no evidence for that, and how that came about is the important historical problem. The first thing to note is that there was no strong French state in existence, not even the strong parliament of Britain; the nation was adding territories and states faster than its own federal government could grow. The only effective regulatory agencies at hand were the states and the local governments, and the evidence is that they tried hard to regulate the railroads.

Even Dobbin's book shows that state and local governments initially used their powers both to promote and to regulate the railroads, in contrast to the "logic" of the Darwinian struggle and privatization.

Dobbin says that for the first three-quarters of the century, "What is most striking about these early ventures . . . is that governments were unhindered by any reticence to intervene in the economy" (34). Initially "Americans gave substantial control over railway planning and finance to local and state governments, as direct representatives of the public will" (35). (This was true initially in all European countries also; the lines were experimental and short, so control was local.)

The rest of his argument in brief is that corruption among railroad officials and public servants emerged; this demonstrated to the public that direct government promotion of industry endangered "private liberties and public legitimacy." This was not a fear of the federal government, almost nonexistent in railroad transportation, but of state and local government. Pubic aid to private enterprises was curtailed, and with it the possibilities of regulation. Instead, "subsequent policies were oriented to sustaining the economic liberties of railroads and their customers" (35–36). The institutional ethos of the American public, he argues, was to protect the liberties of shippers and railway owners. But with control over pricing and competition in private hands, oligopoly emerged after the Civil War, and brought forth regulatory policies to outlaw "restraints of trade." Still, the government would not regulate directly, but merely ensure free-market mechanisms, as with the Interstate Commerce Commission of 1887, and natural selection was expected again to take place as nature designed it and the conservative institutional ethos formatted it.

The Organization Interest Account

Let us exchange this account of nameless agents and cultural logics for one with some concrete actors. I will briefly lay it out in grand terms, without evidence, in this section, and then present the often colorful details and evidence in subsequent sections. Throughout, please note the substitution of organized interests for ethos and logics.

Local merchants and industries needed railroads; railroad entrepreneurs would build them, but needed financing. Local and state governments authorized public funds to the entrepreneurs, but sought control over planning, rates, and safety as a condition of using public debt. Public-private collaboration *was* an institutional ethos, deeply rooted in our culture. (There are such ethos; the question is what historical contingencies and what organizational interests can derail one and promote another, and particularly, whether they explain our railroad history.) The public-private collaboration soon broke down under the pressure of the railroad companies. Attempts at regulation were enfeebled by the lack of a trained and independent state bureaucracy, organizations who would find it in their interests, because of their mandate, to regulate. The increasing strength of the railroad companies and their allies, the shippers, and, after the Civil War, the centralizing banking interests, made regulation difficult. Even the first federal agency, the Interstate Commerce Commission, did little more than encourage self-regulation. Contributing to the ascendency of these organizational interests was the support that they received from the judiciary, and the weakness of the legislative and executive branches of state and federal government, and thus their vulnerability to corruption by organizational interests. The companies bribed judges, legislators, and government officials. The corruption was on a grand scale, and the profiteering and mismanagement resulted in waste and overbuilding, using public funds.

The financial panic of 1837, which was partly due to the corruption but largely due to federal fiscal policies, led to significant losses (20 percent or so) in the public investment in all forms of transportation (canals, turnpikes, and railroads). Legislators, with strong backing from public opinion, as far as can be judged from newspaper reports and referendum votes, passed laws forbidding public investments in transportation policies at the *state* level; the corruption was apparent, the investments were losing money, and those parts of the state that did not have railroads resented the use of their tax monies. Some railroad companies opposed these restrictions on public loans, because they cut back upon free funding; other railroads supported them, because the public funding still imposed some regulations, and the private market for funds was expanding because of the profitability of the railroads. Local funding of railroads increased as local business and agricultural interests sought the access to markets that the railroads provided. (I suspect that local funding was quite particularistic and cozy, and thus more advantageous to the railroad companies than state funding; local legislators would be easier to influence.) Other railroads received private funding, through stocks and bonds; these would be preferable because no controls would be attached.

This takes us through the first burst of building, most of it local and regional, prior to the Civil War. The war brought a second burst of expansion, but it was now more interregional and, more importantly, national, as the lines began to seek out the Far West and the Pacific. Even prior to the Civil War the system was thoroughly privatized, with some exceptions, but the railroad companies were still successful in getting local and state funds. After the war, federal support in the form of direct aid and gifts of land was very extensive. But the companies resisted all regulations that could have accompanied the governmental largess, and successfully fought in court any challenge to their centralized economic power. The new institutional ethos was in favor of heavy federal government support, and increasing competition as the regional lines began to compete for access to the major cities the railroads had effectively built or expanded, and to compete for interregional lines. But free-market competition led to further overbuilding by railroad companies; watered stock by their financial representatives; stock market crashes; high local rates that furthered a national, rather than a regional, system; and oligopolies. A new logic, a taken-for-granted ideology of industrial structure was needed to legitimate the new reality, because it was declared illegitimate by farmers, labor, and reformers. The large, remaining railroads sought government regulation to stabilize the oligopolistic system, promoted the ICC, which did not regulate but just adjudicated conflicts between the giants, and the system was celebrated as the enduring logic of government protection of "the economic liberties of railroads and their customers." This is the substitution of organized interests for institutional ethos. Here is the story in more detail.

The Details

THE LEHIGH PRECURSOR

The clash of corporate and community interests is endemic in U.S. history from the early 1800s on, as we have seen in the case of textile mills. Resources and, in the case of transportation, rights-of-way are given to corporations; using this advantage they can limit competition, make abnormal profits, and ignore local community interests. The Lehigh case illustrates how aware citizens and small entrepreneurs were about the dangers of private interests yoked to state grants of resources. Instead of a railroad rights-of-way, we have a state-owned river, but otherwise there is little difference. Before there were railroads, there were rivers and canals for transport, and the eastern seaboard was blessed with these routes. But coal was up in the mountains, and the rivers were swift. Early in the nineteenth century, anthracite coal was discovered to be a resource of immense importance to the state of Pennsylvania. The "early anthracite canals failed largely because of the hazards of navigating mountain streams," notes historian Louis Hartz in his classic study of economic policy and democratic thought in Pennsylvania in the early century (1948, 58).

To encourage development, the state legislature gave charters to coal companies, in this case the Lehigh Navigation Company, which would have sole jurisdiction of the Lehigh River for eighty-three miles and could both mine and transport the black gold. Organizational power was evident from the start, eliminating the liberties of citizens in the name of liberty. "The Lehigh company, under the effective Josiah White, discouraged the competition of individual miners by charging prohibitive rates for transportation over the Lehigh, and it maintained its own coal prices at a level which evoked criticism in Philadelphia" (Hartz 1948, 59). In effect, the company turned the river into a common carrier, as railroads were to do with their rights-of-way.

Individual operators protested, though rather mildly, noting that a corporate charter with state protection was no longer needed for the exploitation of coal resources because of the unprecedented sums of Philadelphia capital available for mining investment after 1825. A senate committee made a thorough investigation and agreed. The coal trade, in their words, "can now be brought entirely within the control of individual means" (60). Individual enterprise, rather than a corporation, would produce an economical division of mining labor, whereas a conglomerate sitting astride the waterway would lead to inefficiencies and thwart local development. Break it up, they said. The committee held that "the owning of lands, the working of them, the transportation of coal, and its sale were four distinct functions that a single business unit could not combine effectively." As dubious as that argument might be, given the skill by which organizational leaders were able to coordinate different functions, the committee also argued more cogently that this corporate system lead inevitably to monopoly and high prices. The Lehigh company was charged with deliberately overproducing in order to ruin unincorporated competition by flooding the market (60).

Remarkably enough, the senate committee made a quite modern argument for small firms, even if they had to be corporate in structure. They said, "It may become necessary for the purpose of preserving divisions of labor, and to keep down monopoly, for the Legislature to authorize limited partnerships, with limited capital, limited parcels of lands, and so restricted in other respects as to promote the very objects for which individual coal dealers now so laudably and legitimately contend. That even corporations could be erected, and with these advantages, cannot be doubted" (60). In contrast, the large corporation such as the Lehigh one was governed by a distant board of directors and this was held to challenge its economic adequacy. But more important still, echoing the contrast of the big Manayunk and small Kensington firms in Philadelphia textiles, the committee contended that a "community growing up under an incorporate company differs from that created by individual operators," because civic improvements and the living conditions of the workers were neglected in the communities dominated by corporations. Hartz summarizes that "communities at Mauch Chunk, Carbondale, and Tamaqua were declared to consist 'only of the servants and laborers of the companies,' while communities at Port Carbon, Minersville, and other areas worked predominately by individual producers were lauded as examples of civic progress." The corporations were furthermore blamed for the evil of speculation, as the Pennsylvania governor had asserted in 1837, and they were usually motivated "by some plan to dispose of a particular tract of land to great advantage, and not by intention of real investment" in the field (61).

The corporations provided a rebuttal that, not surprisingly, given his overall endorsement of the "master narrative" of our economic development, pleases Hartz: "[H]owever shoddy some of these arguments may have been, the reply of the corporation defenders was obviously sound in substance" (62). Their arguments included the following points: Growth would be retarded as the industry tried to expand, if it did so under individual operators. Furthermore, much more can be known about the capital of the corporations than that of individuals, and this was an insurance against speculation. Moreover, there was less incentive to fraud by the corporation because "such measures with them require too many accomplices to admit a frequent success, whilst no such restraint exists with individuals" (62). The corporation provided steadier work and the corporations did not have pernicious labor conditions. Starting in 1849 there was a series of general industrial incorporation laws, which Hartz sees as promoting acceptance of corporations despite the "heavy criticism of industrial corporations" (62).

The vignette indicates that there were considered attempts at regulation, an implicit endorsement of a strong government; that the arguments are the same ones we hear today; that the positive social welfare consequences of networks of small firms (a hot topic today), were recognized; and finally, Americans did not go into that new future without warning. The "ethos" we were to adopt was debated, even was up for grabs.

A brief comment on the "large organizations versus capitalism" issue, raised in the first chapter: It is possible to argue that capitalist interests shaped the organizational form of the Lehigh corporation, and thus capitalism is the real independent variable. But capitalism had long existed without large, corporate forms, and could neither make the kinds of arguments that the Lehigh one did in justifying its power, or use those kinds of power. The state charter created the conditions for the Lehigh corporation to organize in the way it did. Once organized, its *powers* and its *interests* as an *organization*, rather than as an expression of individual owners of capital, became determinant. The particular powers and interests of the owners existed only because of the organization that they were able to set up. The small-firm alternatives suggested by the senate committee would also involve capitalists, that is, individual owners, but not the concentrated power of the Lehigh *organization*.

GOVERNMENT OWNERSHIP AND REGULATION OF THE RAILROADS

Turning to the railroads, we should note first that the federal government did not expand its powers commensurate with the expansion of its territory and population. But it was taken for granted that state and local government would support commerce and industry for the common good, and transportation was a part of that. Charters were given to companies that allowed them extensive powers, or local and state governments formed "mixed corporations" that received public funds and governmental oversight. In 1844 more than 150 mixed corporations were listed in the official records of Pennsylvania (Hartz 1948, 290). The monopoly given the Lehigh Navigation Company was a commonplace, and public funds usually went with it. Historian Colleen Dunlavy, explicitly states that: "it has become impossible to speak of 'laissez faire' in the antebellum American context" (1992, 117). (Hartz even titles part four of his book "The Myth of Laissez Faire.") Indeed, comparing the United States with Prussia, she says, "Direct and indirect state participation in railroad development proceeded on a much grander scale in the United States during the 1830s and 1840s than it did in Prussia" (121). Prussia had no state-owned railroads in operation through the 1840s. At least the following states built and operated railroads themselves: Pennsylvania, Georgia, Michigan, Indiana, and Illinois. States also invested heavily in private railroads. During the 1830s, state governments alone contributed roughly 40 percent of all railroad capital.

Hartz argues that after 1825, when public works began to expand in Pennsylvania, "public ownership was not only accepted as legitimate but was believed by the overwhelming mass of Pennsylvanians to be practical and desirable as well" (1948, 166). (Public ownership could thus be labeled an "ethos" by Dobbin's criteria, rather than be treated as out of the question.) His account then details how private interests gradually moved the state out of control and ownership. Despite his evidence for the importance of private interests, his general explanation for state withdrawal leans toward a vague change in public opinion, inefficiency of the government, and corrupt legislators. In the 1820s and early 1830s even conservatives favored state ownership of expensive transportation projects, such as Philadelphia's Main Line canal and the Union canals. "The commercial and financial interests in the east did not desire to undertake the works project themselves," but wanted the government to get them built for development purposes (Hartz 1948, 140–41).

The state of Pennsylvania owned the Main Line canal and a section called the Columbia Road. The state passed a bill in 1834 that empowered the canal commissioners to "put locomotives on the Columbia road and operate them for the profit of the state." Contradicting Chandler's thesis that the necessity of common carriers meant privatization, the "state supplied the motive power, while private firms supplied passenger and freight cars." It was an anomaly, however. But what ruined it was the inability of state agents to collect tolls from the private companies. The governor declared in 1842 that for its four-million-dollar investment it received returns of only 3 percent, while the companies using the road received returns of nearly 200 percent on their thirty-thousand-dollar investment (146). But in 1842, contrary to our supposed fear of big government controlling services that private interests could supply, the governor of Pennsylvania moved to have the state run the line outright, i.e., take over the passenger and freight cars as well. He was defeated; "the private companies appear to have had an influence at Harrisburg sufficiently powerful to stifle the scheme of complete state ownership" (147). Here we have some agency other than "public opinion." A suspicious deal whereby the Main Lines' new owners were granted a multiyear tax exemption was challenged in the courts, but predicably the private owners were able to get the courts to hold up for years a decision that would be unfavorable for them (146). The exploitation extended to the workers; "common workers were at a disadvantage in collecting money, being unable to resort to the bribes and political pressure sometimes used by big contractors" (156).

According to historians, there was popular "revolution" against state enterprise after the depressed economic conditions of the late 30s (Goodrich 1960, 148–51). But the shift in policy was by no means final, and Dunlavy notes that "state and local investment still accounted for an estimated 25%–30% of the roughly 1 billion invested in railroads before the Civil War" (1992, 122). There may have been a cultural resistance to the *federal* government financing and running railroads, but it is hard to make even that case because railroads were still quite local projects without an obvious role for the federal government. But no resistance is evident in the case of state and local government. She notes that before the Civil War, states and lower levels of government contributed nearly three-quarters of all canal investments, and four-fifths of the government's share went into publicly owned works (125). Even the federal government proposed national canals and roads, and Congress frequently voted for this on a modest level, which calls into question Dobbin's institutional logic even at the federal level.

The gift to private firms was substantial; state and local governments "afforded powers of eminent domain, donated rights-of-way through public lands, and aided private railways with loans, bond subscriptions, and cash donations." If this did not work, they built railroads themselves. Until 1860, every significant line received state and local aid. At least half of the capital invested in early American railways was provided by states and localities (Dobbin 1994, 40–41). And this excludes publicly purchased rights-of-way and tracts of land granted in lieu of cash.

The courts routinely vetoed any federal role on constitutional grounds. The courts were the most conservative, free-enterprise agency in the country outside of big business. But in support of Dobbin, Hartz, and just about all historians, I should note that the courts' narrow interpretation of the constitution probably had wide public acceptance. Just what the Constitution allowed in the area of public goods troubled many groups in society. There was little precedence for federal support of anything, other than post offices, harbors, a few surveys, the military, and some local canals and highways. Though a General Survey Act was passed in 1824 authorizing military engineers to conduct a survey for canals and roads, Thomas Jefferson was unable to get a plan approved for an interregional road, a presumably legitimate federal responsibility. So I do not want to overstate the case; there was uncertainty as to how much the federal government should undertake, and this was not the case in, say, France. In the United States, privatization of state-financed railroads was more likely than a federal transportation system. But to call the privatization of the railroads and especially their freedom from regulation a "palpable and enduring logic" is misleading. There was too much local and state governmental support, too much advocacy of public ownership and control, and too many attempts to regulate private companies. Had railroad organization interests not prevailed, I would argue, we might have had at least a heavily regulated, well-planned, efficient, and safe railroad system, if not a federally owned one.

GOVERNMENT DIVESTITURE OF OWNERSHIP AND CONTROL

With the economic slump of 1837, states began to pass anti-investment laws and constitutional amendments. Sometimes these anti-investment laws reflected the private appropriation of public goods; as Goodrich notes, "[I]n extreme cases, mixed enterprise came close to representing simply the private control of public investment" (1960, 248). In others there were tax revolts by those who paid state taxes, especially if their sector of the state did not stand to benefit directly. The anti-investment laws forbade state investment in private economic ventures, most explicitly, turnpikes, canals, and railroads. By 1853, when the issue came up in Pennsylvania, such amendments had already been enacted in Ohio, Illinois, and New York. Because government regulation of railroads was weak in Pennsylvania, such that no effective strings were attached to public funding, the proposed law was against the interests of the railroad companies. The courts, predictably, sided with the railroad interests and threw out the legislation. The opponents of public investments then sought a constitutional amendment. The public was not asked whether the powers of the state government should be increased to fight waste and corruption, the roads reorganized, and new taxes passed to cover the losses due to the panic, corruption, and inefficiency. That is what the Bureau of Bridges and Roads did in France when it, too, suffered from the panic. Instead, the amendment merely posed the issue as one of the state getting out or losing more. The proposal to end public investments was overwhelmingly passed by those enfranchised to vote.

Though the railroads opposed the measure, they won in the long run, Hartz perceptively and strongly implies. He notes the irony in the position of the amendment supporters, who were property owners whose taxes would rise with further public investment in the railroads: "[T]he withdrawal of public investment in the transportation field in the 1850s meant inescapably an exclusive reliance upon private corporation." Those opposed to any public investment were implicitly "presenting a defense of the corporate system. Nor is this altered by the fact that corporate attorneys were their main opponents; corporate interest desired to maintain the flow of public funds, even if this meant disparaging the strength of the corporation and disseminating doctrine which, amusingly enough, evoked the charge of Skidmorian socialism" (Hartz 1948, 120). Note that at least a tradition of mixed enterprise was being overturned here, if not necessarily a full-fledged "institutional ethos." Hartz goes so far as to put the following in italics: "the constitutionality of the entire mixed enterprise tradition as it had evolved since the late 18th century was thus challenged for the first time" (117–18).

Hartz is sensitive to the novelty of the private corporation, and has a subtle analysis of another issue, the anticharter movement. This sought to protect the small, unincorporated business from the likes of the chartered Lehigh Navigation Company and its steamroller tactics. The movement, in Pennsylvania at least, was strong as well as colorful in its language. One supporter spoke of the innumerable corporation failures that "now press upon the country with the dead weight of an incubus" (172). Upon the sale of the Main Line to the Pennsylvania Railroad in 1857, a bonanza for the railroad, not only did the pro-sale party get turned out by voters opposed to the sale, but the heavy lobby pressure to sell, which Hartz says "had pretty clearly been involved," invoked a remonstrance. It was argued in the legislature "that this bill was engineered through by the paid borers [lobbyists] of the Pennsylvania Railroad Company, who infested the legislative halls, to tell the representatives of the people that they demand the sale of the public works" (165). But the new corporations subtly incorporated the "ethos" of the small firm and the individual entrepreneur that opposed the granting of valuable charters, Hartz notes. "The corporate system was simply beginning to appropriate for its own purposes the rich individualism of the anti-charter theory. Its defenders either spoke in the name of 'individual enterprise,' or casually obscured the entire distinction between unincorporated and chartered business by speaking of 'private or corporate' enterprise with which the state had right to interfere" (174).

While Pennsylvania railroads opposed anti-investment legislation, because public funds with few or ineffective controls were in their interests, in New York State the railroads took the opposite stance; they wanted government out of the transportation business. By the 1840s there were immense profits available from shipping goods from the Midwest to the East coast, as evidenced by the enormous success of the Erie Canal at the time. But because the state owned the canal, it charged the railroads tolls and restricted the construction of railroad lines that would compete with the state-owned canal. The railroad companies lobbied for constitutional provisions to exclude state funding of internal improvements; capital from the private market was plentiful, so why suffer the regulation that would come from public funds. They recognized the long-term interests of "exclusive reliance upon private corporation" as historian Ronald Seavoy puts it (1982, 100–101; 208–9). But by 1855 there was so much trouble with safety and such extensive profiteering and price-gouging in the railroad industry that a state railroad commission was established. But the state senate abolished it two years later. Seavoy says that the public was "not ready" for a commission, but, as with most accounts that invoke "the public," his offers no evidence of this. In an aside he does admit, "It appears that bribery was involved" (211–12).

While Seavoy generally uses economic efficiency and the public's supposed resistance to strong state action as his explanation for privatization without regulation, and for the subsequent appearance of giant systems, his account (like that of Hartz) is punctuated by the acknowledgment of the power of organized, corporate interests. For example, regarding their opposition to state financing, Seavoy bluntly says of the major companies that had the main (that is, the "trunk") lines, "[T]he director investors wanted the profit opportunities of trunk line railroading for themselves and accepted the constitutional provisions that excluded future state participation in internal improvement projects, just as bank promoters had previously succeeded in excluding the state from participation in the banking business." At this point, the policies of railroad investors and fiscally conservative democrats coincided. It was to "keep the state from subsidizing any more canals or railroads." Finally, he notes that the railroad business was on the threshold of immense profitability due to technological improvements (Seavoy 1982, 201). It was time to control those profits. Later we shall consider the organizational alternatives to the national system that developed, to address the efficiency arguments of Seavoy and nearly all other historians. But as virtually unregulated private interests in the railroads set the stage and form for the great consolidations and oligopoly in much of the rest of industry during the 1890s, it is important, for now, that we detail the overwhelming role of organizational interests.

Chandler echoes Hartz's explanation for the constitutional amendments: the "depression of the late 1830s and early 1840s, however, convinced many disgruntled taxpayers that state supported internal improvements resulted only in high taxes with little improvement in transportation to show for them. Many state constitutions were then amended to prohibit the use of state funds to finance railroads or canals" (Chandler 1965, 43). But his next sentence contradicts this explanation: "in the 1850s, promoters therefore turned to local county, town or city aide or to the federal government." Because the voters had rejected state aid, how were the railroads so successful in getting the public to approve it at the local level? No historian appears to have puzzled over this, so I will venture two reasons. First, local politics were probably more susceptible to influence than state politics. Second, as Hartz repeatedly emphasizes, sectional interests were very strong, and reached their zenith over the question of the railroads. ("So intense was the sectional feeling in the West in 1846 that there were repeated threats that if the Baltimore and Ohio were not given the right of way to Pittsburgh, the western counties [of Pennsylvania] would secede from the state and form a new trans-Alleghenian commonwealth" [Hartz 1948, 43].) Those parts of the states that would not benefit from a line, or from a particular line, would be opposed to funding in general, whereas local interests would support it. Neither explanation, however, accounts for the increase in *federal* funding that followed the anti-investment amendments and laws. It is possible that, especially after the Civil War, the railroads were more influential at the two extremes, the federal and the local level, than they were at the state level.

The railroads were certainly influential at the federal level, as demonstrated when the federal government urged the building of transcontinental links after the Civil War. Economic historian Lloyd Mercer investigated the financing of the seven lines that were to link the Midwest with the Pacific, and finds governmental support for them to be extensive—but necessary. (The seven projects were the Central Pacific, Union Pacific, Texas and Pacific, Santa Fe, Northern Pacific, Great Northern, and one Canadian line, the Canadian Pacific.) Without the largess they would not have been built, or much delayed, he argues, and for national development they had to be built urgently. For example, the federal government gave 6.93 percent of U.S. land to the railroads, and when we add the state grants the government largess totaled 9.46 percent of the area of the continental United States (Mercer 1982, 7). Using the value of the systems in 1863 as a base, he finds that 20 percent of that value came from government grants, and when the even larger loan subsidies are added, 38 percent of the corporations' value came from the gift of public funds (82). For three railroads receiving aid (Central Pacific, Union Pacific, and Great Northern), no aid was required — even without aid, the investment would have been at least as good as other investments (143). The larger lines enjoyed a roughly 10 percent increase in the value of their securities as a result of the aid. Mercer does not consider corruption as a serious matter, and of course, it cannot be quantified for his type of econometric analysis. Land grants were not the most efficient means for financing the railroads, he says, since they involved speculation rather than insurance. (Recall that France in effect used government loan guarantees for private investors as a form of government insurance.) But for political reasons, he says, they were inevitable; it was a case of land grants or no railroads (27, 148).

Mercer's is a thorough analysis of "economic rationality," but that means that it is quite narrow. His estimate of the "social good" of the railroads is based largely on the land brought into cultivation, and of course there is no question that railroads are better than stage-coaches for linking the shining seas. But there were negative as well as positive *externalities*. The amount of corruption was, by all accounts, enormous, but it is not seriously considered in his accounting. The corruption weakened the already "weakened springs of government" that Farnham (1963) describes so well. This had policy implications for other regulatory duties and judicial acts. The U.S. military became an adjunct of the transcontinental thrusts, an expensive proposition for the country and certainly for the Native Americans. Working conditions were frightful for the Chinese but also for the Irish and others. They went for months without pay while the construction companies, owned by the railroad officers, charged inflated prices and pocketed great profits. The haste was expensive and unseemly, dictated by the rivalry for government bonds between the Central Pacific, coming from Sacramento, California, and the Union Pacific, coming from Omaha, Nebraska. The common estimate is that it raised the price of the roads (largely paid by the government in the case of the Central Pacific and Union Pacific) by 25 percent, and justified by economists who reasoned that if the building took twice as long, the loss in economic productivity would have been greater (Mercer 1982, 25). But as we shall see, the most important externality, considered positive by most economic historians, and negative by a few others, was that "nearly all the instruments and techniques of modern finance in the United States were perfected in order to fund the construction of railroads and to facilitate their growth through merger and acquisition" (Chandler 1990, 58), a matter to which we will return.

Self-Interested Opposition to the Railroads

Throughout this book I have pursued an "interest" interpretation, modified by contingencies and happenstance and historical context. The interest interpretation applies not only to the railroads, but to their opponents. I will review the opposition to the railroads since it was often based on very narrow and self-interested actions, rather than a concern that corporate behemoths were at large in the land. Henry Varnum Poor lambasted the railroads for their poor management and corruption, but he was also a most vigorous spokesman for the value of the railroads, and pointed out how opposition to them would halt progress and saddle them with inefficiencies. As a case in point, he noted the inefficiency of rate setting when railroads competed with state-owned canals. The canals suffered the most from the coming of the rails, and they were in most cases state owned and operated, and thus received state protection. Both Pennsylvania and New York required the railroads that competed with state-owned canals to pay tolls to the canals equivalent to what the canals charged. The canal charges, higher than those of the railroads, had to be added to the railroad charges and refunded to the state owned canals! In New York these laws were not repealed until 1851, and in Pennsylvania tolls continued until 1861. The organizations that benefitted were not just the state companies. With reference to the Erie Canal, the flour mill operators, bargemen, and freight-forwarders along the canal agitated throughout the 1850s to reimpose the tolls, according to Chandler. Eastern farmers and their infrastructure were threatened by the competition from the rich western lands. The tolls, of course, hampered economic development, and raised the price of food in the East (Chandler 1956, 188).

Henry Poor also protested the economic particularism of the states. Some states refused to charter a railroad terminating in any town outside of the state; New York would not allow a bridge to be constructed at the northern tip of Lake Champlain to shorten the route from Boston to the West; Virginia tried to block two railroads from crossing its territory; Mississippi insisted that an out-of-state railroad had to deviate many miles to serve a Mississippi town; and Maryland and New Jersey, key territories for one of the nation's most traveled routes, placed a heavy transit tax on passengers and freight moving through their states. Pennsylvania prevented the Erie Railroad from using the most practical route, which carried it for some miles into Pennsylvania, and finally demanded an annual tribute for allowing the Erie to straighten its line. Pennsylvania's legislature passed a law prohibiting the use of six-foot gauges in the state, blocking further incursions from the Erie.

When the New York Central, in 1853, signed a contract to change the gauge of railroads they had just bought so as to be able to run a train from Buffalo to Cleveland without unloading goods and passengers in Erie, "the citizens of Erie met this threat to their prosperity by tearing up seven miles of the new track as soon as it had been laid down" (Chandler 1956, 188–89). The New York Central persisted, defying a municipal ordinance, and a series of armed clashes followed, with two townspeople wounded and much railroad property destroyed. The governor of Pennsylvania cheered the rioters on, the legislature annulled the charter of a connecting road about to be built, and the governor thundered on about the duty of the state "to turn her natural advantages to the promotion and welfare of her own people"—that is, to resist the competition threatened by the two New York railroads (190). Of course, the Pennsylvania Railroad agreed with the governor, but the point is that more than the organizational interests of the railroads were involved in the struggles surrounding the new form of transportation—citizens, workers, farmers, freight forwarding companies, legislatures, and state officials sought their economic self-interests.

Conflicts between towns within states over routes, spurs, the location of facilities, and so on were familiar; this was a new technology, and there were no established means of adjudicating conflicts. In fact, the railroad line, once in operation, increased the difficulty by increasing the speed of travel and communications. For example, New York state had a hodgepodge of contradictory laws and statues, and it retained David Dudley Field, a prominent New York lawyer, to rationalize them. He performed a famous act of codification and standardization, but in some respects, to little avail. Much of the judicial system was in county hands, and once the railroad made it easy to go from one county judge to another, the railroads could shop for a judge that would give them the best verdict. If one side had bribed a judge for a favorable ruling, the other side could quickly travel to an otherwise remote county, and purchase another ruling, and send it back instantly by telegraph. Codification was irrelevant; valid but contradictory rulings were relevant. Indeed, in New York state at one point, there were three contradictory rulings that required enforcement, and millions of dollars were at stake. Into this massive ambiguity and legal fumbling, three factions—Commodore Vanderbilt, and two Erie Railroad factions—moved, and fought battles with all their organizational resources (Gordon 1988, 161–71). Tidying up the law was necessary but far from sufficient; preventing the corruption of judge shopping would require more basic reforms, and the most powerful organizations in the country at the time, the railroads, were not interested in such reforms.

While a variety of groups sought their economic interests, and undoubtably there was some corruption in the government canal and turnpike systems, the corruption in the railroad system, everyone agrees, was enormous. And it is to this that we have to more explicitly turn.

CORRUPTION OBSERVED BUT NOT INTERPRETED

No history of the railroads in the United States fails to mention three patterns of illegal behavior that I will lump together under the term corruption: bribery (e.g., of judges and legislators), illegal or deceptive financial dealings (e.g., watering stock, paying dividends out of stock issues or loans rather than out of profits, getting public funds through deception or misusing the funds and spending them on proscribed projects), and violation of regulatory statutes. (I will use the term "corruption" rather than "illegal activity" because many activities only subsequently were declared illegal; we do not pass laws against unimagined behavior.) While all might be seen as examples of individual failings, they are also organizational in their origin. It is in the interests of the organization that legislators be bribed to do away with legislative oversight of rates and profits; that public funds be received for projects that are not to be carried out; or that, in order to gain market control and drive out competitors, that rebates to large shippers be provided, even though regulatory statutes prohibit them.

A large variety of organizational conditions may encourage corruption (regardless of the character and interests of the individuals doing the corrupting). Ferocious rate wars because of overbuilding is likely to tempt some railroads to break the laws. But even with a secure monopoly or oligopoly with high profits, it may be deemed necessary to secure one's future through corrupt practices. Or, in a secure firm, one department or division, competing with others within the organization, may seek advantages through illegal or corrupt means. (They may justify their behavior because of pressures from the top to perform, and top officers may say they knew nothing of the infractions, and deplore them.) Some corruption may actually sacrifice the organization in the interests of personal gain, as when owners are willing to allow a railroad to fall into bankruptcy after having stripped it of its assets and transferred the assets to their personal accounts. (This was fairly common in the nineteenth century.)

Corruption is important to our story in two ways. First, it involved "social costs." It entailed a waste of society's resources, as in overbuilding or destruction of competing organizations and thus of the social and economic capital entailed in an organization's failure; and evasion of laws that protected workers and communities from negative externalities such as accidents, pollution, and devaluation of infrastructure investments. When a third of a stock is fictitious and half of the trackage must go into receivership, the social waste is enormous. I do not credit arguments that say that some waste was inevitable in such a gigantic undertaking; the waste was enormous and it was occasioned by actions of the organizations that were not "inevitable" but deliberate and avoidable.

Second, and more important for the future of corporate capitalism, corruption played a role in removing legal restraints. By corrupting judges and legislators, organizations could shape the powers and freedoms they would have. Through corruption, laws were voided and new laws enacted, and these cleared the path that enabled large organizations to concentrate wealth and power. Bribing Pennsylvania legislators, for example, enabled the Pennsylvania Railroad to obtain legal permission to hold shares in other railroads, setting the stage for mergers in railroads, and industry in general at the end of the century.

One might ask, would the railroad system have been different if there were no corruption? For corruption to have been prevented we would have needed strong governmental institutions, so the question would have to be "what would the system have looked like if government was not weak?" and the answer to that is "very different." The extent to which the railroads centralized wealth would have been reduced, since the returns from corruption meant more profits for the corporations and bigger dividends to investors (who were mostly large investors). Reducing the social costs of overbuilding, pollution, accidents, and so on would have released more capital for other uses as well as minimizing the displacement of social costs to the less powerful citizens, such as workers. But most important, the corporations would have had less latitude to merge, limit liability, and forestall public regulation. Fairer rates, fewer accidents, less powerful corporations (and investment houses), and less recklessness on the part of owners would have resulted. As we shall argue, the railroads imprinted the corporate structure on the next century, giving corporations powers that were difficult to check. To some extent the railroads were going to imprint future economic development, regardless of corruption; they were bound to be a powerful force. But they would have been less powerful and less destructive, and probably more efficient.

In both cases, social costs and legal restraints, the ability to get away with corruption was a characteristic of the organizations that did the corrupting as much as it was a characteristic of "robber barons" or the emerging capitalist class. Capitalists seek profits, of course, but the kind of organizations that they build determine the social costs that the society will bear, and the powers and freedoms that the organizations will have. With a weak federal state, unable effectively to regulate an interstate activity, and a privately owned industry that needed eminent domain for its routes, railroad routes could make or break communities and economic activities more certainly than weather patterns (droughts, perfect planting seasons) and natural catastrophes (fires, earthquakes, floods). We must therefore add ease of corruption to the usual "factors of production" (land, capital, labor, technology, and organizational form). Because corruption was so easy for the railroad system, due to the weak state and the vital nature of its product, the system was not shaped as much by efficiency considerations as it could have been (contrary to the views of economic historians), as by opportunities of illegal and unethical gain. It is as if a few people (men, as it was) were able to say, "Here is an opportunity for maximizing our personal, organizational, and class interests through illegitimate means that carry scant risk. The product is needed, the regulatory agencies are weak or can be bribed, and the states can be played off one against another because this is an interstate business."

The weakness of the state, in connection with the railroads, is the theme of Wallace Farnham's essay, "The Weakened Spring of Government': A Study in Nineteenth-Century American History" (1963). For a more general statement, see David Vogel's article "Why Businessmen Distrust Their State" (1978). He says, "The relative retardation of the development of national political institutions in the United States has no parallel in any other capitalist nation." While a fair proportion of the Fortune 500 largest industrials were around in 1909, "the modern American bureaucratic state — professionally administered and collecting and distributing a significant share of national wealth — really dates from the presidency of FDR. Not until the late thirties did the annual revenues of the federal government rival those of the assets of the largest industrial corporation. In an almost literal sense, public bureaucracy in the United States is only half as old as its counterpart in the private sector; most corporations are far older than the government agencies of comparable importance" (58). The private sector received its first national bureaucratic institution with the consolidation of the railroads at

the end of the century; the public sector did not become equally organized for another half century (59).

Despite the waste, the railroads were immensely profitable, but corruption meant that the profits were not returned to either the governments that subsidized so much of it, or even to many of the private
investors (shareholders and bond holders), but to a small group of executives and financiers. This concentrated wealth, and the power that
comes from it. The corruption also contributed significantly to two major market crashes, impoverishing many not directly connected to the
railroads, and slowed economic growth. Corruption counts, but few
historians and few social scientists of whom I am aware have done any
counting. As we shall see, they tend to blame the victims, not the per-
petrators — the large organizations.

If scholars see and document so much corruption, how do they explain it? I could find no detailed histories that dealt with the railroads as
organizations engaged in lobbying, joining with merchants and shippers
in getting public funds, fighting regulation and accountability, and generally using the organizational tool to shape the commercial world to
their liking. There is strong evidence that they did, but no organizational studies of the deed nor few details in the secondary sources. The
detailed studies we do have of the companies focus upon internal organization, staff and line problems, relations with subcontractors, and the
like. Indeed, when the issue of government largess and corruption
comes up, it is not the interests served, the railroads, that are considered
the source of this behavior, but elected government officials who "actively and deliberately promoted industrial development in those years
without questioning its efficacy, or the propriety, of doing so" (Dobbin
1994, 42). The railroad companies themselves were presumably passive
targets of this official enthusiasm.

Evidence From the Public Record, and the Outcry

It is not the case that corruption was so commonplace and a part of the
ethos of the time that we, presumably like people at the time, must
accept it as the price of building the economy with the new and unfamiliar tool of the railroads. Corruption was widely discussed, condemned, and legislated against in the state and federal legislatures and
the press and the political campaigns of the time. Indeed, the nineteenth-century counterpart of the Internet and fierce investigatory jour-
nalists existed in the numerous pamphlets and tear sheets of the time. A
research assistant, Mark Zimny, turned up dozens of pamphlets in
Yale's Beinecke Archives on Early America, which thundered, in won-

derfully colorful language, against the railroad monopolies and their control of the political process. One, for example, from Portland Oregon in 1881, quotes such distinguished sources and people as *The New York Times*, the *New York Daily Graphic, Harpers Weekly*, U.S. Senator David Davis, former U.S. Attorney General Jeremiah S. Black, Indiana Governor Gray, and so on. The Anti-Monopoly League had its publications. Most of these pamphlets are long on explosive rhetoric and short on details or evidence.

But not all. A gentleman named Rufus Hatch, for example, issued five circulars in 1871 that exposed the watered stock, exorbitant rates and tolls, and so on of the four trunk lines connecting New York City with the Far West. He concluded that through stock waterings, fictitious construction costs, and profits on land grants, the four roads, all controlled by Commodore Vanderbilt, realized profits of $135 million "in excess of the actual cost of these roads—enough, expended without waste, to build and equip a first-class, double track, road—steel rails and iron bridges—from New York to Omaha, and with a line to St. Paul" (circular no. 5). On one road alone, the Hudson River Railroad, he calculated that Vanderbilt made a profit of $48.6 million and $3.9 million in annual income, yet "refuses to pay to the Government, in the shape of an Income Tax, the paltry sum of 5 per cent, on the amount of his waterings," and was "brow-beating the Commissioner of Internal Revenue" on the matter (circular no. 1).

A series of articles in a magazine by no less than Henry Adams and Charles Francis Adams was so popular that it soon appeared as a book—*Chapters of the Erie* (1886)—and was frequently reprinted. It was a stunning condemnation of wildly extravagant corruption centered on the New York railroads and their masters. The Adams's book and others as well as the press discussed the open bidding for votes. In one example, Commodore Vanderbilt is dismissed by legislators for his "paltry" offer of only $1000 (and only half of that in cash), while Jay Gould was paying between $2000 and $3000 for a vote. (This is a case of extortion by the lawmakers, but for higher fees; Vanderbilt and Gould had long ago subverted the legislators.) That year, 1868, the New York State Legislature, perhaps grown comfortable with this source of illegal income, *weakened* the law on corruption, such that, as John Steele Gordon puts it in his colorful book on Wall Street and the railroads, "as long as a legislator took care to be out of earshot of a third party and took his bribe in cash, there was no possibility whatever of his being convicted of a crime" (1988, 185).[23] Characteristically, when mentioning the book by the Adams, Chandler describes the combatants, Vanderbilt and Gould, as using "ingenious" illegal tactics, thus sanitizing the corruption (1977, 149).

On the other side of continent, the machinations of the owners of the Southern Pacific—Charles Crocker, Mark Hopkins, Leland Stanford, and especially Collis P. Huntington—were detailed in the broadsheet "The Colton Letters: The Inside History of an Infamous Procedure (Huntington 1890) and another titled "How Members of Congress are Bribed" (Moore n.d.). David D. Colton held a fifth interest in the Southern Pacific management. When he died, according to the author of the first pamphlet, Stanford, Hopkins, Crocker, and Huntington "attempted to swindle the widow out her rights in the company, and litigation followed, during which the Huntington letters to Colton were introduced in evidence." Huntington had purchased the Colton residence in San Francisco, and the surrender of the letters was included in the purchase negotiations. Of the 600 letters, only about 200 survived and were part of the records of the Superior Court of Sonoma County, California. They are instructive. The charge is that the Central Pacific, which received government aid of $77 million, absorbed its earnings in the construction of the Southern Pacific, an example of fraud. Though the letters provided ample evidence of the fraud, the United States courts ruled they were inadmissable. Some mention Thomas Scott, President of the Pennsylvania Railroad, under whose tutelage the company achieved the status so admired by Chandler, and who was competing with the Southern Pacific for government grants and legislation regarding transcontinental routes. Scott was apparently every bit as corrupt as Huntington et al. The following few excerpts cover the period Chandler describes as cooperative, rather than the competitive one, when trusts were formed to set the rates that the lines would charge (Chandler 1977, 137–43). Appearing at a time of cooperation, when corruption would appear to be less necessary, the letters, from Huntington to Colton, make the evidence of corruption especially interesting.

Nov. 20, 1874: "Friend Colton: Scott is prepared to pay, or promises to pay, a large amount of money to pass his bill, but I do not think he can pass it, although I think this coming session of Congress will be composed of the hungriest set of men that ever got together, and that the devil only knows what they will do."

Sept. 27, 1875: "If we had a franchise to build a road or two roads through Arizona (we controlling, but having it in the name of another party), then have some party in Washington to make a local fight and asking for a guaranty of their bonds by the United States, and if that could not be obtained, offering to build the road without any aid, it could be used against Scott in such a way that I do not believe any politicians would dare vote for it. Cannot you have [Arizona Governor] Safford call the Legislature together and grant such charters as we want, at a cost of say $25,000?"

Jan. 17, 1876: "I have received several letters and telegrams from Washington to-day, all calling me there [Huntington worked out of New York City], as Scott will certainly pass his Texas Pacific bill if I do not come over, and I shall go over to-night, but I think he could not pass his bill if I should help him; but of course I cannot know this for certain, and just what effort to make against him is what troubles me. It costs money to fix things so that I would know his bill would not pass. I believe with $200,000 I can pass our bill, but I take it that it is not worth that much to us."

March 7, 1877: "I [stayed] in Washington two days to fix up the Railroad Committee in the Senate. Scott was there, working for the same thing; but I beat him for once, certain, as the committee is just as we want it, which is a very important thing for us."

Oct. 10, 1877: "I think I have the bridge question settled for the present (over the Colorado at Yuma). I found it harder to do than I expected. The Secretary of War told me that they had it up in two Cabinet meetings and had concluded not to do anything, as Congress would come together next week, but I got him out of that idea in about twenty minutes. I then saw three others of the Cabinet; then I went and saw the President. He was a little cross at first; said we defied the Government, etc., but I soon got him out of that belief."

Oct. 29, 1877: "I saw Axtell, Governor of New Mexico, and he said he thought that if we would send to him such a bill as we wanted to have passed into a law, he could get it passed with very little or no money; when, if we sent a man there, they would stick him for large amounts."

Oct. 30, 1877: "The committees are made up for the Forty-fifth Congress. I think the Railroad Committee is alright, but the Committee on Territories I do not like. A different one was promised me."

Nov. 9, 1877: "I do not think we can get any legislation this session for extension of land grants, or for changing line of road unless we pay more for it than it is worth."

Nov. 15, 1877: "If we are not hurt this session it will be because we pay much money to prevent it."

March 4, 1878: "I think it would be well if we had more parties in California that were interested with us; there is the Oakland water front; if some of the army officers had an interest in that property I think it would be well for them and for us."

With such purchases of governors and legislators, it is not surprising that efforts by public officials to regulate the railroads were so ineffective. But it is possible that when government bodies, legislative and executive, willfully avoided regulation, they were *not* doing the bidding of large, powerful organizations in the private sector, but rather, were demanding bribes from the railroads. Most of the histories appear to leave room for this interpretation, since they emphasize the corruptness of government, not the corrupting power of the railroads, or merely sanitize the acts or make them commonplace representatives of the low standards of the time. The materials just presented and those that follow do not support this view, but it must be mentioned as a possibility, at least in some cases.

If government officials engaged in extortion, and the railroads complied, I would assume the payoffs to be strictly personal, and not the result of an organizational policy in the government agency or legislature to extract payoffs and distribute them to the bureau or legislature. They would not be "organizational" in that case, whereas if the railroad company did the bribing, it was more likely to be an organizational policy. It is not important to my argument whether or not government personnel were engaged in extortion. The historical record does not document it or even suggest it was common, but it would be hard to discern even if it were. It is important to my argument about the role of large private organizations in the century that the *organizational* interests of the railroads encouraged corruption, and that this not only entailed large social costs but changed the rules of the game for all corporations.

Here are some more examples of government doing the bidding of corporations: The government held three-fifths of the stock of the Bank of Pennsylvania, but the legislators limited directors representing the public funds to four of sixteen directors rather than ten of sixteen, as the holdings would indicate (Hartz 1948, 97). Control responsibilities "were even less effectively discharged" in the transportation area, and "in many cases the legislature failed completely to provide government directors" (100). Hartz reports that in the case of four turnpike or bridge companies, with substantial government finance, "private directors simply refused state agents admittance to board meetings." State agents complained that "the managers refused to let us act." But, avoiding an interpretation that would feature the role of private organizational interests, he does not fault the organizational representatives, the managers or the directors, though it would seem that they had the upper hand. Consistent with his ideological position he blames the state, which "had evaded responsibilities for control too long to assert itself" (102). That is, if business corrupts the state for a sufficiently long time (rendered as the state evading its responsibilities in his account), it is the state's fault that it is weak.

Even when a railroad executive is identified by historians as engaged in corruption it is as an individual, not as a corporate actor. The actors in the following account of one important railroad appear as solo bandits, not masters of an organizational resource that can be put to use for the owners' interests. The president of the Northwestern Railroad Company in Pennsylvania faked 24,994 shares to qualify for public aid, and then spent $40,000 before anyone was the wiser. The directors of the company "distributed twenty-two thousand dollars to themselves for their own services and voted to release their treasurer from responsibility for accounting for private funds that had never been collected" (Hartz 1948, 96). Before the legal revolution starting in 1819, this would not have been possible.

Commentators at the time offered less convoluted accounts of corruption than have historians since. Henry Varnum Poor, crusading editor of *The Railway Journal*, advisor to financial houses, and ideologically conservative but full of rectitude, exposed corrupt practices constantly from 1853 to 1860. Pouring over the meager reports submitted by the railroad companies and comparing them with their dividends, stock issues, and the profits of the construction firms to which their officers were allied, he appears to have dragged every major railroad through the *Journal's* pages. (For an endless account, see Chandler's chapter 6, "Financial and Administrative Reform," in his book on Poor [1956].) Some examples: the Michigan Central carried out no construction but increased its construction account by $4 million, and then paid high dividends. Dividends, Poor sensibly concluded, were paid from capital rather than profits. With a monopoly on the richest route in the country, the Camden and Amboy nevertheless found it necessary to make new bond issues, that is , borrow heavily, and then paid high dividends, using the loans to do so (Chandler 1956, 140). Two New York lines, both charged by Poor with "negligence and inefficiency," were spectacularly defrauded by their directors, and a third, the notorious New York Central, endlessly watered its stock. The worst, in his view, was the Erie. Notes Chandler, "In 1853 and 1854, Poor accused it of violating every canon of sound financial management" (140–1).

Officers and directors speculated openly in the Erie's securities and apparently "were manipulating its accounts to hide incompetence or worse," according to Chandler's summary of Poor's editorials. Its total funded debt had been rising since 1849 at an average of $3.5 million for three years, and as it was unsecured, it must have been paying dividends from borrowed funds (141). Its running expenses were being paid out of the construction account, allowing it to inflate its earnings by more than half. But the Erie was one of New York's main commercial arteries to the West, and "Horace Greeley's *Tribune* and other civic-minded New York papers came quickly to the Erie's defense." In time, Poor's criticisms of the line were to prove to be all too mild, notes Chandler (142).

While mismanagement was a part of the problem, the fundamental one seems to have been corruption. J. L. Ringwalt's massive, fact-filled book on the railroads, published in 1888, is scathing in his criticisms of labor and antirailroad sentiments, and defends the roads on every account. But his summaries of the charges against the roads is revealing. I offer Ringwalt's work to indicate that the charges against the railroads were widespread and came from U.S. Senators and governors of major states as well as businessmen and farmers, and the critics exhibited sophisticated and detailed knowledge of the workings of the lines:

> It was charged [by a committee of the New York State legislature conducting an investigation] that the railroads were capitalized on a basis of two dollars to every one actually paid in providing facilities, and that they could be constructed for one third of their nominal value; that combinations and pools, by which the public suffered, were necessary to their profitable conduct, even with honest management; that in too many cases the interests of stock and bondholders were subordinated to those of the managing ring, who purposely and dishonestly depleted the revenues, so that [the] majority of the bona fide owners got nothing. It was alleged that the railroads of New York were in the habit of discriminating in favor of citizens of other states and of foreign countries to the prejudice of the interests of the people of New York; that individual citizens were given special privileges and rates out of proportion to those charged to the public in general; that the rates of transportation were made unnecessarily high by the maintenance of subsidiary organizations designed to deplete the revenues of the roads before profits reached the stockholders; that fast freight lines, bridge companies, live-stock companies, local lines, leased at exorbitant rates; [that] stock-yard companies, construction companies, elevator and other terminal facility companies, were maintained improperly at the expense of the great roads, and corruptly used to promote the financial interests of members of the managing ring; that the rights of stockholders were in every respect and in the grossest manner disregarded; that the classifications of freight abounded with unjust, unfair, and unreasonable features (263).

And Ringwalt goes on and on. Many of the charges in the above quotation involve personal rather than organizational derelictions — the railroad officials simply feathered their own nest, often at the expense of the organization they headed. One can hear an economist saying in mocking tones, "I am shocked, Professor Perrow, to hear that there was self-interested behavior going on in that part of the economy." It is worth noting that while it is not a terribly strong argument for the power of large organizations in society to note that their existence amplifies greatly the opportunities for self-interested behavior at the expense of others, it is still a consequence that must be placed in the organization box, rather than the boxes for culture, capitalism, class, or economic efficiency.

What is more telling is when illegal behavior by organizations shapes the environment in which they operate. That is the theme in a few of the above charges, and in the following: Governor Patterson of Tennessee in 1883 charged that the railroads "had violated provisions of the state constitution constantly, defiantly, and flagrantly" in order to raise rates and eliminate competition. Secretary of State Jeremiah S. Black "alleged the existence of a combination between the great trunk [main] lines to stop all competition, to unite the power of all into one grand monopoly, and to put the whole people at their mercy" reports Ringwalt (263). Governor Glick of Kansas claimed, in Ringwalt's words, "that the first movements of consolidation among railroads had done away with wholesome competition and all fair and generous treatment of the public, and that an epoch followed during which public interests were shamefully sacrificed." Glick summarized an argument that will be important for us later, regarding the choice between a regional and a national system. He "alleged that

> the result of this [unfair competition] had been to make it unprofitable to develop the manufacturing resources of the state of Kansas; that manufactured goods of all kinds made in far eastern states were brought into [Kansas] and sold at less cost than those articles could be manufactured, for the simple reason that railroads were constantly discriminating against home manufacturers, and exacting excessive local rates under the fallacious plea that a long haul was more profitable than a short one (cited on 264).

The charges were even stronger on the West Coast, Ringwalt notes, and everywhere they led to attempts to regulate the railroads through legislation. Unless the charges were fabrications, and evidence suggests that they were not, we have to explain why the regulation attempts were so feeble. The Huntington letters and other quotes we examined offer a plausible explanation—the legislators, governors, and courts were simply bought out, even while some of their number were thundering antirailroad charges. But that is not the explanation of most scholars.

Scholars Explain Corruption

What have social scientists and historians done with this widespread feeling and its considerable documentation? The issue of corruption has not received its analytical master. There is a small but rich sociological literature on modern corporate crime and price-fixing conspiracies, and economic historians have written about the industry structures that seem to encourage corporate deviance in modern times. (See Baker and Faulkner 1993; Clinard and Yeager 1980; Scherer 1980; Simpson 1986). While addressing organizational issues, they are not useful for the practices of the nineteenth-century corporations. Few legal scholars have addressed the issue of corruption in broad terms, and those that have (Rose-Ackerman 1978) are not very sensitive to organizational issues. I suspect this is because of our tendency to turn away from the power of organizations in our nation's history and instead fix on individuals, culture, and laws. We are also prone to finding a redeeming or exculpatory function for corruption, which is what historian Samuel P. Huntington (1968) has provided.

His argument is summarized by a sympathetic commentator on the functions of corruption, Margaret Susan Thompson (1983). Change creates new sources of wealth and power, and corruption, in Huntington's words, "may be the means of assimilating new groups into the political system by irregular means because the system has been unable to adapt sufficiently fast to provide legitimate and acceptable means for this purpose" (cited in Thompson 1983, 179). We might illustrate this as follows: Railroad companies were a new group that should have been assimilated into the political system, but their profit motives and ruthless competition were not considered legitimate and acceptable, so they had to purchase legislation and judges. The machinery and procedures "adequate to their needs" were not available, says Thompson, so corruption to suit their "needs" was the result. That pursuing their needs should not justify illegal and unethical behavior is an argument not entertained. But with regard to the railroads, there is no evidence that the system did not provide legal and ethical means to their ends; indeed, one might say that government at all levels was very generous. Finally, the ends of the railroads included destruction of rivals; for this I would think there should be no "legitimate and acceptable means" other than more efficient performance.

A second reason is also supplied by Huntington. With the expansion of the public sector, new laws were needed. But, quoting Huntington, Thompson suggests that "the multiplication of laws multiplies the possibilities of corruption" (179). The reasoning here is bizarre; it assumes that if there were no laws to prevent corruption by railroads there would be no corruption! The interpretation by Huntington and Thompson should be just the reverse: the laws were necessary because of corruption; not having them would not prevent it except in the technical sense that if there is no law regarding bribery, bribery cannot be illegal. The fact that the state had inadequate enforcement mechanisms and that the profit from breaking the laws was an "attractive enough incentive to do so" is an explanation that avoids any examination of the corrupters — the railroads. In yet another way our glance is diverted from the important organizations of the time.

A third argument is that behavior is not really corruption if a longer time period is considered. There is a "time lag"; there are no agreed upon standards. (But if so, we might ask why the laws were passed, the laws that under the second argument induce corruption.) New standards, permitting behavior that once had been judged to be illegal, have not yet emerged. So "there will be a higher incidence of activity that does not seem to 'fit'" (Thompson 1983, 179). All we need to do to eliminate corruption is to stop condemning behavior as corrupt, and the corrupt practices will be, in Huntington's words, "accepted as normal and even legitimate [as in] more modern societies." In this way corruption can be accommodated, and critics in the late nineteenth century can be described by Thompson as "naive." She does admit that "some scandals of the 1870s were real" (179), but by and large, new groups had to be assimilated, too many laws were passed declaring practices by these groups to be illegal, and in time they would be considered legitimate (179). Incredibly enough, she says that if people had only "looked more closely at the functional and behavioral dimensions," they might have been reassured that "what they abjured was neither inherently evil nor outside of their control. It was merely new" (187). The title of her article says it all: "Corruption — or Confusion?" In this way corruption as force in history is turned aside.

Corruption plays a big role in Dobbin's account of railroads in the United States, but it is usually independent of, even at war with, his neoinstitutional account. Early on in his book he announces that "government aid to railways was plundered in the United States" (1994, 21), and later on he has extensive and colorful discussions of it. "Railway promoters and public officials were exceptionally creative when it came to defrauding the public," he says (p 44). I would prefer a formulation that would say "owners and managers of railroad organizations were creative in corrupting public officials, and thus defrauding the public." But at least his formulation employs an interest argument that has little to do with culture and logics. Three of his main examples (taken from Hartz) are instructive. "First, railway promoters [read "organizations"] often won public assistance to build lines that had no chance of making money." The example is a line that received $5.7 million from scattered municipalities, and thus meandered across New York, avoiding all major cities. The line was built; there was an organization hiring workers, laying the track, and disturbing the land, we should emphasize. But "the line was bankrupt almost as soon as it was opened, but not before its directors compensated themselves handsomely" (Dobbin 1994, 44).

They were able to do this, we should note, because organizations had long ago lobbied for limited liability laws, making such acts easier. It was not just a matter of corrupt individuals.

Dobbin's second example describes the embezzlement of public funds, concluding that "a common ploy was for the directors to disappear with public funds before laying a single rail tie (44)." The third also focuses upon directors, rather than the capacity of the new organizational form, in this case those who authorized their companies to print new stock and gave it to themselves without adding any capital to the firm to justify the increased capitalization. For example, at one point Cornelius Vanderbilt voted himself a bonus of $20 million as the majority shareholder in the New York Central, in effect reducing the value of all other stockholders and claimants by that amount; Jay Gould added $54 million to the book value of his Erie railroad over eight years without adding any new funds or value to the line. The practice extended to politicians and government officials. This milking or draining off the assets of the publicly traded companies was so widespread that Dobbin reports estimates that by 1885 fully *one third* of railway capitalization was fictional — "water," or "watered stock" (44–45). (Watered stock allowed a small group to gain control; it did not directly affect efficiency or profits.) The wide-spread use of this deception invites an emphasis upon the role of organizations rather than individuals, that is, corrupt directors or corrupted officials. If there are large organizations with convenient laws protecting them and scant regulation, it is possible to practice deception. It would be quite difficult to do these things in small organizations because they would have fewer and more attentive stockholders.

Another major explanation of corruption is government failure to prevent it. In this regard, Dobbin has two explanations: lack of state capacity, and then a cultural explanation for the lack of capacity — government is seen as evil. Regarding the first, he notes that in regulatory matters the government was very weak, even at the state level. Dobbin notes and endorses the "widespread agreement that railway aid schemes were rife with corruption because state and local governments failed to exercise administrative controls over railroads" (45). Dobbin quotes one historian writing in 1913: "[P]ractically all public officials and employees were selected, retained and dismissed for political reasons. Grafting in public office was common" (46). Note the passive construction; it is almost as if the railroads were the victims, trying not to defraud the public but forced to do so. This curious view is reinforced by his next observation: Even after the railway scandals began to appear, "policy makers refused to expand public controls and even to exercise the controls that *were* at their disposal" (46). One is encouraged to think that the railroad companies were behind this refusal to have themselves regulated, but that would be an organizational interest argument, and it does not emerge.

Instead, we find that public officials "operated with a model of governance in which government intervention in private matters was tyrannical." (Why, then, were any controls at their disposal?) As examples of preserving the economic liberties of citizens, he gives these illustrations: Legislators in one state passed a law forbidding their state representatives to hold a majority on railroad company boards, regardless of the extent of state investment. The majority owners — the public — could not have a majority on the board because it would restrict the liberties of the minority owners, the railroad directors! In another state, which owned the lion's share of the railroad company stock, lawmakers refused to accept a majority of seats on the board, and never asked to review the company's accounts. When representatives of the citizens' investments did try to stem the flow of money to private owners and directors, they were thwarted. The city council of Baltimore ordered their representatives to vote against a stock-watering extra dividend to private shareholders of the Baltimore and Ohio railroad, but the representatives refused; they were censured for selling their votes to the directors, but the courts ruled that the dividend was to be paid (46–47).

These machinations were justified on the grounds that controls over government representatives on the boards would interfere with the economic liberties of citizens, or subject private firms (using public monies, recall) to the influence of that dirty word, "politics." Remarkably, Dobbin believes in the force of these all-too-convenient and transparent arguments (without accepting their legitimacy). "Political culture" is the explanation. It was "government's determination to keep out of the management of private concerns." This, he says, is an example of "the American notion that state expansion — in this case embodied by public aid to enterprise — is inescapably evil," and "their state institutions depicted concentrated authority as a danger to the polity" (46–47).

One can be sure there were such sentiments, but direct evidence that they were at all representative of the public's view is hard to find. Instead, as evidence of public sentiment, we only get rather casual and marginally relevant quotations from interested parties such as that from the *Vermont House Journal* noting that salaried state offices are "in all cases, an evil" (cited in Dobbin 1994, 70). Or a quote from historian Charles Francis Adams (before he became director of the Union Pacific Railway) that "the American mind is not bureaucratic." State control over interstate tariffs would be irrational, and according to Dobbin and other historians we have cited, contrary to supposed "American sentiments" (70). (Recall that we have previously documented the great degree of "public aid to enterprise," and the vigorous support of, and many examples of, government regulation of business.)

In Dobbin's cultural account, the American people did not find corruption a sign of unregulated private power; it "generated tremendous publicity because it seemed to shake the very foundation of the political order," and to restore that order "states reacted with constitutional amendments prohibiting all public investment in private enterprise" (73). This cultural account says that there is an institutional logic declaring that the legal powers that go with majority ownership by the state of private organizations will not be exercised because state power is "evil." Why did they bother to set up the legal powers and the provisions for public representatives in the first place, one wonders. Only once in a while is Dobbin's cultural account salted with the much more sensible, straightforward organizational interest account. For example, he notes that laws were passed in several states, but ignored by the railroads; because enforcement depended upon the courts, railroads bribed the judges (Dobbin 1994, 73). Burton Folsom gives accounts of judges who were lawyers with large business interests and often served as bank directors — accounts that provide some insight into the conservatism of the judiciary in the nineteenth-century United States (Folsom 1981). If "American sentiments" were so opposed to regulation, how do we account for this: "Public anti-railroad sentiments ran so strong that governors could not appoint experienced railwaymen to their commissions." (Experienced railwaymen probably meant those employed by, or with strong financial interests in, the railroads of course!). Upstanding but naive citizens were appointed, and "were easily fooled by the railroads" (Dobbin 1994, 74). Here is one final and telling example from Dobbin that contradicts his main theme but instead inserts railroad organizations as an agent in this history: The railways "bribed legislators to relieve them of the public obligations they had incurred in exchange for government aid. . . . As long as railwaymen could purchase relief from public controls, in one way or another, regulations alone would be ineffective" (47). Just so.

Finally, I will cut short our journey through tales of corruption with a mention of two extensive and graphic accounts of railroad corruption by historian Mark Summers. One deals with corruption in the pre–Civil War days, and we learn that the railroads were the prime venue for prewar corruption scandals (Summers 1987). The other focuses on Southern railroads in the post Civil War decades (Summers 1984). In both accounts there is an endless stream of colorful corruption examples. Major subsidy laws for railroads were written by railroad executives. The head of the Texas Pacific wrote the bill granting his railroad large amounts of cash and land, and it passed just as he wrote it. Another vice president of a line did the legislators a service by writing for them a bill endowing his line with $10,000 a mile for track laid (1984, 65). The editor of a Little Rock, Arkansas. newspaper would not take $12,000 from the president of the railroad who sought his support, judging the stock not worth a "picayune," but did accept $6,000 in cash (101). Summers also deals with corruption on a less picayune scale, involving the search for national market control. "[T]he most significant cases of corruption had out-of-state capitalists and consolidation schemes mixed in them somewhere" (179). Railroad companies and their investment bankers in Boston, New York, and Philadelphia carved up the rest of the country and controlled the trunk (main) lines and bought legislators. Consolidation "was almost an obsession among Southern railroad executives, as it was among Northerners," and where the two competed, the Northerners generally won. The owner of the Pennsylvania Railroad, so praised for his organizational genius by Alfred Chandler in other connections, envisioned a network of lines joining the Northeast, South, and the Pacific. Under the corporate title of the "Southern Railway Security Company" and "with a lot of argument and a bit of bribery," he and his business associates bought up the state of Virginia's railroad stock in two railroad lines, on "easy terms." By 1873 the company was operating thirteen lines in most of the Southern states (Summers 1984, 176). The Reconstruction South, Summers demonstrates, offered fertile ground for most forms of corruption in the service of market control (1987, 183–84). The bribes of the Southern Railway Security Company are not mentioned in Chandler's account of these events. Instead, he sees it as a part of great movement from competition to cooperation that characterized the 1860s and 1870s, and enabled the major "administrative innovation" of a decentralized management structure (Chandler 1977, 137, 143, 155–56), which we shall consider in the next chapter.

SUMMARY AND CONCLUSIONS

I have argued that the central issue regarding our second big business in the nineteenth century, the railroads, is why were they privatized so quickly and unregulated so long? A quick comparison with railroads in Britain and France indicated the key role of the state and state bureaucracies. France had a centralized government that was familiar with controlling public goods, and its Bureau of Bridges and Roads, while allowing private investment and guaranteeing the returns, planned and ran the roads. In Britain, with rule divided between the crown and parliament, the crown kept capital pools restricted, and so there were many privately owned small railroads, and the parliament set up cartels to insure that the track gauges matched, the trains were safe, and the rates reasonable. The United States started out with a well-established tradition of mixed public-private ownership or government ownership, with substantial regulation. By the time of the Civil War it was a privatized and largely unregulated industry, in contrast to that of all other industrial nations. Economic historians and sociologists have put forth the following explanations: common carriers must be privatized; private industry was the more efficient form; the "institutional logic" (American culture) opposed big government and government control; and our tradition of economic individualism and freedom entailed privatization and little regulation.

Instead, I have argued that aggressive railroad corporations turned the public representatives out, and campaigned for private ownership. Where states did not regulate, the railroads succeeded in getting public investment (without representation), and where states did regulate, the railroads argued against public investment. In either case they found convenient "institutional logics" to back up their arguments. By the 1850s it was clear that everyone wanted a railroad, and the states and then the Federal government were willing to cover around half the cost. With enormous profits in sight because of privatization, European capital poured in to help.

I have argued that corruption was a major force, on a par with the factors of production (land, labor, capital, technology) in the case of the railroad industry. The social costs of the corruption were substantial, but more important for my argument, it was driven not just by the propensity to seek gain, which is endemic to economic systems, but by the organizational forms that were being invented (socially constructed), including devices that emerged from the legal revolution we discussed in the first chapter. The forms were neither "obvious" nor "inevitable," but contested and in every instance opposed. These forms of corporate organization meant they would be free of public responsibility, and of personal liability for debt, accidents, and social costs to workers and communities. The corporate form was to include provisions enabling organizations to own and control other organizations, increasing their market power and political power. The country needed railroads, but the privatization and freedom from governmental oversight allowed the organizations to hold communities and states hostage to remarkable amounts of public financing and land grants with little accountability. In all this, and more that we shall consider (in particular, an economic nationalization that stifled regional development), corruption played a significant role.

Other commentators have focused upon government officials and legislators as the corrupters, extorting bribes from the railroads. While acknowledging that reality, I have argued that seeing the railroad corporations as the corrupting agency makes much more sense, and the historical details support this view. Though historians blame the corrupted, rather than the corrupters, or blame the standards of the time, or rationalize corrupt practices as "new ways" of doing things, they still detail the corruption, and there was a lot. For example, over one third of railroad stock was watered, half of the track was in receivership, and the Credit Mobilier scandal was the biggest of the century. But historians and social scientists have missed the implications of corruption: large organizations had arrived on the scene and they wanted public funds, and needed legislative acts, new laws, and judicial rulings that would consolidate their power. We are not talking about a few promoters and directors, that is, corrupt individuals, but about the biggest organizations of the time. If we examine our history as increasingly driven by large organizations as the century moved on, the importance of organizations as corrupters is revealed.

Chapter 6

THE ORGANIZATIONAL IMPRINTING

T HE RAILROADS were more complex than manufacturing, mining, or maritime enterprises in the nineteenth century, and they
quickly evolved administrative structures to handle the complexity; the structures are celebrated as the basis of modern organizations,
public and private.

The large textile mills were complex in many respects. There was a
substantial hierarchy: the owners delegated to the superintendent, who
delegated to men who headed the repair shops, raw materials handling,
and the production steps such as carding, spinning, and dyeing; and
these men had foremen of a sort who helped them supervise the machine tenders, runners, teamsters, and so on. A large textile mill had a
fairly complex structure, but in contrast to the railroads it existed in
one place only, and though many different production operations were
involved, production accounted for most of the employees. Most manufacturing was like this in the nineteenth century — a single location, little
staff, and mostly production personnel and a few foremen (or inside
contractors). When firms began to integrate forward to marketing and
sales, or backward to getting their own raw materials or making their
own equipment, staff was required for records, coordination, planning,
and so forth. But long before manufacturing firms did this on any scale,
the railroads were already awash in staff and bureaucracy, as befitting
the prototypes of our modern organizations.

From the beginning, the railroads operated in different locations, had
a large machine shop and maintenance operation, a stable of locomotive drivers, firemen, and brakemen. A separate group was in direct
touch with the consumers — freight men, ticket takers, conductors. And
finally they had the intrinsic problem of tight scheduling to meet posted
times and to prevent trains from colliding en route. Later on, all organizations would take on functions and technologies that made them as
complex as railroads, but initially it was the railroad that led the way to
achieving control and action at a distance through delegation — that led
the way to modern bureaucracy.

Divisionalization

Though celebrated, the evolution of modern bureaucracy was initially quite straightforward and obvious. The first delegation, indeed, the first step in "divisionalization," was to assign a station master to each end of a line that went from A to B and back again. That was simple, and we can see it in an 1838 report by two civil engineers. They were employed by the first railroad in the country, the Baltimore & Ohio. It commenced service in 1830 with horses drawing the carriages along thirteen miles of track. Steam locomotives came two years later (Licht 1983, 6). The two engineers surveyed the operation of a few railroad companies that were operating by 1838, and found at least two cases where station masters were appointed for the management of the depots, and a master engineer appointed to oversee the machine shops and the locomotive drivers and firemen, thus decentralizing both by place and by function. This was done without the fanfare Chandler makes and probably without much effort or thought.

Divisionalization into sections came next. It was not initiated originally as an efficiency measure, but in response to a state investigation. A spectacular collision on the Western Railroad (Massachusetts) occurred in 1841 and the state demanded a reorganization. Chandler and Salsbury (1965, 134) say that "Western's management responded spontaneously to the crisis of the moment," but this is a typical Chandlerian gloss; the railroad was investigated by a state committee and ordered to change its management, as Chandler and Salsbury themselves note (133). And the wreck that precipitated the crisis (two killed, seventeen injured) was only one of a series of wrecks with fatalities, and no spontaneous response was forthcoming after any of these occasions. The railroad's response to the investigative report was to set up a special committee and use the occasion to review the whole management structure, set up three divisions, and establish clear authority in the divisions. That was no doubt needed; with 160 miles of track, this was a long line for the time. But the matter of collisions was simply handled; it had been a problem of "general confusion and laxness" in giving orders, but from then on, "to prevent collisions, exact timetables were published and placed in the hands of conductors with detailed instructions to follow should breakdowns or other factors delay trains" (134). It doesn't sound like a big task; indeed, it is rather obvious, and was probably implicit in the previous rules governing the twelve passings that took place each day between Worcester and Albany.

The three divisions handled a section each, and each section had a master to oversee the track maintenance and a second master to handle the stations — again, decentralization by place and by function. Most important, the main office set up the full-fledged embodiment of the bureaucratic Zeitgeist — the manual, specifying every employee's responsibilities — and appointed a staff specialist, a master mechanic in charge of all shop work for the three divisions. The military had long had a staff-line distinction, but this may have been the first formalized one in private enterprise. Strict rules were laid down regarding schedule changes and breakdowns and delays, and the lines of authority were more clearly specified (134).

Finance Takes Charge

The next major development came from a cost-cutting president of the Baltimore & Ohio who declared that the railroad would need "a new system of management." It was thoroughly planned and took a year to devise. We are now into the kind of innovation that so excites Alfred Chandler and business historians: something both new and not obvious at the time, "one of the very first functionally departmentalized, administrative structures for an American business enterprise," as Chandler and Stephen Salsbury pronounce it to be (1965, 137). It also is the first serious divergence from the organization of other industries at the time, including the big textile firms, which had only the rudiments of divisionalization and staff specialization. The business was now decisively split into the "operating" and the "financial" sides. We might date the 1847 report of the Baltimore & Ohio as the certification of the bean counters.

Finance was not just to collect money and pay bills and wages. The office of the treasurer looked inward and meticulously controlled the way fares were collected — an obvious source of what economists like to call, without conscious drollery, "interface leakages" — and the way freight was received and receipted, what records were to be kept to judge hourly performance, how the nickels and dimes were to be transmitted, and how bills and wages were to be paid (late, whenever possible, and in the case of wages, frequently months late). Whereas other industries looked for better machines and production processes, the companies had no office for keeping records and thus had little notion of how the machines and men performed on a daily basis, what was wasted, and what the productivity of different machines, people, and arrangements might be. That casual approach would not do with the railroads. Unlike most industry, railroads were in direct, hourly contact with their customers, their customers were many in number and were both repetitive (freight) and nonrepetitive (passengers). Much could be learned about machines, workers, and customers by the newly powerful finance office. Bureaucratic control is indirect control, through rules, regulations, and reports. The railroads were probably the first to develop fully these unobtrusive, inexpensive, pervasive, and impersonal control devices, the best elites have ever discovered. It is a virtually unmarked turning point in humankind's history.

INFORMATION AS CONTROL

The innovations on the operations side were more developmental than radical. The work was now divided into three parts: the roadway, machine shops, and transportation (engineers, firemen, conductors, station masters, and agents for fuel and lumber and depot upkeep). The head office specified monthly reports from the three divisions. The Baltimore & Ohio was still rather small at the time it made these innovations. By the mid 1850s the New York & Erie Railroad had more than four thousand employees; with this size it needed more than just two main office departments, finance and operations, along with the familiar divisionalization into regions. Over a number of years the general superintendent of the Erie, Daniel McCallum, expanded the head office's control. He brought some functions into the head office that had been in the divisions, but mostly the head office was to set the standards and review the reports of those in the divisions. The purchase of fuel, the handling of freight and passenger business, machinery and repairs, and running the telegraph became head office functions or was subject to close control. Chandler and Salsbury well characterize McCallum's contribution:

> His great strength was in sharpening lines of authority and communication, and in stimulating the flow of the minute and accurate information which top management needed for the complex decisions it was increasingly being called upon to make. Hourly, daily, and monthly reports, more detailed than those called for earlier on the Baltimore & Ohio, provided this essential information (138).

As the authors note, such minute and even hourly information was vital in eliminating bottlenecks and other troubles, and McCallum's use of the telegraph to achieve not only safety but better coordination and administration was noted by other railroad managers.

THE DUAL AUTHORITY BOGEY

There was a thorny problem from the start, however, as McCallum knew, and it is the classic thorny problem of administrative design to this day. With operations of such size and complexity, and thus with massive record keeping and surveillance, what had always been a residual difficulty, to be solved informally, thrust itself into prominence: a manager might have two or more bosses, one at the division, his immediate superior, and one or more in the head office. Licht, whose account draws, as all have, on Chandler, puts it this way: "Whether a station master, for instance, was directly subordinate to the general freight agent, the general ticket agent, or his divisional superintendent remained uncertain" (1983, 16).

The next innovation—to avoid this uncertainty—came from the Pennsylvania Railroad in 1858, when it was half the size of the Erie. The station master would have only one superior, and the head office, with its divisional superintendents, would keep its hands off of direct control. The head office would have no direct role in the daily supervision of operations and employees; it would develop plans and strategies, set standards and procedures, inspect, and advise, advise, and advise. (All sorts of head office proliferation accompanied the change—accounting was separated from the treasury department, purchasing was established, a secretary's office set up, and a legal department.) Planning was to be kept separate from operations; operations would be kept free of daily intrusions by top management, or so it was hoped. Under this structure the railroad grew to over fifty thousand employees in the 1880s, the biggest in the nation, and its form was copied by almost all the others. A lovingly dense chart with some nine levels of authority and wide spans of control appears in Chandler's *Visible Hand* (1977, 108), representing the railroads of the 1870s and the scholar's awe.

The idea that the head office plans and monitors, but does not supervise, and the divisions act almost as independent companies, produces a structure that is taken for granted today, with one elaboration and only one serious violation. The elaboration comes with divisionalization by products rather than geography (the multidivisional firm, which can also be a multinational multidivisional firm). There are two or more hands-off head offices now, one over the whole company, and one over each of the product divisions. This is celebrated in Chandler's early and truly path-breaking work on General Motors and a few other large firms, *Strategy and Structure* (1969). The violation comes with the remuddling of responsibility with the "matrix" structure in firms with changing technologies and products. Here a manager intentionally has two or more bosses, as he or she runs a small business, so to speak, with supervision from a direct superior (project group leader), but also from production, marketing, engineering, and finance representatives of the head office, who just might meddle. The cost that is paid in the confusion of authority—which boss do I answer to—is apparently justi-

d with a fully centralized structure, where, for example, a direct line
uthority meant that the vice president for maintenance of equipment
:rvised the chief master mechanic at each division or sector of the
oad. Though we have no details on other American railroads with-
the decentralized structure, there were apparently some. More im-
ant, this was the structure British and continental European rail-
ds used, and they were notably efficient organizations. Chandler
s explicitly argue that the decentralized, divisional structure "was
her natural nor inevitable (1965, 141). But this is not a path-depen-
t argument; as he makes clear, it really is inevitable if you have cre-
e people and a long railroad and are going to be efficient. He dis-
ses the British centralized departmental type of organization as due
'the shorter systems in Europe and in Great Britain." He even says
 this departmental system is "less practical" on railroads of great
ance, "as the New York Central found out" (143). Because the New
k Central was profitable for a long time, and Chandler does not
ghten us as to when or how it "found out" that its structure was
ficient, the argument is still open. Furthermore, the "great distance"
ument is not developed. What is the difference between a London to
nburgh, or Paris to Marseilles line and a comparable one in the
ted States?

ut my argument is not for the superiority of either the divisionalized
he centralized structure; it is that at this point in time, for railroad
fits, it did not matter much which structure was adopted (though it
uld matter for the future). Two alternatives were possible. A central-
l, departmental structure, without significant divisionalization,
uld have served *regional* lines quite well, and as we shall see later, a
ional system of railroads was not only advocated by a few railroad
ders and most businesses outside of New York and Chicago, but
ually was in practice for a number of years and promoted innova-
n. A second alternative was the cultivation of much smaller organiza-
ns in the system through the practice of contracting out, which also
s tried and deemed profitable. This would produce organizations
all enough so as not to need divisionalization nor any great separa-
n of planning and execution. This leads to the second argument
inst an inevitable path toward efficiency.

ntracting Out

.e second argument, that a broader view of efficiency would have led
 a different turn, is not a "counterfactual" one; U.S. firms tried and
dorsed this alternative, but abandoned it for reasons that are unfor-

fied if the technologies and products are complex a
than routine and stable.

Inevitable, or a Chance Path?

Whether the railroads were the first to divisionalize
headquarters that just planned and monitored is no
argument; the form was quickly adopted by most or
grew large and looked about for some way to handl
lems. Was it all inevitable, a straight line trajectory c
trial revolution (the transportation revolution) as m
or even assert? Or was it, as I shall argue, a part o
process, whereby some or all firms might have tur
right? And what difference would it make if all did
divisionalized form allowed very large organizations
many different functions and very large markets. In
ized form could be big, as the New York Central was
form probably put a limit on its ability to manage
efficiently and to control markets that were wide sp
sense divisionalization allowed a greater centralizat
power.

Only two bits of historical evidence support a pa
ment, wherein nondivisionalized firms and smaller
contractors might have emerged, but that is enough
bility and thus counter the inevitability argument
others. Both would have been efficient, but for the l
than individual firms, though these would also have
If alternative structures were possible, and they were
have the possibility of an organizational, rather than
torical driver. It is hard to conceive of a cultural exp
the values of the nation favored centralized bureaucr
one (e.g., that there was heavy regulation from the
centralized bureaucracies in the private firms), whic
support for the premise of this book—that the mos
of our society in the last century has been one part
large organizations.

The first argument for saying that something otl
was at work is the weakest—but still important. The
Railroad did not set up the head office form of the c
divisionalize as they had. As obvious as the form se
not deemed all that necessary for the New York Cer
to install it were repeatedly frustrated. For some ni

tunately quite obscure. This was the "contract form," as Licht correctly labels it (1983, 19), though it has come to be called the "subcontracting" form. Two forms must be distinguished: subcontracting, or contracting out, where an independent firm is hired to perform the service; and second, "inside contracting," where the contractor works on the customer's premises, renting the space and power, and supplying his or her own personnel, tools, and materials. This second form is familiar to us from our discussion of textile mills in Philadelphia. Either form of subcontracting, as we have seen, distributes wealth and power more widely, can promote flexibility and innovation, and localizes ownership. For those who emphasize transaction costs, stemming from opportunism with guile, contracting out is inefficient; the costs of external transactions are high, because of guile and cheating, while internal transactions can be policed and settled by authority. For those who emphasize throughput, as does Chandler, it is a slow and uncertain mode of production, and Chandler rejects it as inefficient. But as Licht points out, contracting out was widely used and widely praised in the early days of railroading.

The remarkable Henry Varnum Poor, crusading and liberal editor of the leading railroad journal of the time, had a brief love affair with the contract system, according to his great grandson and biographer, Alfred DuPont Chandler, Jr. As Chandler notes in his biography of Poor, he was more organizationally astute than his contemporary commentators. Instead of preaching moral virtues as the solution to the problems of efficiency and mismanagement, Poor recognized that owners were increasingly diverse and necessarily uninformed, and their agents, the managers of the roads, were unaccountable to them. He recommended that directors, representing the stockholders, be full time and even live along the roads rather than in Boston or New York. Furthermore, he recommended a thoroughly decentralized contract system, wherein the contractors would have the incentive to increase efficiency as they would retain the profits from improvements (Chandler 1956, 164). The directors could then concentrate on the financial aspects. Several English and continental roads operated their locomotives by contract, as he observed first hand in 1858, and at least four major railroads in the United States did so. The Philadelphia, Wilmington, and Baltimore reported in 1858 that contracts had replaced fixed salaries except for the repair of bridges, and for managing the conductors and the supervising offices. Poor recommended that the mismanaged Erie should follow this practice, but the financier heading the board of directors, Daniel Drew, refused, shortly before the road went into bankruptcy.

Poor blamed the speculating directors for failing to adopt the system; they wished to retain control to carry on their stock market manipulations, he argued. Chandler disagrees with such an interest argument. Though Poor was "probably partially correct," Chandler concedes, the real reason was that the vigorous competition required "adjusting rates, rescheduling trains, granting concessions to shippers, and so forth" (166). It would be "hazardous" to separate the directors from management. Moreover, there might be "incompetent or dishonest contractors." And finally, the coordinating problems would be "an obvious weakness in the plan which Poor failed to consider." Indeed, as the president of one of the roads noted as his reason for abandoning it, there was an absence of "a community of interest"; contractors maximized the interests of their function rather than the whole. The party managing the roadway had to take an interest in the locomotive or car departments for it to work (167). Poor himself advocated the plan for only a few months, according to Chandler.

Chandler rejects the contract system too easily, I would argue. All the problems he raises are fundamental problems of the hierarchical system as well — inflexibility, incompetence, and dishonesty, and parochial departmental self-interest. It would appear that the incentive advantages of the contract system — spreading the profits more widely and linking effort to reward more directly — would minimize rather than maximize these other enduring organizational problems. Regarding flexibility, the cost of rate wars should be a temporary corporate cost, with the company's affected lines being subsidized by the unaffected ones, and contractors thus compensated. The penalty for incompetence and dishonesty would be extracted more quickly, through loss of contractor profits, than in the hierarchical system, where they will be undetected for longer periods. Parochial self-interest is probably less likely to surface if the profits of the line decline, affecting all contractors in the next round of contract setting. At the least, the problems would not seem to be greater in the contract system, and the quality of maintenance and rate of innovation should be higher. The one major problem with the contract system, though, is not addressed by Chandler — it redistributes profits away from top management and directors and spreads them through the many contractors.

Contracting was widely used in the building and construction industries, machine and tool industry, garment making, and "inside contracting," was used in such leading manufactures as Eli Whitney, Robbins and Lawrence, Brown and Sharp, Colt, Remington, Singer, Pratt and Whitney, and Winchester (Licht 1983, 19). (The major work on inside contracting is by Dan Clawson 1980.) So we should not be surprised to see it in railroading. From 1849 on (not the "few months" that Chandler reports), Henry Poor reported on successful experiments in England and the European continent, where locomotive drivers received a set fee for driving the firm's engines, and kept the engines in good repair, supplied their own fuel, oil, tools, and labor. They did all this, Poor testified, more efficiently than the company managers did, and saved the companies a good deal of money (Licht 1983, 21). It is not hard to see why: the profits went to each engine driver, increasing his incentive to keep the machines and his workers in order. Indeed, the driver absorbed many transaction costs (buying fuel, finding and supervising and paying workers, etc.) that the company might have paid, and because of the possibilities for building trust in these transactions, because of their decentralized nature, they probably cost less than if the company had assumed them. It is our familiar theme, the benefits of the deconcentration of wealth and power, in contrast to the theme of most economic historians, the efficiency of concentrated organizational power.

Other railroad journals called for the extension of contracting to all aspects of railroad operation, and some of the leading railroads used it and reported positively. The Fitchburg Railroad noted that under the old (bureaucratic) system "service, if performed at all, was rendered grudgingly," while the contracting "mode of transacting the business of the company" resulted in savings (Licht 1983, 21). The Pennsylvania Railroad, the largest, contracted conductors; a Southern line contracted engineers, and so on. But the most revealing case occurred in 1857 when a Philadelphia line introduced it in all phases of its operation. For six years the profit reports supported the wisdom of the decision. But in 1863, with wartime inflation, the contracting system, which "had resulted in great savings in expenses," was given up "temporarily." The logic was that with rapid price increases, "it was deemed more for the interest of the Company to take the risk of future prices, than to pay an amount for service which would cover all the risk that the contractors would be liable to" (Licht 1983, 22–23). The following year the Philadelphia line reintroduced contracting in the track maintenance area, and hoped that prices for labor and materials would stabilize and allow them to reintroduce it throughout the company, because they still believed it was "the best system." As Licht notes, this was the last mention of contracting in their published reports; we do not know why they failed to reestablish the much-praised system throughout the company.

It seems likely that the contractors sought the suspension of the system in a period of rapidly rising prices; they would have been stuck with set prices for a year, whereas the company could have raised rates and increased profits freely. Their prices would be sticky, those of the company would not. If prices rose rapidly between yearly contracts, the contractors were at a distinct disadvantage. No labor or commodity price indexes existed, which would have allowed the contracted price to rise commensurate with the rise of these prices. The solution would have been six-month contracts, or a yearly adjustment based upon rising contractor costs and rising profits from the firm, which could have raised its prices while contractors could not. It does not seem to have been at all impossible. But the practices of using yearly contracts was widespread, and though the contractors may have argued for monthly contracts, they were probably not in a position to judge their inflationary losses over a short time — or even over a year.

All pricing — for services, materials and the product itself — was vulnerable to rapid inflation, not just subcontracting, and thus inflation may not necessarily have been the cause of its disappearance. Indeed, today sophisticated governments cannot anticipate, let alone control, bursts of inflation (generally occasioned by wars). The Nixon administration, during the Vietnam war, imposed price and labor controls to try to mitigate the kinds of problems that the railroads and their contractors were facing during the Civil War. But why did the Philadelphia line not reinstate it if it was as beneficial as the company reports indicated? There was certainly a convenient ideology available to justify it. As Licht says of the many celebrations of contracting, it reflected "a noncorporatist or Jeffersonian vision of an American nation of autonomous producers and citizens" (Licht 1983, 24), something Frank Dobbin could label an "ethos." We don't know why it was abandoned; historians have celebrated the rise of bureaucracy so assiduously, that they have not unearthed the evidence that might help us understand the demise of an alternative.

I would offer one explanation: contracting, including both contracting out and inside contracting, attracts too much attention if it is too profitable, and the owners quickly seek to "appropriate the profit stream," as economists would say, under beneficent environments. The profits of railroads soared after the Civil War. Indeed, by 1880 they took in $613 million and paid out a whopping 30 percent of that in dividends to stock holders and interest payments to bondholders. The additional profits the owner (stockholders, bond holders) received because of the efficiency of the contract system — let us say a 10 percent increase in profits — was swamped by diversion of profit streams to hundreds of contractors. Even if efficiency declined, and profits declined by 10 percent, when contract work was taken over or folded into the firm, the owners may have seen their profits swell because, for example, the engineer now was getting a salary or a daily wage, rather than, say, a 30 percent return on his investment and effort. One authority on the inside contracting system notes that it began to disappear in manufacturing when contractors rode to work in top hats and carriages, and were making more money than the owner (Buttrick 1952). (Since a firm typically had many contractors, were this to happen at times it would have still spread wealth more widely; replacing the contractors with salaried foremen would have concentrated the wealth, as well as reduce contractor's incentives to be efficient.) But of course there is no logical reason that capital should hire labor (convert the contractors to foremen) rather than labor hire capital (the contractor hires a capitalist with a railroad on which he can perform his skills).

We have reviewed two bits of evidence that the divisionalized bureaucratic structure adopted by most railroads (and then by most industry) was not inevitable. Some profitable railroads in the United States and in Britain got by very well with centralized structures, but I have argued that were they to become huge through acquisitions, the centralized structure would have probably been very cumbersome. Still, if profits had depended more on market control than internal efficiency, it probably would not have made much difference. The second, and more interesting reason why the path we took was path-dependent and not inevitable, is that for a time some of the leading railroads in the United States experimented successfully with extensive subcontracting, as did European roads. Rather than just keeping a railroad small in order to manage it centrally, this alternative broke up the road into several separate "profit centers" as we might call it today, with the profits going to the contractors. It would have meant a wider distribution of wealth and power, which is why I believe, but cannot prove, it failed.

If the divisionalized structure was not inevitable, did any particular structure matter? Was it not the economic and political hegemony of the larger railroads that determined success, rather than efficiency or service? The thrust of most historical work on structure and performance would deny this (though not all of the work), particularly Chandler. In a symposium on Chandler's work, most economic historians had nothing but praise for it. For example, David Teece, one of the most interesting of economists for sociologists, said that "it was the development of effective professional management and organizational systems to support the development of vertically integrated business enterprises" that counted for Chandler, in contrast to the conventional economic literature on growth and development; and Teece agrees with Chandler. So power is marginalized by even one of the most sociological of economists (Teece 1993). But even with Chandler there is a lapse. He was too good a historian to ignore organizational power completely, but in his brief but most extensive reference to it, to which we turn, he denies its importance.

While celebrating the managerial revolution of the railroads, Chandler himself appears to admit that during the building period, the management of the roads was less important than market control, and efficient service was quite secondary. Commenting on Henry Varnum Poor's major reform effort, which sought to foster publicity and disclosure, he notes that "by providing the maximum of information either through voluntary means, financial pressures, or state legislation, Poor hoped to make economic self-interest and competition a force for social progress." But this view, Chandler says, only "hampered Poor's understanding of the new railroad problems and limited the usefulness of his suggestions for reform." It would be silly, Chandler notes in a remarkable observation, for "the railroads to compete for traffic by improving service rather than by cutting rates." Improving efficiency rather than aggressively working for new traffic "invited bankruptcy" (1956, 177). Listen, then, to this uncharacteristically *real politik* view of management's problems and tactics:

> More certain ways of obtaining immediate traffic than the improvement of service were to build or purchase feeder lines; to undercut competitors by offering special rates to shippers, cutting all rates on routes where competition existed and raising them where it did not; and, when competition had brought rates too low, to make treaties with competitors dividing the traffic and maintaining rate schedules. To survive in the competitive conditions that came into existence during the 1850s, the roads resorted to competitive methods which from their point of view made any very detailed presentation of their accounts or activities almost an impossibility. And if a road was determined not to give information, it was extremely difficult for any outside agency to get accurate data about that road no matter what laws were passed. These were the same conditions, requiring as they did a flexibility in management, which made impractical Poor's plan to have the policy-making board of directors contract out the day-to-day operation of a road to a separate company of railroad managers (177–78).

This passage is in marked contrast to his celebration of efficient management, low rates, expanding volume, and all the other ingredients of the "master narrative." Were these the dynamics of the "first big business?" They were exactly what the Grangers, many lawmakers, and very many shippers were in an uproar about. Put more bluntly, market control through oligopoly, secret kickbacks, monopoly pricing, cartels, breaking treaties secretly, and violating disclosure laws is what the railroads had to do. All of this is summarized benignly in Chandler's last sentence as the "flexibility" management needed that made decentralization of profits and operations impossible. The railroads that pursued these measures, we may safely conclude, were the ones that survived; survival depended on such predatory tactics, not on the management structure that Chandler celebrates in his other writings. Of course, perhaps he would claim that after the 1850s, efficiency and service came into their own, but the next three decades were characterized by oligopoly, kickbacks, monopoly pricing (high prices where the competition had been eliminated, low prices where it persisted), cartels, and nondisclosures.

I have argued that administrative structure — the decentralized structure that many roads adopted — was probably not important for survival and success, since other successful roads in the United States and abroad did quite well with centralized structures. However, the decentralized structure accomplished one thing quite well and it was to be important — it permitted very large organizations through acquisition of competitive railroads and the linking of lines into regional and then national networks, a matter to be taken up shortly. I have also argued that regardless of centralization or decentralization, the successful experiments with subcontracting and inside contracting indicated that smaller or less hierarchical organizations that dispersed wealth and power were quite efficient. All this suggests more than one path was possible, even within a privatized industry. We will now turn to two other important organizational characteristics that were also in flux in nineteenth century railroading: leadership style (autocratic or participative) and the treatment of labor.

LEADERSHIP STYLE AND WORKER WELFARE

Whereas Chandler and others deal with the formal structure of the "first modern business," we have Licht to thank for pulling together materials on the more evanescent matter of management styles and workers experience. Despite the presumed imperatives of technology and their convergence on bureaucratic administration, management styles varied greatly. Nothing in the literature explains why some managers were strict or lax, indifferent to workers' welfare or concerned with it. Rationales were plentiful for any style. For example, it was argued that concern with welfare improved productivity and thus profits, whereas others said it just reduced profits. Some managers were strict disciplinarians, citing the need for precision and the accident risks of the business, and others believed that a disciplinary style destroyed work incentives and morale and did not ultimately benefit efficient operations. The nature of the technology could be invoked to require either obedience or initiative. Some took no interest in their employees' welfare and others had company-sponsored welfare measures such as group health and life insurance and even profit sharing. It could be that the rapidly emerging bureaucratic structure entailed no particular management style, and there were benefits to indifference as well as concern, to strictness as well as latitude. (Something called "contingency theory" today, to which I have contributed, would be shocked to learn that technology dictated no particular structure or leadership style.) More likely, however, is the possibility that the comparatively trivial effects of differences in style were overwhelmed by market and route strategies, financing, government subsidies and land grants, and the behavior of competitors.

Licht does not address the issue of whether management style matters, but judging from the following quotation, I think he would agree that other things matter much more. Speaking of the executives, he says, "Although they occupy the common position in the productive process they did not forge a common or coherent philosophy; in fact, labor related matters occupy little of their attention" (1983, 29). Only strikes, of which there were an abundance in the late 1800s, seemed to catch executives' attention, and even then the strikes were often treated as if they were unrelated to the executives' behavior, much as a mud slide or a flood might be. A business that brings annual returns of 30 percent and can count on the state militia to keep the lines running during strikes might not be concerned with fine tuning either its management style or its labor relations.

In his book on Poor (1956), Chandler notes, "To the laboring force, Poor, like most of his business and editorial contemporaries, paid little attention" (197). This is true of Chandler as well, and it is customary to fault him for leaving out labor. In his *Visible Hand*, he declares that he cannot deal with everything, and will leave it to others (1977, chapter 1). But he need not take that position. Labor, in fact, does not seem to have mattered much for railroad performance until the great strikes near the end of the century, after railroad consolidation. (That the railroads had a great deal to do with the labor relations inherited by the twentieth century is a different matter; we will redress Chandler's neglect of this issue in a moment.)

However, organizational structure and leadership style are another matter. My view that they were of only marginal significance for performance will be rejected by both the economic historians, who are mostly conservative, and by labor process theorists, who are all radicals. The former would reject the implications for efficiency theory, believing that, at least over time, the most efficient form prevails. Although it is true that, until Chandler, little attention was paid to internal structure and process, there still was universal agreement that a bureaucratic form was a functional necessity. They simply did not detail, as Chandler did, the way it came about or its multidivisional refinements. The radicals would reject the thesis I have proposed because their view of capitalism requires that owners and managers suppress workers and exploit them.

If, as Licht shows, some did not, there is the messy matter of why. It cannot be because labor policies were not an important variable to the managers and owners; for radicals, extracting the most "surplus value" from workers preserved the class system.

I rather suspect labor policy was in most respects inadvertent; some owners and managers saw "driving labor" as profitable, and others saw cooperation as profitable. Either would not make much difference due to the extraordinary prosperity of most railroads — despite the waste, abandonments, failures, and bankruptcies. The search for efficient forms, for refinements of the emerging decentralized bureaucratic structure, came later in less prosperous and more competitive industries. But the decentralized bureaucratic form, with its inadvertent labor policies, had far-reaching consequences. When the railroads became large, centralized, and national, labor had the opportunity to wreak much greater havoc; the large railroads had government support for breaking strikes, and more interest in suppressing strikes than they had in realizing small efficiency gains by treating their workers well. When that happened, the labor policies of the roads were no longer inadvertent and inconsequential, but were deliberate. The policy of calling in federal troops and strike-breaking private agencies (a policy of confrontation rather than negotiation) and creating propaganda facilities, all quite successful, set the tone for new giant firms that were created in the great merger wave. Railroads imprinted labor relations for most of industry, and in examining how this happened, we can see how organizations matter. They created a new "culture" of industry-labor relations.

Work in General

A few other observations about work at this time are useful, as the interpretation of most historians, and my own account, favors a view from the top. Recall that we are a long way — many decades and many big organizations — from a "society of organizations." We are witnessing the appearance of a hundred or so organizations of over 1000 in size from the 1860s to the 1880s, most of them railroads. Apparently personal and family connections were extremely important in finding jobs, as they are today. People moved freely and got their first job easily, sometimes on the basis of very slight skill, connections, or requirements; patronage, favoritism, nepotism, and even extortion were common; employment of family-based groups of workers was also common. One might expect railroad workers to move a lot, and they did, but so did most of the people in the nineteenth century. Summarizing the work of Stephan Thernstrom (1969) and others, Licht says that "in any given community in any given decade, upwards of 60% of the inhabitants moved" (1983, 69). But he goes on to say that, for railroad employees, this was not a picture of rootless, atomized, and disassociated managers and workers; "railway men moved frequently but often only to re-establish contacts with relative, friends, fellow employees, and former supervisors. Family and personal connections remained important factors in securing jobs, and their influence within the industry quite often transcended geographical distances" (59).

Although the topic of labor shortage is controversial, with some economists saying there was one and other economists denying it (Licht 1983, 60), in the case of the railroads "the overall pattern [was] one of adequacy and even surplus of labor" (61). Turnover was very high (73). Even for managers, only about half remained over two years, and only a quarter of the lower-level employees did. (There is no adequate data, Licht says, on how this pattern relates to the rest of industry.) "The real question of labor supply was not whether a large and competent pool of workers existed to staff the industry, but whether railroad labor once mobilized could be retained" (77). He concludes that "America's pioneer railroads, thus emerged under conditions of labor surplus and not scarcity, but more important, within the context of high employee turnover" (78). During the time of its great expansion, up until the 1890s, this was probably a somewhat less wage-dependent industrial population than most, but that is hard to judge.

Licht's chapter "Working to Rule" documents not only the extensive rule books at the time, but also the difficulty of bureaucratizing actual tasks, which were varied due to special circumstances; this account moderates the "bureaucracy ascendent" thesis of labor-process theorist and others, but does not refute it of course. His chapter "The Rewards of Labor" documents high wages and the many rewards of working for the railroads. American railway workers made twice the rate of British counterparts (129). In the chapter "Perils of Labor" we learn that "prior to 1880 and even 1890, railroad companies resisted all attempts to introduce safety devices like the automatic airbrake and the automatic coupler." Laws were passed, but few roads abided by them, and in many states railroads joined forces to block passage of safety device measures (188). Even the state railroad commissions opposed new safety legislation, as did for example, Charles Francis Adams, Jr., the head of the influential railway commission of Massachusetts (188). Even locomotive engineers opposed the introduction of air brakes. Operating the brakes was an extra task, and they were not paid extra to do it. But by 1874 the engineers came out for this safety feature. The Westinghouse brake was first tried in 1869 and was well improved by 1873. Throughout this chapter I have argued that in terms of safety the industry was most inefficient. Licht notes, "It was not until 1893, a full 25 years after the invention of both the automatic brake and the couple, that Congress narrowly passed the Safety Appliance Act" (189). Regardless of the act, "In 1889, for every 117 train men employed, one was killed; for every 12, one was injured. The Interstate Commerce Commission found these figures distressing too, for in England the corresponding statistics were 1 trainmen in 329 killed and 1 in 30 injured." Licht goes on to say, "During the 19th century approximately 3.5% of the nation's railway workforce at any given moment were disabled." The brakemen led the most precarious lives. For a ten-year period, 1874–84, one company found that one in seven men in the "switching service" — which presumably included brakemen — suffered a disabling injury, and one in ninety were killed. With returns of 30 percent, such carnage has an especially melancholy ring. The second big business was big in many ways, and the inattention to safety may have been related to its size and power.

We get some sense of this in the way that the courts responded to the appeals of railroad corporations in the matter of safety, and how they imprinted labor relations for the rest of industry. Legal historian Morton Horwitz notes, "The introduction of railroads after 1830, however, not only magnified the risk of serious employment injuries; it also seems to have established the first really impersonal system of employment in America" (1977, 208). In the textile mills we have discovered that the workers injured by machinery were at the mercy of the paternalistic system of employment current at the time. But limited as its benevolence was, the paternalism was disappearing. Workers did not often seek redress in the courts. But in an 1841 railway case, and in a landmark railway case in 1842, workers tried to sue. The courts acknowledged what came to be called "agency theory" today: there could be "no question, that, in general, the principal is liable for acts of the agent, performed in the execution of his agency." But the court held that it did not apply if there was a contract, such as an employment contract, because the parties to any contract were equal and had freely entered into it. Before the nineteenth century, Horwitz notes, the principle that the principal (owner) is liable for the acts of the agent (employee) did not have anything to do with contracts, or private agreements, but was imposed by a normatively superior customary law. It was taken for granted. But with the 1841 ruling, it was suspended when there was a bargaining relationship, a contract. No prudent man, the court said, would engage in perilous employment unless higher wages compensated for the risk. This was a market conception of legal relations, ratifying "those forms of inequality that the market system produced." Equal bargaining power "inevitably became established as the inarticulate major premise of all legal and economic analysis" (209–10).

Of less importance, but worth mentioning, were the pension programs, where, like safety concerns, the heroic harbingers of big business were distinct laggards. Notes Licht, "While European railroads began establishing structures for inclusive insurance as early as mid-century, interest and acceptance of such proposals came only very slowly in American industry" (1983, 207). "In France, Germany, and England, carriers at an earlier date introduced super-annualized funds to which both employees and employers made contributions. In America the idea was little discussed." Only the Baltimore & Ohio had a pension plan at the turn of the century (212–13). Of course, most industries did not, but "the first big business" was not leading the way here, either. Despite high wages and other rewards, then, "working for the railroad" had little retirement security and many dangers. It was the nonwage issues that prompted the great strike waves of the late century, and in this, as in organizational structure and control, the railroads were also pioneers. Wages were less an issue than the externalities of the firms, such as late wage-payments (months late) and numerous working-condition issues. The issues, and the behavior of the two sides, tells us much about what was to come in what was just beginning to be a society of organizations. The pattern for labor-management accords was laid down by the struggle of labor against rising industry and government troops.

Chandler and others are often criticized for leaving labor out of their accounts, but if their concern is the administrative structure of the industry, they are probably justified. But if the issue is the impact of the biggest industry with the biggest and richest organizations of the century, then labor issues cannot be ignored. First, there is the distributive issue, the concentration of wealth. At a minimum one can say that increasing labor's share of the large profits probably would have reduced the accumulation of surpluses in the hands of top management and major investors somewhat—though not by an equivalent amount, because the firms would have increased the price of goods and services somewhat to compensate for their loss. (Still, I don't think there would have been a great deal of redistribution since railroad profits depended most heavily on inflated construction contracts and watered stock and monopoly pricing, rather than driving down wages and thus increasing operating profits.) With lower profits, the economic power of elites would have declined, they would have not been able to waste as much, bribe as much, and shape other institutions as freely. A more affluent working class could afford more time and resources for addressing the

political questions of power and the economic questions of such externalities as pollution, crowding, health and safety, and retirement.

Next, with the government and especially the courts on their side —
but not often local communities (despite the disruption caused by
strikes, strikers got sympathy from communities fearful of corporate
power [Montgomery 1979]) — and with their great economic power,
railroads were emboldened to confront labor rather than bargain with
it. It seems likely that in this respect, confrontational labor-management
tactics were quite successful, and that the railroads set the pattern for
the large organizations in other industries that were coming into being.
Because labor largely lost its battles and thus was weak, management
did not have to explore the possibilities of labor-management cooperation. It seems quite likely, and was argued as such by many at the time,
as noted earlier, that cooperative relations would have improved productivity; a larger share of the surplus for labor would have meant a
larger surplus for both management and labor or cheaper goods and
services. In this view, management's labor policies were both socially
inefficient and inefficient for the enterprise.

Next, the evolving pattern of big enterprises begat the counter-force
of big labor in the next century. As unions grew very large indeed in the
twentieth century, as they had to in order to deal with large corporations and large government, labor organizations themselves generated
inefficiencies and externalities, and the staff and employees of the big
unions began to *absorb* civil society just as big corporations did. Finally,
the pattern that the railroad industry developed reinforced the drive
toward the centralization of the economy, the bureaucratization of enterprises, and the criminalization of many forms of labor activity such
as the right to strike and the right of advocacy. Had economic historians
not neglected labor issues, or not simply treated them as a constraint or
side issue, but instead seen them as outgrowths of the rise of big business, the full measure of what big organizations such as steel, mining,
and the railroads did for half of the work force that was wage dependent at the turn of the century would have been assessed. One did not
have to be employed by a big corporation in 1900 to feel the effect that
those corporations had on labor-management relations. The script for
even the small firm was well established.

NATIONALIZATION AND CENTRALIZATION: THE FINAL SPIKE

Privatization with light regulation was the first major organizational
triumph of the railway age. Bureaucratization was the second. But these

two alone, as significant as they were, would not satisfy the elites who were shaping the system. Privatization meant private, rather than collective (societal) rewards would predominate. Bureaucratization afforded unobtrusive control over the huge work forces that even regional lines were acquiring through consolidations, and it created narrow production efficiencies with "driving" labor and unsafe working conditions. In 1880 the railroads were big indeed, and for the times, they were the biggest organizations around. There were eighty-four firms that had over 1000 employees; the average number being 3,714. While representing only 12 percent of all firms, they employed 74 percent of all employees (Licht 1983, 35).

But how much more manageable and profitable the system would be if the system could also be centralized, and serve national, rather than local and regional markets. Privatization itself did not necessarily entail a few centralized, national corporations; some railroad executives and quite a few labor and farmer groups fought for a regional system and against a national one. Indeed, the Interstate Commerce Commission, established to regulate the railroads in 1887, initially sought regionalization. Nationalization was not technologically inevitable, nor a result of the huge capital needs and the "lumpy" nature of the railroad investments, though that had always been the only argument until the work of Gerald Berk (1994). National interests won out over regional ones because of a "market failure" in the railroad industry. The abundance of capital and governmental subventions allowed too many weak lines to be built, and in the reorganization of bankrupt lines, centralized capital sources in New York exercised their preference for big (thus national) over moderate-sized (thus regional) organizations. They lobbied the courts in order to weaken the act establishing the Interstate Commerce Commission. It took time, because regional interests were strong too, but it seems clear, though it cannot be proved, that increasingly the interests of large capital held sway over the consciences of a majority of Supreme Court justices, and produced a rather bizarre but fatal ruling in favor of nationalization, as we shall soon see.

Organizational Versus Political Interpretations

This is an *organizational* interpretation: organizations—the large investment banking houses and commercial banks and the railroad corporations—made the decision as to how our transportation system would be organized. The judiciary sided with them rather than regional organizations and interests, which were not powerful enough to ensure regional control of the system. This view is in contrast to an *efficiency* interpretation, which sees a national system as more efficient, and a *political* interpretation, which argues that political actors either thought it in the best interests of either the nation or their constituents to have a national system (political ideology), or felt that to get reelected, or reappointed, they had to act in terms of the interests expressed by their constituents (the behavioralist and rational-choice political theory that is favored today).

Throughout this work we have been at pains to emphasize the role of powerful organizations in shaping national policy. Dartmouth College, pressing for independence from the constraints of representatives of the public, was not powerful, of course, but the ruling it got was an important step in allowing gradually larger and more powerful ones. We moved on to the contrast of the Lowell mass-production textile mills — a unified interest, shaping public policy and market structure — with the Philadelphia flexible-production mills — a plurality of decentralized interests that reflected representative social as well as economic concerns — and then on to the regulation of the railroads. It is now time to try to disentangle two essential "drivers" of public policy: the political and the organizational. Both involve power and organizations and consequences for the polity. But just as we contrasted Lowell and Philadelphia, we now will contrast the national and the regional organization of rail transportation. The proponents of a national system were the large railroads and large capital sources (banks, investment houses). Though they used politics — Supreme Court decisions favoring a national system were essential — the leverage was organizational power: the allocation of capital resources, concentration of ownership, support of elite class interests, governmental largess, and financial corruption and bribery. Politics, in the sense of elected representatives and appointed officials acting out of ideology or acting in terms of the interests of electors, was not greatly evident, though, as we shall see, some politicians were eloquent about the defeat of the public interest by monopoly.

The proponents of a regional system were a much more diverse group of organizational interests — the smaller railroads, merchants, local industrialists, farmers, and such labor groups that existed. Their leverage had to be political more than organizational, because their organizational interests were diverse and conflicting. It was through a political process of bargaining, compromise, regulation, and electoral platforms (and the ideologies the platforms formulated) that their interests would be represented. Organizational interests were sufficiently diverse and deconcentrated such that political processes at the legislative and administrative level were needed to reconcile interests and select winners and losers. At the regional level, then, politics reigned. At the national level, where a national system was being proposed, organizational power reigned. The national interests won out, and thus I would characterize this as organizationally driven, and emphasize an organizational power interpretation. Had the national interests not won, the regional victory would be characterized as a political one. (I acknowledge, but cannot avoid, the logical dilemma here of selecting on the result, the "dependent variable." If the result favors national interests I assert the cause to be organizational, if it were regional, then I assert it to be political.) Politics could have been triumphant, but it was trumped by organizations.

This seemingly recondite and even tendentious distinction between a political and an organizational process allows us to use both political and organizational explanations where appropriate. The political sees diverse organizational interests mediated by politics, the organizational sees concentrated ones controlling politics. (Though the former tends to be local and the latter national arenas, local areas such as one-industry towns invite an organizational view, and highly competitive national industries, such as the early computer industry, invite a political interpretation.). Our approach is not inconsistent with the interpretation of our indispensable guide in this historical moment, Gerald Berk, for it recognizes the political. But it does not call it a "constitutive moment" and a "political" decision, as he does. Decades of pressure by railroad interests makes it neither a constitutive moment nor a political decision.

More was decided by the large organizations than just the length of a railroad, as we shall see later when we turn to the work of William Roy. For when overinvestment in the railroads brought about a crash in 1893, the now-centralized capital markets needed someplace to invest other than in railroad consolidation, and in the industrial age it would not be in agriculture or marine shipping, the previous consumers of capital. Money poured instead into the mining and manufacturing industries, so fast that in five short years (1898–1903) more than half of the book value of all manufacturing capital was incorporated, the aggregate value of listed stocks and bonds going from $1 to $7 billion (Roy 1997, 5). The firms were made giant by consolidating the assets of several firms in the same industry and market. Naomi Lamoreux notes that "from 1895 to 1904, 75 percent of the firms that disappeared into mergers joined consolidations of five or more enterprises" (1985, 1). More than 1,800 firms disappeared into consolidations. (Lamoreaux, however, attributes the consolidations to "abnormally serious price wars" at the time [12].) By 1904 most of the giant firms that would remain giant until the present (after further mergers in some cases, of course) were formed, in a vast intoxication with market control and oligopoly. As a result, very big organizations were to be our lot and to determine our fate.

Thus, the importance of the railroads goes far, far beyond the consequences for modern management structure or the consequences of economic integration celebrated by historians, and even beyond the labor-management discord that a few have addressed. The railroads' twisting historical path—with its path dependencies of ownership (public, then joint, then private) and path dependencies of regulation (from close to almost none to some) and with its scope (local to regional, then decisively national)—prompts an organizational view of history. This twisting path made the modern multidivisional multiproduct corporation possible, and once the national versus regional issue was settled, it did it virtually overnight.

Where Did the Money Come From?

The first major railroad boom was in the 1850s, and it fueled some novel devices that we need not dwell on here: an extensive call loan market (short-term credit), a spot market for corporate securities handled through the New York Stock Exchange, which dealt primarily in railroad securities, and a new class of private investment bankers, drawing on seaboard merchant funds and those of European investors. In contrast to Europe, there was no crown to challenge the accumulation of private capital or to regulate the variety of devices employed to insure its rapid flow and risky fictionalization. The various markets and "instruments" expanded greatly during the Civil War, that great stimulus to private profit, and private banking grew rapidly from 1862 to 1870. Railroad construction collapsed during those years (perhaps because of the war and its aftermath), but recovered in 1869 and then doubled its prewar rate of growth. Vast new funds were available for construction, many from the seaboard merchants, the very group that had opposed internal development heretofore, when they had favored instead the export of raw materials and the import of manufactured goods. These seaboard merchants had lost the political battle to Hamiltonian manufacturers, who passed protective tariffs that would favor local manufacturing and created a shaky national banking system. The seaboard merchants then capitulated to the Republicans; they certainly were not going to join farmers and labor. The Republicans made sure that the war loans the merchants had made were paid off rapidly.

Flush from profits on their war loans, a new class of private bankers began to invest in the development of the trade across the Alleghenies and into the west (Berk 1994, 26–28). As the nation tried to evolve a national banking system, complex restrictions and regulations governing banks in the hinterland reduced the capital available to agricultural and city and town interests, and perhaps inadvertently, channeled it to New York City capital markets (33–34). National policy kept money tight, despite protests and despite domestic economic and population growth, and prices actually declined near the end of the century. This attracted enormous overseas capital, and it went to the only place at the time ready to use such sums, American railroads. We can add the fuel of the government subsidies and land grants, and revitalized commercial banking firms with money to lend, to the economic stimulus. (As an attentive reader, you will notice more than organizations at work here; political and ideological forces were at work; but so were organizational interests, and they were able to capitalize dramatically on the confluence of forces.) The result was the pouring of money, from 1870 to 1890, into railroad construction. Just between 1870 and 1872, as many new miles of track were added as had been built prior to the Civil War. Berk summarizes this rapid transformation:

> By design and unintended consequences, the New York money market became a magnet for domestic and international savings; and by far the largest portion of that credit went into the railroads. In sum, the pace of rail construction doubled after the war for politically contingent, not technologically necessary, reasons (35).

Although technology was clearly not the reason, as we shall see, we should qualify Berk's conclusion a bit, as to what was intended and what was political. To some extent the consequences were unintended by federal regulators; attempts had been made to prevent the centralization of capital, but they backfired. But the reason they backfired is neither accidental nor do to political actions; organized interests, such as banks and railroad companies, thwarted the regulators' attempts to disperse capital among the major cities. A dispersion would mean more players and more competition; a concentration would mean fewer. Who, then, could be for the dispersion? Would not all financiers and railroad owners and executive favor concentration, if they might be one of the concentrators? Yes, but if they were in Des Moines or even Chicago, they had little chance to be one of the concentrators. Capital markets were being centralized in Boston and especially New York since the Civil War. If financiers and railroad owners were in Des Moines, their best bet was to argue for regionalization, and to band together with the merchants and farmers and manufacturers who would benefit, and secure the acceptance of public representatives.

Once again, to elaborate on our earlier distinction, this is what is meant by a *political* process, as distinct from an *organizational* one. Those pushing for regionalization did so in a political marketplace. Those who sought nationalization avoided that marketplace as much as possible and exercised concentrated organizational power. To venture a definition of the political process, it requires diverse organizational interests capable of checking the power of any one of the organizations, or any one group, such that bargaining and alliances take place, and these require ratification by political actors such as elected or appointed officials and / or political party leaders. Although the settlement will affect organizational interests, these are diverse, and it will also reflect to some degree the interests of groups of citizens. Citizens thus have at least a presumptive role in the process. The process tends to be public, as well.

An organizational interest process, on the other hand, requires one or a few allied organizations using economic power (economic and political threats, bribery, public officials that primarily represent their interests, or governmental largess) to secure legislation, rulings, and favored treatment to achieve their goals. The clearest difference is in the number of parties actively involved, and the extent to which public representatives who are not serving the interests of one party are involved. The interest of others, organized or not, public or private, are accommodated to the minimum extent necessary, and may not be accommodated at all, and settlements as well as any necessary negotiations are likely to receive as little publicity as possible. In both cases, organizational interests are being served; they are among the actors. But in the former they are diverse and include governmental and political organizational interests. In the latter, they are more restricted to a particular set of organizations (and any political or public representatives whom they control or with whom they have allied themselves). Political processes include as their drivers ideology as well as voter interests that need some representation, and their output is public development. (Of course corruption can erode the political process, too, and turn it into an organizational or personal-interest process.) Organizational explanations have owner interests and the interests of powerful segments of the organization (which may not mesh with the owner's interests) as their drivers, and the content of these interests is largely made up of the ways in which organizational power and control can be used. Like many distinctions of this type, there is a serious weakness here: it is hard to imagine how it could be tested. As already noted, it tends to rest too much on the outcome rather than the process; it pronounces "political" when there is no clear winner and much compromise, and "organizational" when there is a winner and not much compromise. But it is a beginning attempt to distinguish the organizational from the political.

The consequences of organizational power also appear to be quite intended, rather than unintended. New York financial interests lobbied for the legislation that would benefit them, clamored for quick debt reduction, and once they had invested in railroads, softened their opposition to greenback inflation. And although these events are "political" in a very broad sense, they are organizational in the quite specific sense that a few organizations brought about the events. But the larger point is the main one: the country wanted railroads, certainly, but the timing, growth, and centralization of the capital market was not because railroads were capital intensive such that our financial markets had to respond as they did. It is, rather, that circumstances and interests created a pool of easily available capital that needed a place to go, and the railroads and their bankers were ready to provide that place. The best evidence for this is how dramatically they overshot their mark. Between 1870 and the turn of the century virtually half of all railroad mileage collapsed and fell into court-ordered receivership — half the mileage was bankrupt and a good part of that was to rust away (Berk 1994, 26). This gross "miscalculation" suggests an abundance of capital and a free market to play in.

REGIONALIZATION VERSUS NATIONALIZATION

As the capital markets of East grew large, it favored big customers, the twelve or so lines that could be national, over small customers, the three hundred or so local and regional lines. The small railroads pushed for a regional system, as did their local customers, whereas the big lines and big customers favored a national system. The Interstate Commerce Commission and its act of 1887 favored a regional system, wherein competition would be regulated through regulating rates, but successive Supreme Court decisions favored railroad concentration and the regulation of monopolistic lines through other means than the rates. The Supreme Court justices won the struggle on behalf of the big railroads and big capital, and regional development was thwarted. Berk (1994) treats this as "constitutive politics" — a confluence of interests and ideologies that is settled by political means. This is a better interpretation than a crude self-interest argument (the struggle of railroads versus merchants and farmers to maximize profits) or a simplistic economic rationality argument (long hauls and cars with only one product in them are more efficient than short hauls with mixed goods — which is true only if the measure of efficiency is that of railroad profits, rather than the larger economic system of which they are just a part). But Berk's characterization leaves out the other significant actors, or agents, other than the railroad companies — the financial houses and banks. The interests of these organizations is not simply profit, as a crude interest group theory might put it, and it is not just any kind of power, as a crude class analysis might put it. The controlling organizations and the railroads they controlled appear to have wanted a type of economy that favored large units of all sorts — manufacturing, mining, transportation and communications — with limited competition. These would have created the markets most suitable to them, mass markets, which in turn would have permitted the most suitable form of output — mass-produced goods — that would have fostered the preferred type of customers — standardized customers.

The organizational interest, once you have the possibilities of dominating a market and have few network constraints, includes not just wealth or profits, but the institutionalization and reproduction of a form of economic structure that favors large, oligopolistic organizations. Profits per se are a goal of course, but profits are also a means to insure the long-term generation of profits in a system with minimal economic and social instability, and controlled change and minimal change, one that will bring stability of family and ethnic membership in the elite that manages the economic system. If we can explain behavior in these expanded terms, we avoid a "simplistic" economic interest explanation, and even the vague "constitutive politics" one.

What lay behind the regionalist interest was not narrow sectionalism (as argued by Elizabeth Sanders and effectively countered by Berk [1994, 80]), which resembles a cultural argument, nor was it the narrow economic self-interest of farmers and merchants and subnational railroads, but a view (Berk inflates it to a "worldview," but that is a bit grand) of how an economy would function without the "ruinous" competition that would easily lead to oligopoly. If most of the essential manufacturing was centered in the East, there would be big firms and oligopolistic profits, and little room for independent local manufacturing. What local manufacturing there was would be dependent on the big national firms and would be servicing them. If there were viable independent local manufacturing along the Mississippi River, which had the resources for it, the local firms and their merchants would prosper and grow as independent units, not as appendages. It was a developmental issue — how should the economic development of the nation proceed — but the alternatives were national development through centralization, or national development through regionalization. As we got the former, we have to present evidence that the latter "ethos," regionalization, existed, and was viable, and show specifically how it was defeated. That is our task in the rest of this section.

The Debate over the Ethos

As with other turning points of decision in the Republic, the one concerning national versus regional development was well debated and evolved over decades. The issues were muddy and the interests of various groups could be unclear, shifting and cross-cutting. The overall issue turned on novel circumstances — short-haul and mixed carloads were more expensive than long-haul unitary carloads, but how much more, and what were the *externalities* or costs of long-haul unitary carloads? There was little competition for the short hauls, one or at most two railroads might serve a middle-sized town, so that the railroad firms could "extract monopoly rents" — charge high prices on these. There was much competition between large, interregional cities, such as Chicago and New York, or St Louis and major southern cities. Because of the greater "sunk costs" of these long hauls (big investments in track and right of way and rolling stock), the railroad companies wanted them as fully utilized as possible. So they cut rates to attract long-haul customers. Long-haul shippers thus benefitted. Indeed, rates were cut so much that the long hauls were losing money, and railroads had to raise the rates of their short hauls to "cross-subsidize" or pay for the losses. There was little competition for the short hauls, and much for the long ones.

A few ways were possible to avoid the transparent inequities associated with cut-rate long-haul charges and expensive short-haul charges. Government regulation could declare that it was unfair to favor long hauls, where there was competition, and unfair to penalize short hauls were there was monopoly. The Grange, a powerful pressure group of farmers in a few Midwestern states (then called "Northwestern" states), sometimes called for identical rates, regardless of distance or the mixing of cargoes. But more often they favored a second possibility; they called for simply decreasing the spread between the short and long haul rates without eliminating it. Long hauls were cheaper, but at present they were under cost; raise these rates and lower the short-haul rates. The short hauls, with rates lowered but still well above cost, would increase in volume, as more goods were produced for and sold to regional markets rather than national ones, and thus generate more profit for the railroads. Farmers, at one regional conference, went so far as to demand that the federal government replace its heavy subsidies with both public ownership and operation of selected railroads, setting competitive standards for the remaining private carriers (Berk 1994, 79). So even the privatization issue was not dead in 1873.

The railroads and the financiers (and liberal intellectuals, including Charles Francis Adams writing in the mugwump journal *The Nation*, and Arthur Twining Hadley, a Yale University president and economist) claimed that the railroads would go bankrupt and that this would be the forceful confiscation of private property if the rate equalization laws that the Grangers were getting passed in several states were allowed to continue. But there was no evidence for this whatsoever (84). In fact, studies at the time and later on showed that in the states where the Grange laws were passed, thus equalizing rates or reducing the spread, the railroads performed a bit better on all measures (profits, growth, and return on investment) than in non-Grange states (86–87). Rate equalization apparently promoted traffic, as predicted, thus providing evidence for the viability of a regional system. This evidence has been ignored by most historians.

Another alternative to the uneven long-haul and short-haul charges was to allow pooling, whereby competing railroads divided up the business under government price regulation. Pooling was practiced, but without strict regulation it led to collusion between railroads and the cartels in livestock, oil, and anthracite coal, with large profits and distortion of rates and distorted economic growth. The weak Massachusetts commission that was to regulate pooling, sponsored by Charles Francis Adams, was reduced to just publicizing the grossest violations; they were not given the power to stop them. It was questionable as to whether commissions such as this, representing the public, could counter the power of the railroads. One critic at the time noted the dramatic shift of Charles Francis Adam's position, from a devastating critic of Jay Gould and railroad corruption in 1875, to a supporter of ineffectively supervised pools. "The power of the railroads," wrote the critic, "cannot be conquered by any body of 9 men at salaries of $7500 each" (98). In theory, with strict regulation, pooling should have worked, and did in some instances, but this alternative soon disappeared. Our old bogey, culture, in the form of "American equalitarianism," is brought forth to explain why there was such strong opposition in the House of Representatives to state-supervised pools. Historian Martin Albro, writing in 1974, argues that the opposition in the House was irrational, rooted in a "deep-seated mistrust, hatred and fear of large, insulated aggregations of power," public or private (cited in Berk 1994, 96). Eminent historian Stephen Skowronek in 1982 echoes this explanation (127–30, 141–50). But it is hard to equate, as he does, "large, insulated aggregations of power" with a low-salaried government commission supervising the pooling arrangements of private business; the "aggregations of power" are better represented by emerging national railroads with paid retainers in Congress. And the "equalitarian" American citizens in several states, reportedly so fearful of centralized power, strongly supported even more drastic aggregations of state power — the strict and crude Grange laws. The pooling schemes were clearly pro-business, compared to the Grange laws, but they were not clearly pro-nationalist; as such the pooling schemes would not receive the support of legislators receiving the ample railroad favors from the big lines with national ambitions that so characterized the period.

There was ample evidence to support an argument that the public feared big business more than it feared commissions of nine men on modest salaries. In Pennsylvania, Standard Oil colluded with the Erie Railroad to monopolize the trade in crude oil, through the use of secret rebates, industrial sabotage, and strong-arm tactics. In this way J. D. Rockefeller gained control over more than 90 percent of the oil industry by 1890, and there was ample and graphic publicity and outrage. (In relative terms, he was far richer than any of our billionaires today, and this occasioned more outrage.)

In fact, despite the "efficient scale" justifications of Alfred Chandler for Standard's strategy (no one actually defends the secret rebates and the sabotage and violence, historians merely justify it), Berk notes that the independent producers had lower costs in many respects, were able to control overproduction and periodic price wars, built the first successful oil pipeline across the Alleghenies to the Atlantic Coast—cutting out the railroads and increasing efficiency. "More important, by sharing transportation and collectively regulating the flow of crude to seaboard refineries, the independents claimed external economies equal to Standard's internal economies." Rockefeller, however, forced the independents to abandon the pipeline, and Standard regained control of the industry (Berk 1994, 90). Politics was certainly involved. As Berk says, regarding the larger struggle wherein national market rate-making was able to undermine "constitutional sensibilities of fairness and the moral economy of regionalism, . . . the outcome would be determined in politics, mediated through Congress, the Interstate Commerce Commission, and the Supreme Court" (91). But rather narrow, even crude, organizational interests seem to have been at stake, and the public was aware of it. (Narrow and crude organizational interests are evident in the recent biography of John D. Rockefeller by Ron Chernow [1998].) He offers extensive evidence, ignored by previous biographers, of deception, dishonesty, law-breaking, threats, ruthlessness, and violence, though comparatively little corruption. It is a striking portrait of amassing and using organizational power, but Chernow is not concerned with our issue of centralizing power through nationalization, at the expense of regional development.)

Regionalism was a clear interest. From the beginning, prior to the Civil War, Chandler, in his biography of Henry Poor, notes that "the editors of all regional papers feared New York financial domination of their region" (Chandler 1956, 130). The historians of the Grange laws, Solon Buck and George Miller, although differing on whether the laws should be attributed to farmers or merchants, agree on the regional basis of the arguments. The founder of the Grange, notes Miller, long championed the "promise of the Mississippi Valley as a distinct region" with the North and South bound together by the great river along whose shores "every crop can be raised and everything manufactured." Many, Miller continues, "believed that the valley . . . had become too dependent on outside markets and thus it should be allowed to develop its own economic destiny. . . . This spirit of regionalism remained and was an essential part of the Grange movement in the Middle West" (cited in Berk 1994, 79). The area could make all the clothes, boots, and shoes it needed, and had the iron and coal and the skilled labor to make implements from iron. "Why not do it," asked the journal *Industrial Age* "and save the heavy freights from the East?" (79).

One Congressman argued that the railroad had colluded with major shippers to establish a system of "forced combination and centralization . . . a vast concentration of capital and work, and workers in the ponderous cities." Another said they had the power to "build up or tear down towns and villages, even cities, just as they please." Population and business enterprises were driven from the country and towns to the big cities, impoverishing the former. The system, said another, keeps producers and consumers far apart, forcing goods to be carried long distances, and then claims that low long-distance rates and high short ones are necessary (93–94). Berk concludes, "It transgressed the republican ideal of a society of small producers, located in a network of moderate-size cities, engaged primarily in regional trade" (95).

A report to the Interstate Commerce Committee by its conservative chair, but friend of farmers, Shelby Cullom, filled in the details: the railroad policy had resulted in the most efficient service and lowest rates in the world, but its effect had been "to give the large dealer an advantage over the small trader, to make capital count for more than individual credit and enterprise, to concentrate business at great commercial centers, to necessitate combinations and aggregations of capital, to foster monopoly, to encourage the growth and extend the influence of corporate power, and to throw the control of the commerce of the country more and more into the hands of the few" (95). It is a good summary of the argument of this section, drafted at the time by the chair of the ICC.

It is also an organizational, more than a political or cultural, account of what was to happen in the United States; there is no mistaking Cullom's emphasis on railroad interests rather than "constitutive politics." Nor can the political argument be saved by saying, as some do, that the policy favoring national lines *necessitated* the combinations and aggregations of capital. The argument says that the political policy determined organizational form. Once in place, the policy did; but why was it put in place? I would argue that the big financial institutions and the big railroads made sure that such a policy was established so that it would insure the combinations and the aggregations.

A Political or an Organizational Interpretation of the Struggle?

In Berk's analysis, the defeat of regionalism is clearly not due to any economic necessity; as we shall shortly see, regionalism was a viable option. Nor does he believe that cooperation and civic humanism was "overwhelmed by the hardened class and factional conflicts of industrial society" recently celebrated by leftist scholars (114). Presumably the leftist account errs because elites of the emerging class structure were on both sides of the debate, though Berk is not explicit on this score. Finally, it is not because of the gradual, adaptive process of "state building" in an era of rapid economic change, as celebrated by scholars such as Skowreneck and Skocpol. Neither scholar sees regionalism as a viable and intended alternative to "corporate liberalism" (maximum liberties for corporations). When regionalism is recognized as existing by such scholars, it is seen as an expression of private interests, an expression of the advancing division of labor. Instead, Berk offers "a genuinely constitutive account" of the modern corporation (115). Between 1887, when the ICC was established, and 1898, when Supreme Court Justice Field (who had earlier tried to tidy up New York state statutes) had led the court to disembowel its key provision, we have a constitutive moment, a reconstitution in favor of corporate liberalism. Here is how it happened, and here are the materials to decide on a political or an organizational interpretation:

The key issue was whether railroads could charge higher rates for short hauls to compensate for the losses on the long hauls necessitated by competition and large sunk costs. The ICC had been set up to say no to this practice, and by the end of its first decade, it had nearly eliminated the worst cases of rate discrimination. It also served the goals of rate stability and increased railroad revenues. Rate wars had devastated the industry from time to time, but policing by the ICC had increased the costs of cheating, thus stabilizing trunk-line rates (106–7). One might think that the railroads would have been happy with this state of affairs, but the more aggressive ones were not; the policy favored regionalization, and that meant many railroads rather than a few big ones. The federal judiciary began to chip away at the doctrine, and in the Alabama Midland decision of 1897, they in effect ruled that the provision that Congress had set up was not to be enforced.

The case involved a Southern railroad that charged a substantially higher rate from Florida to Troy, Alabama, than to Montgomery, Alabama, even though Troy was en route to Montgomery. Greater competition at Montgomery justified the lower rate, said the Supreme Court, and thus Troy, with no competition, should subsidize the loss (107).

Because the major intent of the ICC regulations had been to prevent this form of rate discrimination, and as it had been doing so effectively without harm to trunk-line profits, the Court's decision was certainly puzzling. Berk treats it as a consequence of "intransigent carriers" and a "corporate liberalism" ideology, but one is not satisfied. Would not the carriers who were not intransigent have realized that the law, when policed, was in their interests, and would not their presumably majority voice have carried the day with the court? Were the justices such ideologues that they could not see that unfettered competition was ruinous, and could only lead to oligopoly? Or were there other interests involved, that used the intransigent carriers and the conservative drift of the court to foster a nationalization of the roads, which is what the case tended to do? These interests could have been the "capitalist class," to put a loaded and dangerous name to it — the banks and investment houses and those individuals with large investments in potentially national enterprises — including but not limited to, railroads — who would benefit from local subsidization of their national enterprises. At least, this is what some thought at the time, and it is curious that scholars today generally fail to entertain or even discuss this proposition.

Progressive Wisconsin Senator Robert LaFollette was clear. The traffic managers of the railroads sought only to secure "the long haul, the big tonnage, the large revenues, and the dividend." It was of no concern to them that there was a *social economy* "of serving a given territory from the center which would serve it best and cheapest, the economy of the multiplication of convenient centers of trade and industry, of the building up of many small cities well distributed over the country" (cited in Berk 1994, 112–13). Instead, LaFollette said, it was centralized at four points: the Atlantic coast, the head of the Great Lakes, the Missouri River, and the Pacific Coast. Senator LaFollette's remarks cannot constitute the persuasive evidence that I need to argue that it was not an aggressive outlier, or a constitutive political moment, that decisively settled the issue of regionalism versus nationalism. In the nature of the case I cannot bring forth the evidence that would prove my point that those behind the court's decision would have had to be the banks and investment houses and corporate leaders of both the railroads and emerging industry. It was they that spectacularly benefitted, so they must have been among the suspects. It is not even clear that speculation about the interests of the Supreme Court Justices would help prove the point — their ties to the "capitalist class" interests, perhaps their personal investments or family connections. All I can offer is the insistence that organizational interests matter more than even such acute and perceptive analysts such as Berk have allowed, and are a more concrete explanation than "constitutive politics," just as they certainly are more concrete than "culture" or "efficiency." Regional republicanism "was defeated within the chambers of the state," Berk says (116), but I suspect it was in the board rooms of the dominant financial and industrial firms of the day.

The "constitutive moment" actually spanned the period 1870 to 1897. It was initially made possible by the 1870 legislative act in Pennsylvania allowing the Pennsylvania Railroad to own lines in the states stretching to Chicago and the South. (We will return to this important decision later.) Then there was the 1887 ICC formation, and then the 1897 Alabama Midland decision of the Supreme Court. The railroad sought an interregional reach, and achieved it. The "moment" then, was not a short period of ambiguous economic interests but three decades of concerted effort by the Pennsylvania, and then other major lines, to establish a national system.

Berk sees two conflicting camps, the regionalist greenbackers and the nationalist corporate liberals, locked in an ambiguous struggle wherein economic interests were unclear and conflicting. This gives rise to the "moment," when the issue was settled, and *then* we have normal power politics and clear interests to consider. To quote from a student's memo (James Cook) from a remarkable sociology seminar at the University of Arizona that Professor Marc Schneiberg and I tried to manage, "Berk is stubborn in his assertion that economic interests had nothing to do with the pattern of conflict between regional republicans and corporate liberalists, that 'the battle over regulation, then, is better understood as one over world view and program than economic interest narrowly conceived or a struggle between 'parochial' and 'cosmopolitans' in the state'" (cited in Berk 1994,18). But, Cook goes on to note, if local markets pay more for agricultural products and are more stable than national markets, and if short-haul rates in the corporate liberal system will be higher per mile than long-haul ones, one might expect the interests of the farmers to be unambiguous. They were; they sided with the regionalists. If corporate liberal organization leads to the dominance of Eastern urban centers, whereas regional republicanism leads to the dominance of regional agricultural centers, one might expect the intellectuals in the urban East to side with the corporate liberals, which they did, even the radical *Nation* magazine. And, of course, the big railroads with interregional tracks opposed the regionalist solution.

Finally, other students (Wade Roberts, Michael Mulcahy, Richard King) raise the issue of just how the federal courts were constituted (those favoring nationalist solutions appear to have been the dominant appointments), and even the possibility that their distinctively organizational interests played an "interest" role. (Their federal orientation might dispose the courts to rulings favoring national, rather than regional, interests that would have delegated their judicial power to states). Unfortunately, I have not pursued the lead that the courts had organizational interests and that the appointments reflected economic (and class) interests. There is already enough circumstantial evidence for an organizational interest account of the regional versus national systems stretching back to the 1860s to question an argument about a confusion of interests in a constitutive moment. Berk's account is crucial and unique in its consideration of a fundamental conflict between regionalists and corporate liberalism, and he effectively buries the economic rationality account. It is the marginal status of power and interests that I am contesting.

WAS REGIONALISM VIABLE?

The Chicago Great Western Railroad is Berk's centerpiece for illustrating the efficiency of a regional railroad (Berk 1194, chapter 5). Interestingly enough, the hero, A. B. Stickney, started out as a speculator. One newspaper editor described him, and the railroad business of the time, thus: "Of the many railroads he built, not one of them did he build with the intention of operating them as independent lines, but built them for speculation, and he has made money by doing so." But for unknown reasons, this time was to be different. He built and successfully ran a profitable hub-and-spoke system with terminals in Minneapolis, Omaha, Kansas City, and Chicago. At the center of the web was the little town of Oelwein, and his first innovation was to move all his shops there, and to introduce the first use of electric power in railroad shops in the nation—a much admired and copied innovation. Next, he violated the doctrine so celebrated by Alfred Chandler by doing away with a multidivisional organization. He eliminated the four divisions in the four major cities, thus substantially reducing the hierarchy. He introduced what we might call today "project managers" who worked directly with employees in the field. Station agents, dispatchers, and freight handlers gained discretion and had their lines of communication with headquarters shortened. With this structure, flexibility rather than high-volume mass production was possible, and it enabled the railroad to handle diverse mixes of freight, variable daily loads, and short hauls. (Contingency theory works here.) Compared to the major trunk lines, it is rather like our comparison of the mass-production Lowell and the flexible-production Philadelphia textile mills.

The Maple Leaf, as the Great Western Railroad was called, worked well for several decades; it was profitable, efficient, and served the region well. Why then was it sold at an auction in 1909? (J. P. Morgan controlled it for a time after that, but it remained an independent line for a half of a century thereafter, presumably integrated into the national rate structure.) The proximate cause was "a series of events (that) overloaded the carrier" (Berk 1994, 145). One line required extensive renovations in 1906, and in 1907 there was a wage dispute. Stickney was unable to secure further financial support, and J. P. Morgan moved in and briefly took it over. But the basic cause Berk gives was that it ran counter to the "prevailing norms at the turn of the century" (145). We may question this normative explanation; indeed, Berk does so at times. "The Maple Leaf was precisely the sort of road Morgan had tried to bring to heel" (147). "Once the national systems had committed themselves to a high division of labor and extensive operational hierarchies," that is, once they had chosen this form rather than a flexible form such as Stickney developed, "the regional shippers' demand" for equal pricing "became costly." That is, with a national system in place, reducing the high short-haul rates would affect profits too much. It was the national organizational form, rather than any inherent technology of economies of scale, that required "long-term relational contracts with large-scale, long-haul shippers" (124).

It would be too much to say that if the modern multidivisional organizational form had not been invented, we would have had a regional railroad system with a more decentralized and flexible economy. A lot of other things could have happened, such as fatally ineffective governmental regulatory bodies that stifled development, or a centralization of ownership without any accompanying economies of scale and long-haul single-freight economies. Still, as the with the textile mills, and even with the experiments with subcontracting in some railroads, the causal role of organizational form should not be neglected, if for no other reason than it offers a more concrete explanation than ones based on "constitutive politics" or "American ethos."

CONCENTRATING CAPITAL AND POWER

Railroads were the first organizational powerhouses on a national scale, far more influential in creating a society of organizations than were the organizations in the textile and other local or regional industries. Their significance is that they pioneered the organizational forms that were to spread throughout industry, and then throughout government and nonprofit organizations. We have examined the railroads' internal structure (divisionalization, records, surveillance, etc.) via Alfred Chandler, recognizing the novelty but treating it as less remarkably innovative than Chandler did, and seeing some of it as even fortuitous and accidental. But the corporate structure — ownership, liability, and strategic control — is only lightly treated by Chandler. Berk goes into it substantially, with discussions of "friendly receiverships" and the critical decision to treat the corporation as a natural entity. But the most extensive discussion, drawing in part on Berk, is by William Roy. For him, the corporate structure put in place by the railroads becomes the essence of capitalism; the history of the railroads decisively shaped our form of capitalism. His remarkable book, *Socializing Capital: The Rise of the Large Industrial Corporation in America* (Roy 1997) will be our indispensable source for the final and most important part of the story of the railroads in America. The title, *Socializing Capital*, refers to the dispersion of ownership and its attendant risks through widespread stockholding. "Instead of each firm being owned by one or a few individuals, each firm became owned by many individuals, and individual owners in turn typically owned pieces of many firms" (10). At issue was the nature of property, and it was the corporate structure (rather than the more narrow organizational structure) that determined this. That structure changed dramatically in the late nineteenth century.

Roy's analysis is what might be called, with apologies to Alcoholics Anonymous, that of a "recovering leftist"; there is no ruling class, but there are class interests among the organizational and financial elites; labor has been left out of the equation completely (though it often is given too much agency in leftist accounts; it is as inconspicuous here as it is in Chandler, unfortunately); there are no conspiracies, but rather, the inexorable use of financial power in the interest of financial accumulation that hardly needs elite conspiracies; corruption is not a significant dynamic, but shows up in power struggles among different interests; power is central (it is a power analysis) but is ever hedged with neoinstitutionalist constructions, giving the whole a disembodied atmosphere and a script with only marginal roles for concrete organizations. My use of Roy will, not surprisingly, be to reinstate concrete organizational actors and to convert the "socialization of capital" theme to something I am more comfortable with, the "definition and legitimization of big organizations." But there is no question in my mind that in terms of relentless scholarship, tight argument, and explosive findings, there is nothing to match this book for understanding the transformation of property relations under capitalism. Would that more leftists had recovered as well as he has!

The Corporate Form Triumphs

Roy's early chapters cover much of the same ground we have already covered, and I have cited him in connection with these. Where he begins to build on the narrative I have laid out so far is in his distinction between entrepreneurial and corporate forms of governance (and thus of property relations). This is important enough to review closely. The noncorporate firm was owned by an entrepreneur, or by partners, or a few joint stock holders, and run by these owners. Owners had first claim to the assets, including profits, but they were liable for any debts or failures or lawsuits, not just to the extent of the firm's assets, but their personal assets as well. If the firm failed, creditors had first claim on the assets that the firm held when it failed, including the personal ones of owners. All this caught the attention of owners, and linked the fate of the firm they owned and presumably managed, with their own fate. In addition, tightening the link of performance and reward, revenues and expenses were tightly coupled. This coupling provided quick indications of problems and emphasized productive efficiency. Owners were limited to owning only those businesses they held full title to, and in practice, because of these restrictions, the businesses would be only modest in size, and thus no more than regional in scope. These limitations, Roy decisively demonstrates, would not make them inefficient (chapter 2). Indeed, I would argue, from the industrial districts literature, that the productive efficiency of firms of this size and nature is higher and their social efficiency much higher than that of large, corporate firms.

The form that replaced this, first in the railroads and then in other major industries, was the corporate form. Ownership was widely dispersed, but control was centralized in the hands of one of three groups, which often overlapped: owners of large blocks of stock, top managers, or investment banks. Owners, whether large or small, did not risk any of their personal wealth in the event of failure or lawsuits, they risked only their investment; controlling managers might not even have any investment to risk. Dispersed owners and creditors are disenfranchised; dispersed owners lack voting power and control over major financial decisions, and creditors' claims are subordinate to the claims of investment houses; dispersed owners and creditors thus become one of many "interest groups." Because stocks and long-term bonds provided capital, sales revenue might fall below expenses for years without triggering inquiry or corrective action; this, I would stress more than Roy does, opened a large door for inefficiency, and for corruption. Competition could be controlled by buying stock in competitors' firms, and a controlling interest obtained by an investment of 5 to 10 percent might eliminate competition and lead to profitable price rises without the costs and responsibilities of full ownership of the supposedly competing firms. As the corporate form encouraged much greater investment capital than the noncorporate form, which was limited to a small circle of owners (family, friends, partners), corporate firms could be much larger.

TABLE 6.1

Characteristics of Corporate and Noncorporate Firms

Noncorporate Form	Corporate Form
Single or few owners	Dispersed ownership
Run by owners	Run by managers/major stockholders/banks
Full liability	Limited liability for owners
Owners retain first claim to profits, creditors to liquidation	Owners and creditors lose power to managers, major stockholders, and banks
Direct link of revenue and expenses, maximizing efficiency	Stocks, bonds, and mortgages break the link between revenues and expenses, permitting inefficient performance
No ownership of shares in other firms	Own controlling interest in other firms
Small to moderate size	Large
Local or regional market	National market
Limited monopsony opportunities unless geographically isolated	Large monopsony opportunities
No oligopoly unless isolated	Oligopoly
Decentralized wealth and power	Centralization of wealth and power

Controlling competition would also increase their size. With large size, they would have an interest in national rather than regional markets, and would be able to dominate suppliers better than a local / regional firm of smaller size. This would invite a greater centralization of wealth and power. I have listed the characteristics of each in Table 6.1.

Every one of these characteristics was subjected to close examination and controversy in the nineteenth century, as Roy makes clear. No national character, no technological imperative, no efficiency drive was responsible for what emerged. What lay behind the change from the noncorporate to the corporate form as the dominant mode of economic organization was a series of legal decisions by the courts, statutory laws by the legislatures, and administrative rulings by governmental bodies. It is these that he seeks to explain.

THE CORPORATE FORM AND CORRUPTION

First, however, a note on the corruption issue. In addition to a weak national government, and competition between states and between local communities for railroad service, we can add the structure of the organizations as part of the context that gave the organizations the opportunity to corrupt officials. Under corporate capitalism, if the return from revenues is insufficient, the firm can go into the stock or the bond market and obtain funds to keep going; capital is "socialized." Mortgage bonds can be sold offering a fixed interest rate and a fixed due date, and this money will be available regardless of the "profitability" of the firm, that is, regardless of its revenues and expenses. This may allow an inefficient firm to survive for years, especially if bondholders have little information about its performance, or are given, as was common, deceptive information. Or, additional stocks can be sold, bringing in the money needed to cover the gap between revenues and expenses. The amount of stock sold may far exceed the liquidation value of the firm (one basis of "watered stock"), further masking the link between performance (revenues) and survival.

As valuable as this form of financing — corporate capitalism, involving the sale of stocks and bonds — was for capital intensive industries and new industries, it greatly reduced the discipline of the marketplace, and invited fraudulent practices. When over half of the trackage went into receivership in the late nineteenth century, boosterism and over-building was certainly involved. But even where fraud was not intended, the corporate form of finance with limited liability, and with dispersed and uninformed owners, contributed to it. I believe that a good portion was due to fraud and corruption, though it is impossible to quantify the amount, or even clearly to define what was illegal.

Because of corporate financial devices used initially by the railroads then by other industries, Roy estimates that until the 1890s the enormous profits of the railroad companies came at least as much from constructing and merging railroads as from operating them. We think of railroads as being profitable if their operating revenue exceeds their expenses, and thus it depends on the efficiency of the firm. This, at least, is the economic and the Chandlerian historical point of view. But it appears that very inefficient firms could be considered profitable because they could convince those with the capital to buy stocks or bonds that the corporation would survive, and could convince the government to give them grants, loans, and free land. In fact, one might conjecture that the efficient operation of the firm was less important for survival and for profits than securing capital and governmental largess. If so, the link between efficiency and survival is greatly loosened, thus encouraging fraud and deception.

Perhaps even more important is the fact that when the survival of a railroad is threatened, whether because fraud is disclosed, or because of poor planning or even inefficient operation, whether the railroad actually disappears or not has little to do with the source of its difficulties. Railroads did not fail for these or other reasons so much as they were "reorganized" in order to put them on "sound footing." The master of reorganization, the firm that did most of it, was the investment house of J. P. Morgan. But with the separation of performance and survival, who survived and who failed did not depend on processes linked to efficient performance, but linked to other criteria — political patronage or influence, or the interests of large investment houses. When J. P. Morgan reorganized a sizeable proportion of the industry, his investment house decided which lines would close and which would get a competition-free lease on life on the grounds of return to his organization, the investment house. Picking and choosing which railroad companies would emerge as the dominant ones was based on his organizational interests, not efficient operation of the line or efficient layout of trackage or efficient development of regional resources.

It is here that we see the blurred line between an organizational and a "capitalist class" interpretation. Morgan's interests, as Mark Mizruchi reminded me in an extensive and penetrating critique, was certainly in the organizations that he controlled, but he was also the steward for the American capitalist system; his organizations were the means to control, and, as Neil Fligstein (1990) might emphasize, to stabilize that system. Another version of the stabilizing thesis can be found in Dobbin and Dowd, who maintain that bursts of "predatory" behavior (buying or bankrupting weak lines) that interrupted the "cooperative model," were ended by financiers, "who stood to lose the value of their diverse holdings in small firms" (2000, 636). But the financiers were the big investment houses, such as the House of Morgan, interested not so much in seeing that every firm they held an interest in was protected, since those interests were small, but in seeing that their much larger interests in a few big firms were protected and extended. Promoting consolidation would not only do that, but increase their wealth and power by centralizing the system in their hands.

Explaining the Arrival of the Corporate Form

To interpret the change from entrepreneurial organizations to the corporate form, Roy explores several explanations. The first, the efficiency explanation is quickly and neatly disposed of. Chandler and other economic historians would predict that the corporate form would predomi-

nate in industries that were rapidly growing, technologically sophisticated, efficient, and that had mass markets, and those with the most
amount of these characteristics would be the ones that survived. The
data do not support it. Analyzing firms and industries from 1901 to
1904 to see the degree of incorporation, and the survival of firms eight
years later, Roy finds that size alone, not even scale economies, is the
principal predictor of incorporation and survival. His measures of efficiency (productivity and growth in productivity) have *no* predictive
power (1997, 28). "Scale, not economies of scale, accounted for the
creation of corporations" out of the entrepreneurial form. "Any economies of scale, at least as indicated by productivity, had little influence"
(31). And survival of the biggest was striking; the top 200 firms in 1912
were the top ones in 1973 (26).

Throughout the book Roy repeatedly challenges the efficiency explanation as he lays out the process of incorporation. For example, a stunning chapter on pools and trusts in a variety of industries also negates
the efficiency argument (1997, chapter 8). Most manufacturing was primarily entrepreneurial until 1890, with very few large "socially capitalized" industrial corporations; by 1905 the latter dominated the
economy (221). Constructing a statistical model that explores consolidation, he concludes, "The results are consistent with the argument
that firms with initial advantages use those advantages to reproduce
their prominence" (37). Roy's measures of efficiency accounted for very
little of the variance. His model explained a striking 42 percent of the
variance in incorporation — mostly from size and capital intensity. To go
into these key examples of consolidation and monopoly in tobacco, paper and pulp, sugar, food, and finance itself would illustrate our argument but take far too long.

Part of the explanation is historical accident. One of Roy's favorite
examples is the sharp recession of 1837, which occurred just after states
and localities had made large investments in turnpikes, canals, and a
few railroads. The recession triggered political processes that led to statutory restrictions on public investment by states. Losing some 20 percent of their transportation investments, states passed laws forbidding
public investment in transportation (1997, 72–73). (As we have seen
earlier, I would argue that railroad organizations played a key role here;
after the depression, they refused public investments that meant regulation, but accepted them when no effective regulation would accompany
the public monies. This removed the last feeble occasion for effective
regulation of routes, rates, and safety, privatizing fully the growing railroads, in contrast to Europe.) Neoinstitutional theory then enters Roy's
account, because privatization, he says, quickly becomes taken for
granted as legitimate. (I would stress the effort of organizations and

elites to legitimate privatization, and the resistance by merchants, labor, and communities. All that was "taken for granted" by the latter was that they had lost.) After the Civil War, he goes on, there was no need to consider the public interest in any industrial or transportation or mining operation, even if public funds were utilized. Political processes—the actions of the state legislators and the judiciary—were combined with historical contingency, and, in his account, the two generated the construction of social legitimacy.

A second confluence of historical contingency and political processes is the sharp depression of the late 1890s. As a result of overbuilding and corruption, railroad stocks and bonds suffered two setbacks after the Civil War, and the second one sent European investors—and U.S. investors, who were less important—out of railroads and into looking for alternative uses of capital. Coincidently, the railroads and the growing investment houses had pioneered the new corporate form and they allowed the investment houses to turn to manufacturing firms, convince them to reorganize as corporations, buy up their competitors or merge with them, and thus centralize several of the major industries, with the investment houses continuing to exercise control (1997, chapter 8). Dispersed stockholders were made passive, liability was limited, inefficiency could be masked with new infusions of capital, competition could be controlled, and national, rather than regional markets favored, resulting in uneven development of the nation. Supreme Court decisions were crucial in making all of this happen, a political interpretation in Roy's scheme. But once it was in place, neoinstitutionalism is invoked to explain the taken-for-granted acceptance of what was once bitterly opposed by a good part of the public and perhaps most of the merchants and smaller noncorporate firms. The neoinstitutionalist spin on the incorporation and merger movement, what Roy rightly insists was "an event" rather than a "process," seems unconvincing. After all, it all happened in one stunning four-year period, setting our industrial structure for the next ninety years, and thus not leaving much room for crescive social constructionism, habit, and taking things for granted. Unfortunately, I know of no data on the wealth shares of the very rich that covers this short period. R. E. Gallman has calculated the share of the nation's wealth held by the top .031 percent, and it rose from 6.9 percent in 1840 to 14.3–19.1 percent in 1890, more than doubling in fifty years of industrialization, and this is before the great consolidation (see Williamson and Lindhert 1980, 43). The merger movement was more of an event than a process, but it is more like an imposition that is well defended and sticks, than a construction. There is plenty of agency in Roy's account, it just needs to be highlighted and made explicit. Let me attempt this.

An Organizational Agency Account

It is perhaps ironic now, at the beginning of the twenty-first century, when the attack on strong governments and the praise of free markets is so strong, to recall that the bastion of these sentiments, Wall Street, was a creation of our government. In the early 1800s the U.S. government needed to borrow money and states needed funds for transportation projects and public utilities (Roy 1997, 122). The institutions of Wall Street—the stock and bond markets, clearing houses, credit raters, stock and bond sellers—gradually appeared, with governmental blessings and encouragement, to serve these needs. Initially, and until the railroads appeared, the Street dealt primarily with government securities, and secondarily with bank stocks and insurance company stocks, as did similar and more advanced institutions in Europe. Industrials were not listed or traded in any number until well after the Civil War.

The war gave a big boost to the financial institutions housed on Wall Street. It stimulated the first large-scale securities market in the United States when Jay Cooke copied techniques of mass marketing used by Napoleon III to finance his Crimean War, socializing finance capital by bringing together scattered pools of capital. The war syndicated underwriting, bringing together a group of investment houses that purchased and then sold government securities, thus centralizing finance capital. The war established Wall Street as the center of the securities market and strengthened links to the all-important foreign capital (127–31). The government obliged corporate and financial interests and created a national currency and banking system with the National Banking Act of 1863, and by creating the mechanism for drawing money from rural and hinterland areas into the New York market of finance capital, it further centralized wealth (132).

The rapid changes were not unnoticed. Wall Street institutions became targets of political criticism. After the war, President Andrew Johnson charged that "an aristocracy based on nearly two and one half billion of national securities has arisen in the northern states to assume that political control which was formerly [only] given to the slave oligarchy" (cited in Roy 1997, 134). He was a bit off in his geography; the aristocracy that financed over half of that was European, not Northeastern ($1.4 billion in 1870, to rise to 3.3 billion in 1890), but those foreign finances were increasingly controlled by Wall Street investment houses. The European investing community hardly needed the meager American business, notes Roy, but the United States was a poor nation, and the investment was crucial.

One unwitting consequence of massive European investment was that it helped redefine the nature of property, and thus of organizations: did the railroad belong to stock holders, who had purchased shares in it and presumably could choose the leaders of their organization, or did it belong to those who just lent money to it, by purchasing its bonds? Both had legitimate claims. Those of the bondholders proved stronger because the law, reasonably enough, gave them first claim to assets if the company was liquidated. The stockholders bore the greater risk but would reap the gains of dividends and appreciated net worth, gains not available to those who merely leant money. Thus the interest due the bondholders had to be paid before any dividends on stock. European investors overwhelmingly preferred the more secure bonds to stock. It is estimated that 90 percent of all international capital before 1914 was in bonds (or nonvoting preferred stock, which was similar). With more and more of the financing coming not from the owners — the stockholders — but from the lenders, "stock ownership lost many of the rights of ownership, including a much weakened right to manage," says Roy, who adds that they "even lost some of their right to profit insofar as interest on bonds took priority over dividends on stock." Bondholders, and more importantly, the investment bankers that represented them, "often gained the upper hand in directing the corporation" (138). Control was being centralized in Wall Street institutions, not dispersed throughout the nations' stockholders.

Again, the shift was noticed and controversial. The Pennsylvania Railroad Company, controlling 13 percent of the nation's railroad capital, was doing well in 1874, having paid an average of 9.9 percent in dividends per year over the past twenty-one years. But nonetheless when management developed an unprecedented $100 million bond issue, a committee of stockholders was formed to protest. They owned the company, they said, and were "the original and only source of power and authority." They were losing some of their rights of ownership, such as the amount and terms of borrowing money, leasing the property of other companies, guaranteeing rentals to other railroads, setting the interest and principle on bonds, and incurring nonincidental liabilities — all of these arrangements affected the interests of stockholders as distinct from those of directors. Most specifically, tracing their diminution of power to the increased use of long-term bonds that had first claim on assets and profits, they strongly resolved that bonds be issued only temporarily and only for expansion and construction (138). They lost, just as stockholders, unless they were very big ones, have lost continuously until the stirrings of pension funds in the 1990s.

It is important to note the cause-effect relationship here, identifying the independent and the dependent variable. Roy is not particularly concerned with who or what disenfranchised stockholders; whatever it was it became embedded in legal practices ("institutionalized") and people's expectations ("construction of reality" as our ponderous phrase puts it). But the stockholders' suit identifies the "agency," or source of the disenfranchisement that was taking place throughout the country—it was the directors of the railroads. It was they who substituted bonds and nonvoting preferred stock for the more conventional stock offerings.

It is important to unpack the catchall, "directors," particularly because of the image created by Berle and Means (1932), in which dispersed and powerless stockholders, and a few professional managers, with insignificant amounts of stock, run the business. This was greatly overstated for the 1920s companies that they referred to, because families controlled as much as one-third of the big corporations; and the image was even less applicable at the end of the nineteenth century. (For the first of several studies criticizing Berle and Means, see Zeitlin 1974). In the late-nineteenth-century directorship we find three major interests: (1) the top operational managers, such as the president or chief executive officer and key vice presidents including the finance director; often they were also sizeable stockholders; (2) major stockholders not affiliated with investment houses and other financial institutions, such as wealthy merchant families; and (3) those directors who were representatives of the major sources of capital, the investment houses. These three groups, I would argue, the top operational managers, major investors, and representatives of finance capital, were the agents of the legal revolution that made the corporation a distinctive, and model, organizational form. As they deliberately built the law that was to separate the corporation from the entrepreneurial firm and the partnership—always against opposition—they built the major outlines of our economy and pulled our political values toward their organizational vision.

The burgeoning economy, swelling along the tracks of the railroads and heated by combustion engines and then radiating electricity, needed all sorts of devices to raise and distribute and profit from capital. The "institutional structure" that emerged in the second half of the century bypassed the noncorporate form, that is, the entrepreneurial firms and the partnerships and joint-stock companies. These noncorporate forms were hobbled by restrictions and limited to the cash economy. Although they certainly remained the preponderant form in sheer numbers, because they required little capital, and were effervescent and flexible, if they were to grow they had to incorporate. Large corporate firms could use the growing stock market with its growing number of laws and governmental enforcement and backing; the friendly states that allowed one corporation to buy the stock of competitors and control competition; the brokerage houses that turned hard money into paper, allowing it to be packaged in easily accessible and transferable piles; investment houses that reorganized firms and concentrated markets to make them less competitive; businessmen's associations that created the legal means to inform, organize, and discipline industries; credit rating houses that "institutionalized trust"; and a specialized mass media that informed the nodes of the complex network of corporations and their service organizations as to what was doable and needed doing, and who was paying. Of course all these developments required an infrastructure legitimating them, and this was the government, guaranteeing the reality of the paper money, enforcing liability laws that the corporations drafted, and punishing those who breached the practices the corporations wrote into laws. But the government responded to the agents, it was not itself the agent.

LIMITED LIABILITY

For the corporate form to emerge as it did, the top managers, top stockholders, and the agents of the investment houses required legal changes to make the institutional structure responsive to their desires, which, I believe, were simply organizational growth and the centralization of wealth. One legal ruling they sought was limited liability. The joint-stock company had all the powers of corporations, but liability could not be limited. It would be very convenient if the failure of enterprises could be, as Roy loves to phrase things, "socialized" — that is, if the *costs* could be spread as widely as possible and as far as possible, protecting the major investors. The limited liability afforded the corporate form served this purpose. Investors could lose their investment, but not any of their personal wealth. Legislators in some states objected; they said that the consequences of ill-advised undertakings, mismanagement, corruption, and fraud should not be so heavily visited on innocent communities, workers, and suppliers that went unpaid. The cause or source of the disaster, the investors, should bear the brunt of the damage, and several states required this. As Roy puts it, "Limited liability basically shifts the risk of enterprise from the owners to the creditors, including construction companies, suppliers, lenders, and laborers. So it is not surprising that limited liability was not accepted without debate" (160).

For example the author of a widely cited legal treatise on corporate law, William W. Cook, published in 1891, was alarmed by it all and reasonably argued that stockholders of banks should be liable for twice their investment so that depositors could be compensated if the bank failed; the stockholder enjoyed the profits from using the deposits, and so he or she should suffer from insolvency. Cook noted that Michigan and Ohio required that stockholders be liable for debts to laborers when a business failed; New York had such a law for railroads; and California required the same liability for stockholders as for partnerships. But, as Roy notes in discussing this, Cook acknowledged that corporations avoided chartering in such states, and chose the ones that allowed limited liability for corporations (160–61).

The corporate arguments for limited liability seem less persuasive than the arguments against it, but states such as New Jersey accommodated them. Herbert Knox Smith, who might fit Seller's description of the early-nineteenth-century lawyer as a "hired gun of capital" (see chapter 1 of this book), argued that because the mass of capital was "necessarily" dispersed, efficiency required that it be centralized in a few hands. Roy dug out Smith's *Yale Law Journal* article from 1905 and quotes him: "The many small investors, necessarily thus deprived of personal responsibility, control and supervision over the use of their individual contributions, must in equity also be relieved of personal responsibility for mismanagement" (Roy 1997, 161). Having lost out to the big investors for efficiency's sake, they should not be held accountable. Fair enough, but look who else was not to be held accountable. The big investors on the board of directors and the representatives of the investment houses placed on the board of directors were also relieved of responsibility. They did have control and supervision and thus would be the source of any mismanagement. Appropriately, Mr. Smith went to Washington as the U.S. Commissioner of Corporations.

Production, Roy notes, is a collective activity, and neither directors, stockholders, nor investment banks holding securities should be considered the "essence" of the corporation any more than suppliers or employees. Legal definitions of the role of each are something to be explained, not taken for granted, and in the nineteenth century the definitions were "up for grabs." "Why is a strike seen as the workers against the company rather than as an intra organizational conflict?" Roy asks. "Why are workers considered a creditor when the firm goes into receivership? Why aren't the promising ideas of technicians considered an asset in bankruptcy proceedings, especially because 'goodwill,' a quality at least as elusive, is frequently considered" as an asset like capital? (162). Indeed, we could add, why doesn't labor hire capital? (It does in a few professional firms.) We can push Roy a bit further than he seems willing to go with his reflections on institutionalization as a "historical force with a momentum of its own," in the presently popular formulation of DiMaggio and Powell (1991). Corporate interests needed the Mr. Smiths in Washington and in the state houses to obtain legal authority for the centralization of business and wealth; it had as little to do with "institutional ethos" as it did with efficiency arguments. Reality had to be *deliberately* "constructed" and "institutionalized" by persons, agents, and groups with interests.

The issue of liability was not an academic one, though it was debated academically. Between 1875 and 1897, seven hundred railroad companies representing more than half of the country's track went bankrupt (108). In the famous Wabash decision the owners were treated as just another interest group, like labor or creditors, whereas managers were considered the representatives of the corporation — which now was no longer a fiction, but a *natural entity* that had to be preserved. The managers of many bankrupt railroads became the managers of still larger, consolidated corporations built out of the failed ones mainly by J. P. Morgan; the managers were preserved. Judges, under the pressure of railroad managers and investment banks, discarded the contract theory of the corporation, in which a contract existed among investors, and "adopted a natural entity theory, treating corporations as collective bodies best directed by managers rather than owners" (109). (See also Berk 1990, on whom Roy relies heavily.) We can see the natural entity theory in operation with the case of the Southern Railroad, which bankrupt, needed reorganization. J. P. Morgan's investment house agreed to handle the reorganization (they did most of those concerning the railroads) but only if a majority of stockholders put voting rights in trust, not only during the reorganization, but for some time afterward. According to Berk, Morgan used his power to gain enormous concessions from bondholders: debt was cut by about a third and the participating railroad companies were consolidated in one large holding company (Berk 1990, 146). Out of these reorganizations, by the turn of the century, the railroad companies had coalesced into six major communities for the whole country (Roy and Bonacich 1988).

THE HOLDING COMPANY INNOVATION

There was one major impediment to the centralization of wealth and power through the railroads: there were too many of them and they competed. The last thing capitalists want is competition; most of what they do is directed toward eliminating competitors entirely or preventing them from taking their customers. One alternative is to simply buy out one's competitors, which is what happened rapidly in manufacturing and mining with the four years of intense mergers at the close of the century, once there were pools of money to finance them. But it was very expensive, and in the 1880s there was not the wherewithal to consolidate thousands of railroad lines into a few. One agreeable alternative would be to purchase stocks of other lines, of either competitors or extensions of one's own network of lines. This would limit the capital needed, and limit the liabilities of outright ownership, while still enjoying both returns on the stock in the form of dividends, and the much greater returns of limiting competition so that rates could be higher, and extending the reach of one's lines to bring in additional business. Not surprisingly, many saw this as the equivalent of reducing competition, and thus raising prices and profits at the expense of the public.

The debate about whether a company could own other companies was intense, and would continue for decades as holding companies appeared, and were outlawed, followed by trusts, which were then outlawed, and finally by multiproduct firms (the forerunners of today's conglomerates), which successfully completed the redefinition of the nature of corporate property. (The classic work on this sequence is by Fligstein [1990].) In the beginning, the debate was over what the corporation was—an activity of individuals, or an entity, like an individual, in its own right. As an activity of individuals, it represented the pooling of resources to do things that a single individual could not do, an entirely reasonable conception. But "as a contract among individuals, they should not be entities that themselves could hold property other than their physical assets" notes Roy (1997, 150); individuals agreeing to pool their resources could not own an interest in the resources of other individuals that were pooled; they would have to buy them out completely. As most states strictly defined the circumstances under which a corporation could sell its assets, often requiring unanimous stockholder approval, and almost always requiring a majority vote, buying up a part of another corporation was not feasible. But to control another company required only a controlling interest, generally much less than a majority of the stock. Therefore, a conception was needed that allowed the individuals of one company to own an interest, even if not a controlling one, in another company. This would permit the first company to reduce competition.

Such a conception was quickly conceived by the corporations interested in controlling competition. They argued that the corporation was an "entity in itself," not just a legal fiction as in the first view, but a social reality, an entity that acted. It was, in legal terms, an *individual*, and given the power to do things that individuals could do, including owing stock in other companies. A partnership could not do this, nor even an entrepreneur, a single owner of a company. For a time and in many states, the courts would not allow a corporation to own stock in other companies, but the notion of the corporation as an entity with the rights of any individual was plausible enough that eventually one state, Pennsylvania, managed it through a special charter for the Pennsylvania Railroad. A few years later, New Jersey allowed any corporation that incorporated in New Jersey to own interests in other companies. Corporations flocked to New Jersey to register, and soon we had a new form of the corporation, the "holding company," which existed solely to own other companies (Roy 1997, 150–51). Competition could now be controlled.

Legitimating the holding company, where one firm could own stock in another, was not easy. Many states foresaw the oligopolistic implications of this and forbid it. But transportation was vital for states. Philadelphia, Baltimore, New Jersey cities, and New York City in particular saw their economic future linked to the control of routes from the dense Eastern corridor to the grain heartland (which were being increasingly controlled by Chicago), and later to the control of routes to the Pacific Coast. The Pennsylvania Railroad was probably the first to legitimate holding companies on any scale, but it required special legislation that the legislature was quite willing to provide (295). We have no record that Scott, vice president and then president of the corporation at this time, had to spend any of his bribery money. (Recall that Huntington complained in the Colton letters about the high prices Scott was willing to pay for legislators' votes.) But it would have been worth a lot to him. To get to the Chicago lodestone the railroad had to pass through Ohio, Indiana, and Illinois, and each could impose tariffs. Allowing the Pennsylvania Railroad to own stock in connecting lines would insure its health, which became increasingly robust as it soon became the biggest corporation in the world.

Chandler provides some details in a matter-of-fact, functional account. "To assure legal control of their many properties, the Pennsylvania perfected the modern holding company." In 1870 it got the legislature to charter a holding company for the northern holdings they sought, between the Atlantic coast, the Great Lakes, and the Mississippi River, and the next year one for the southern ones. The northern company purchased stock in several lines and in the fast-freight firms (shipping firms), and solidified its empire. The competing Baltimore & Ohio did likewise (Chandler 1977, 155–56). But these were ad hoc accommodations that required legislative charters and perhaps attendant fees. Until 1888–89, when New Jersey essentially legalized the holding company for anyone wishing to incorporate there, other states had restricted it. Firms rushed to New Jersey; the state was able to avoid income taxes because the revenues from the incorporation business were so great. By 1901, 66 percent of the U.S. firms with $10 million in capital or more, and 71 percent of those with $25 million or more, were incorporated in New Jersey. Incredibly enough, as Roy notes, "despite their historical impact, these laws were virtually unnoticed when passed, with not a word in the financial press or national newspapers" (Roy 1997, 152). A zealot might cry "conspiracy," but that is going too far; it is enough to say that it was the result of obvious organizational interests in market control and empire building.

Although it is disingenuous to phrase the drive behind the Pennsylvania's interest in holding companies as Chandler has, "in order to secure legal control of their many properties," it is not much of an improvement to cite the "taken-for-granted" mechanisms of neoinstitutionalism. Roy has a regrettable tendency to do this. When Roy travels the path-dependent route he goes too often by the way of vague atmospheric "institutions" rather than the organizational mountains. The infrastructure of corporate capitalism—banks, investment houses, brokers, the stock exchange, and the money system—so brilliantly analyzed, are, he says, "the fertile soil in which corporations are rooted"—just lying there, not put there, not a contested terrain—and, he continues, "these institutions shape the taken-for-granted categories that reify frequently repeated social practices into things like money, markets, corporations, and institutions themselves" (140). In this quote the House of Morgan disappears, even as it reorganizes the bankrupt half of the railroad trackage and we get six major noncompetitive systems. The long struggle in the Supreme Court about regulating railroads is replaced by a reified social practice.

Roy adds, "These practices, when they become reified as things, acquire ideological power by appearing as inevitable supra social developments" (140). They didn't appear to be inevitable supra social developments for the Grangers, for much of labor, the ICC commissioners, or even a minority of the Supreme Court justices. The practices were constantly contested and corporate leaders did constant battle to further their interests and extend their control. Dobbin notes that in the rate discrimination cases of 1867, the Granger leaders "argued in stark terms that the monopoly powers exercised by railroads posed a threat not only to rural livelihood but to the polity itself" (1994, 72). Roy continues, "Institutionalization becomes a historical force with a momentum of its own" and "becomes the default means by which people do things just because they are there" (141). This statement ignores the progressive era, resurgent labor, third party candidates, and bloody strikes, all involving people who challenged the institutions, rather than taking them for granted. I don't think that Roy's work would lose even a tiny bit of its cogency and power if such passages invoking neoinstitutional theory were simply excised. They mislead, obfuscate, and distract the reader from the recognition of organizational power that is otherwise so abundantly documented in his great book.

Summary and Conclusions

How have the railroads carried our organizational freight forward into the twenty-first century? First, the groundwork was established in chapter 1, the transformation of law that allowed the corporate form to emerge with its scant trappings of public responsibility. Railroad legislation carried this thrust further. Second, the discussions in chapters 2 and 3 on alternative forms of small- and moderate-sized organizations, versus large organizations with oligopolistic market control, found echos in the railroad account of divisionalization and inside contracting. Thus law and organizational size and form kept driving the narrative, making the railroads, at the end of the century, the prime example of the corporate form that would dominate the next century.

Then we asked why, alone among industrializing nations, would the United States allow a common good, a common carrier in this instance, to become the private property of capitalist owners and also be so lightly regulated? We rejected the answers of most economic historians: that common carriers had to privatize in order to operate efficiently; that only private industry, largely free of public regulation, could manage the centralized control over their complex operations. That was clearly not the case in Britain, Prussia, and France. We also turned aside the historical explanation that the panic of 1837 drove public and public-private ownership—the prevailing form at the time—into private hands as the states voted to cease investment and to sell off their interests. Local governments and states, instead, continued to finance the roads and even kept some publically owned ones running profitably. What happened after the panic was that private interests could more easily prevail if they were determined. Finally, we challenged the neo-institutionalist explanation that the culture of the nation so feared big government that it tolerated big corporations. The culture, we documented, was on both sides of the question, with compelling arguments drawn from traditions and ideologies commodious enough to support either forms of ownership.

Instead of these explanations, we argued that the railroads came along at a time that we needed, not to transport goods more cheaply from one established urban or agricultural center to another, as in Europe, but to serve a larger undertaking, to open up new territories and exploit new resources. Railroads were to build, not just link, the nation. As such, their growth was so urgent that the towns and cities were, with much reluctance in some quarters, to give away land, lend money freely, and tolerate overbuilding, destructive competition, and graft and corruption. The federal state was small and weak, and when the roads were small and rarely crossed state lines, it took no interest. Into this fertile "historical moment," private interests could easily move. As the profitability of the roads increased, drawing in European capital, the private owners were quite agreeable to local and state funding if no regulations were to follow, or regulations could be ignored, but if regulation seemed immanent, existing railroads supported legislation that no public funds be used, reducing the risk of both regulation and competing lines. Public ownership, or public-private ownership with regulation, evaporated after 1837 and by 1850 privatization with little regulation was the accepted fact.

The most important agents of this process were the roads themselves, that is, organizations. Initially, they were not big enough economic enterprises to shape their territory with threats of moving away — railroads do not move away in any case — and harming employment and infrastructure investments. Their organizational power was the promise they presented of development, of getting to a coal deposit, timberland, cotton field, granary, or river trading post. States and towns clamored for their tracks. But, being private, for-profit enterprises, the railroads lay down steep terms. They included control over rates, routes, standards of construction and operation, construction profits, eminent domain, and the terms of public subventions. To gain these they used their organizational power, based on the promise of development, to influence the judiciary (all kinds of novel legal problems were involved) and government legislators. For some observers, the focus has been on the corrupted, the lawmakers and judges, almost implying that they extorted the defenseless railroad corporations. But we saw ample evidence that the railroads sent their agents, loaded with gifts of stocks and money, into the legislative and judicial halls, and badgered the weak public railroad commissions and public representatives on their boards, even forbidding them from voting. When the transcontinental lines were being built with government funds, there was little machinery for supervising the expenditures. For example, the reports of the inspectors "were usually prepared by company clerks rather than by the commissioners, and often were signed before the inspection took place" (Farnham 1963, 665). Supervision of the immense project fell chiefly to the secretary of the interior. One secretary held stock in one of the companies and was personally associated with some of its promoters (Farnham 1963, 664) Railroads played off towns against each other, extracting higher donations, and leaving worthless track behind on occasions. Nearly one-tenth of the nation's land was given over to the railroads, much of it to become the most valuable land because of the railroad. Special charters and then novel state laws allowed speculation free of liability, allowed a line in one state to buy a small but controlling interest in competitors in another state, or allowed the joining of lines through holding companies, all of which promoted consolidation and monopoly. Occasionally the favorable legislation went unnoticed for a short time, but more commonly the judicial rulings and the new laws were denounced from the start by the (weak) farmer and labor parties, and then vigorously fought as rural interests organized on their own in movements such as the Grangers. The biggest financial scandal of the century, concerning the Credit Mobilier company, involved railroad construction and legislative bribery.

The railroad organizations soon were the biggest and richest organizations in the country, and then the world. They set organizational forms that would dominate all of industry for the next century. Some of these were creative solutions to the problem that haunts all organizations — accountable delegation — or how do you delegate your authority but maintain control and accountability. It had been faced by the first big business, the Lowell textile mills, and the result was the same, an organization of bureaus, reporting upward in successive and narrowing steps. But the railroads had more offices and more complex ones and very dispersed ones, and so their innovations in bureaucracy were more important. Andrew Carnegie copied the organizational structure of the Pennsylvania Railroad, where he once worked, to great effect in his steel mills. Along the way one innovation became especially important for the future: breaking the organization up into divisions, with separate heads, rather like smaller organizations owned and run by a superordinate organization. Some big railroads did not divisionalize, with no apparent ill effects, nor did the privately owned but cartelized and heavily regulated British railroads. But if a railroad were to expand to a national line, to be one of the six that controlled the national system, it would probably have been too vast and complex to run without divisionalization. This innovation enabled large organizations to become giant ones, and the form, with variations, is the dominant one for big enterprises today. At the end of the nineteenth century it enabled the railroad system to jump from a regional one, fostering regional development as some national leaders sought, to a national one, as the major railroads and the banking interests sought.

Along the way another innovation that showed great promise disappeared, for reasons that are lost to us. This was the contract system, wherein, in one of its most imaginative applications, locomotives were leased to engineers who then maintained, housed, and fed them, and drove them to the stipulated destination. (Other functions were also contracted out, or turned over to "inside contractors," which is what the engineer essentially was, since he was using the capital resources of the organization.) The more efficiently and innovatively the engineer did his work, the more money he made, and the better service the railroad received. Conceptually, this arrangement is akin to the small-firm network form that we reviewed in the Kensington textile district. Had it spread more widely, we might have had more efficient and more innovative railroads, and certainly smaller central organizations running them, since independent or semi-independent organizations would exist in conjunction with them. I suspect it disappeared, despite its touted efficiencies, because it deconcentrated wealth and power, and those are more important than efficiency.

In the area of labor policies, the railroads joined with steel and mining, two other big industries in the last two decades of the century, to drive organized labor to the wall. Huge strikes, with violence, private police, and federal troops, were won by the railroads. A pattern of confrontation was established, and when union activity again emerged in the twentieth century it had to be big union organizations against big corporations. The railroads were not solely responsible for this, other industries took the same stance, so our pattern of labor relations might well have occurred even if the railroads had been nationalized. But they did their bit.

The "final spike" in our nation's railroad system was to nationalize it. Again, it seems that a period of turmoil was important, as it was after the 1837 crash that furthered privatization. Over-built and over-extended lines failed, as did those that were plundered, and those driven out by the power of larger railroads to reduce rates to levels ruinous to smaller lines. Over half of the trackage went into bankruptcy and reorganization. The firm of J. P. Morgan did much of the reorganizing, on terms which gave the firm control over the surviving companies. "Destructive competition" — all competition is unwanted by capitalist firms, and sometimes it is so ruthless that it will destroy some firms — gave way to cartel-like accommodation, and most importantly, to a national system. The Interstate Commerce Commission, farm and labor organizations, and progressive politicians, and some railroad executive that had mastered short-haul transport, all favored a regionalization of the roads and the economy. The Supreme Court undercut the ICC, and the large railroads won.

A national system favored centralized production of goods to be shipped, and thus a centralized economy. Shipping goods long distances, not short hauls, was the route to profits, provided that competition was controlled. With nationalization, a regional area should not try to be as self-sufficient as possible, but should specialize, and ship its goods out to other regions specializing in something else. Such an economy would require very large producing organizations and favor mass-production techniques. And it would require the final actors in our organizational journey, large investment houses and banking facilities, which now had significant organizational interests in their own right. By 1905 the economy had been shaped. The few large firms that disappeared in the twentieth century were obsolete or supplanted by new technologies. But most of the 200 largest at the beginning of the century were, in one merged form or another, dominant at the end.

Chapter 7

SUMMARY AND CONCLUSIONS

HOW DID IT COME about that the United States developed an economic system based upon large corporations, privately held, with minimal regulation by the state? Two hundred years ago there were none. Until the 1890s there were only a few large ones, in textiles and railroads and the steel and locomotive industries. Then there was a spurt at the turn of the century; in about five years most of the 200 biggest corporations of the time were formed, and most of these still rule their industries.

Nothing comparable occurred in Europe. Until the 1950s the corporate structure of the United States was unique, and it was dominant in the industrialized world. Some of the reasons for this American "exceptionalism" are familiar: the industrial revolution found fertile ground in a resource-rich land with mass markets and democratic institutions and a culture of individual freedom and entrepreneurship. But two things have not been emphasized enough: in the United States a weak state did not prevent large concentrations of economic power and did not provide strong state regulation, in contrast to Europe's stronger states. Second, concentrated power with large-scale production was also possible for organizational reasons: organizations changed the legal system to give organizations sovereignty, and they had a wage-dependent population that permitted a bureaucratic structure with tight labor control.

For large corporations to spring into existence at the end of the century, the legal structure of the commonwealth had to be reworked. It had to favor the accumulation of private capital for large-scale production for national markets, rather then the dispersion of capital into smaller enterprises with regional markets. It appears that the United States centralized private wealth and power a century sooner than Europe did. Our global success then forced our solution upon Europe in the last half of the twentieth century.

The weak state and the organizational arguments are interdependent. Assuming a minimal degree of democracy, we can argue that (a) weak state will allow private organizations to grow almost without limit and with few requirements to serve the public interest; and (b) private organizations will shape the weak state to its liking (this requires state action, in the form of changing property laws). A strong state, however, would have sufficient legislative independence of private economic organizations, and sufficient executive branch strength and will to check the power of private organizations. Together these could limit their growth and require some attention to the public interest. This happened to a greater degree in Europe than in the United States.

Capital, labor, and technology are the main variables needed to understand the rise of organizational power. In Europe, in the sixteenth to the eighteenth centuries, agricultural production increased, leading to better diets, and, with greatly improved disease control, Europe had a population increase. Stronger states appeared as the agricultural surplus and the first technological stirrings brought some prosperity, and strong states reduced the power of war lords and bandits, providing stability. With stable states, the new inventions of the industrial revolution could spread and develop. The population increase provided the manpower for the artisans, craftsmen, and small "man-u-factories." Wealth increased, but it remained centralized in political / religious hands, resulting in even stronger states. These states restricted the size of private power sources, just as the states beat down the nobility and sought to control the church.

Private economic organizations emerged anyway, because there was an industrial revolution and notions about a market economy to exploit the revolution in technology. But labor was still tied to the land, whereas industry was urban. The labor power had to be moved. In England, the state allowed the nobility to reduce its historic obligations to the peasantry, and removed them from the land—the enclosure movement—creating a small urban population wholly dependent upon wage labor. Newly created profits from manufacturing began to be centralized in private hands, and private power that might challenge the state and the church appeared. In England, the crown simply confiscated the estate of the newly rich upon their death—the mortmain, or dead hand laws—and limited capital investment to the financial resources of business partners or a few stockholders. The primary means of raising capital had to be through joint ownership or joint stockholders. The sums were small, and the size of economic organizations were correspondingly limited throughout the nineteenth century and into the next one. There were some big organizations, such as the East India Company, but it had a royal charter with government representatives, and some like the pottery giant, Wedgewood—but there was not a free hand for private investment in big organizations. It was the United States that allowed that to happen.

The United States was blessed with a fear and hatred of two gigantic organizations the immigrants had experienced in Europe: the official church and the state. No national church was established, and the federal state was kept small, weak, and divided. With no significant state, there was no nobility. Without a nobility, there was no feudalism and all those immobile peasants. With no strong state, there could not be a strong church; it takes a state to impose one. Without a crown, church, and nobles to be jealous of the rise of private economic power, large organizations were able to flourish, though resistence to them was strong through much of the nineteenth century. Farmers and laborers and some politicians objected to the lack of regulation and the lack of public representation in the new corporations, and objected to their market control, but the strong demand for their goods, and their ability to corrupt politicians, gave these objections only a limited effect.

Initially there were a few legal impediments to organizational power that had to be removed. Since organizations make use of all sorts of public services and benefits, the common law from England required that charted companies serve a public interest, and have public representatives on their boards. In 1819, in the Supreme Court's Dartmouth decision, New England merchant elites hired lawyer Daniel Webster to strike out that provision. That year also saw the dissolution of two other restraints upon the private accumulation of power. One was limited liability: an entrepreneur who went bankrupt and could not pay his workers or his creditors did not have to pay them out of his own pocket—he could be very rich but his personal wealth was separated from the assets of his business. It was inconvenient for workers and creditors, who subsidized the failure of the business, and it encouraged mismanagement and lack of planning, but it certainly encouraged risky business ventures.

The Supreme Court also declared that the federal government acted for the people directly, and its laws would prevail over any laws of the individual states regarding the conduct of corporations. But the executive branch of the federal government hardly existed at that time, and the legislature was easily bribed, so local control was removed over internal improvements, banking, and significantly, the railroads when they appeared. The economy was to be largely unregulated.

The final check upon private power to be removed was the limited ability of partnerships and joint-stock companies to raise enough capital to build really big organizations. In a quirk of history, Robert Lowell, when he went to England to steal the technology for building the new waterpowered looms, spent much of his additional time in Scotland, where he encountered a unique legal fiction: the corporate company, one where any number of people could invest small amounts of money in one firm, and the officers were subject to few restrictions from the investors. There were few such organizations; Scotland was not industrializing fast and the heads of the state had little to fear from the small organizations that did incorporate. Lowell saw the advantage immediately and took it back to Boston, and formed a series of true corporations, interlocked.

The manufacturing elite that was emerging was a motley bunch — there were gentlemen with landed wealth and wealthy merchants, but there were also farmers, small businessmen and craftsmen, and clever and ambitious immigrants. Indeed, the emerging elite could be almost anything as long as they were white and not Irish. This is important because, in contrast to Europe, no particular culture shaped them; lineage was scant so wealth was more often gained than inherited, thus favoring the industrious; background culture was varied leading to more chances of cross-cutting fertilization of ideas and practices; there were few established traditions that might be blindly followed. There was widespread fear among rural and labor interests that their freedom would be curtailed by large, private centers of wealth as these emerged. But the openness of organizational opportunities in the United States probably increased the legitimacy of the new forms.

Two additional things were crucial, beyond a small state not interested in limiting the private power of organizations, and a elite that was neither hereditary nor ethnically and religiously homogeneous: these were capital and labor. Regarding capital, it was initially scant and local. The Napoleonic Wars and our own War of 1812 shut off the import of cheap manufactured goods needed for a rural, colonial nation. New England capital was diverted from trade in the extractive industry to manufacturing. Had this not happened the continent could have been like India, ruled by colonials who extracted the raw materials and shipped them abroad and shipped in the manufactured and consumer goods made in England. For a time this was Canada's fate, until the British empire began to break up and Canadians gained some economic independence.

In the United States, with independence, and then with restrictions on importing European goods, the major center of wealth — New England merchants — turned toward tariff — protected manufacturing and internal transport. With high tariffs, ample natural resources, and a steady labor supply from exhausted New England farms, and most important, from immigration, European capital flowed in, investing in manufacturing and transport. European capital (along with state and federal land grants, gifts, and secured loans) was especially important in satisfying the giant demands of the new railroad industry from mid-century until the end.

But there were important variations in capital formation among the states. In Massachusetts, the state government allowed a free reign to banks, and the textile elites were able to put together the large sums needed to establish mass-production mills of unprecedented size. These were in company towns that further centralized wealth and power. They used the corporate model, borrowed from Scotland, which allowed passive, remote investment from many stockholders. In contrast, in Pennsylvania, the state closely regulated banks and favored investment in transportation, and this limited the ability of elites to raise the capital for local enterprises; their wealth went into railroads, mining, and shipping, and ironically, New England textiles. The conditions in Philadelphia were favorable for the first major industry in the first half of the century, textiles, but the lack of capital insured a decentralized textile industry of small firms. By the 1880s its production was bigger than New England's, even with small firms drawing upon half the capitalization of the New England firms.

Regarding labor, the towns along the mid-Atlantic and New England coast soon filled with workers dependent upon a wage for a living. This was new in the early nineteenth century. Many were immigrants, but many were also the younger sons of the farmers who could no longer subdivide the land into viable plots for all sons, or who found their New England soil exhausted and discovered that easy migration to the West was no longer possible as the distances increased and Native Americans blocked movement just east of the Great Lakes. As with England a few decades before, a wage-dependent population became available for manufacturing. Where there was not wage dependency, that is, where workers could choose farming, skilled trades, or a mix of these and some casual day labor, factories could not find workers. As in England, a generation earlier, the first factories were staffed by orphans, paupers, and criminals; no one else would accept "wage slavery" as it was called, so new was it. When the New England textile mills were built in the 1830s, they were in remote areas where waterpower was available and land cheap. But there were no wage-dependent workers there. They had to recruit farmers' daughters, who worked for three or four years until they had a dowry and could marry, and the mills had to treat them well. They were not wage dependent, they could always go back to the farm. But once the famished Irish came over and a railroad could bring them from the Boston port to the inland mill towns, a dependent work force was available. Wages were cut, the New England daughters left, exploitation increased, and the handsome mill towns became slums. Profits soared, the companies were returning 25 percent per year on their investments.

This was one path of development available to the industrializing nation—centralized capital, high wage dependency, mass production of cheap goods, little technological development, and large externalities, or social costs to be born by workers and communities. It did not become the dominant path until late in the century.

A quite different path, but also not the dominant path, is illustrated by the textile mills of Philadelphia. Though there were a few mass-production mills with unskilled and exploited immigrant labor, the lack of large amounts of capital for manufacturing, due to the state's restrictions on banks, meant that textile mills would be small. Unable to compete with the Lowell mills in the low-end market, they developed high-end goods, where quality and innovative styles ruled, and could not be copied by Lowell. The firms were small, spreading the profits over many owners; they exchanged personnel regularly, spreading the skills and innovations; they didn't build big integrated mills, but rented rooms with power, spreading the capital investment; they cooperated with each other as well as competed, and workers easily became owners and then workers again when another shop got the contracts. Wage dependency was reduced because there were many firms to choose from (there is no evidence of blacklisting employees who left a firm, while that was standard in New England), and higher skill levels also reduced dependency. Status was not as fixed as in Lowell mills. The small firms were profitable and prospered, and when owners achieved their modest financial goals they often retired, further spreading the wealth, and spending it locally. Labor policies were crude by our standards, but not for the time; there was child labor but the high level of skills required meant less child workers than in the mass-production Lowell mills. And the small firms invested in their communities by demanding paved streets and clean water and sewers and trade schools, and paying the required taxes. Today, we would describe these Philadelphia communities as small-firm networks, similar to the celebrated ones in Northern Italy.

There were a few communities in Philadelphia that had large mills, and they did not invest in infrastructure improvements. They fired workers for voting for the wrong candidate, fought public schooling for children, and centralized the wealth in their communities. They also eventually lost out to Lowell, whose mills were more massive and whose control of the communities was near absolute.

It is hard to generalize, since data sets are so scanty and we have to rely upon case studies, but the industry that grew from 1820 to about 1880 appears to have been midway between these models, except for the railroads. Mass-production techniques were surprisingly slow to develop for most industry, and were often resisted by owners (Hounshell 1984). Firms grew by adding more identical modules, or small shops, rather than reorganizing work on a Fordist assembly line model. Batch, rather than mass production was the rule, and skills were reasonably high (Hershberg 1981). Markets were small and local for most production, so economies of scale were not important. Of course, this all changed late in the century, and for an industry such as petroleum, well before that.

This economic structure of even small- and moderate-sized firms produced substantial inequalities in income and wealth in the nation. Economic historians Jeffrey Williamson and Peter Lindert demonstrate that wealth inequality was low through the colonial period, substantially lower than in Europe, started to increase with industrialization in the 1820s and 1830s, then experienced a sharp rise by 1860. Most of this, however, was due to the increasing returns to skilled labor, and the shortage of skilled labor. While increasing wealth inequality, these factors did not *centralize* wealth as much as spread it more widely in the middle class. In the 1860 to 1890 period, there was a rise in wealth inequality, but not a spurt. However, as we have seen, in this period there was a spurt in the percent of wealth held by the very richest, the top .031 percent. Their share of the wealth more than doubled since 1840. This top strata is where the industrial magnates would reside. By the eve of World War I, wealth was as unequally distributed in the United States as it was in Europe. As Williamson and Lindert note, "Tocqueville was right; less than a century after his visit, the American egalitarian 'dream' had been completely lost" (1980, 52). Wealth inequality fell off markedly in World War I, rose to peak in 1929, with the shares to the top 1 percent rising especially high, fell sharply in the depression years, and stayed there, and even declined, until 1970, when their book ends. The appearance of the income tax in 1913, and the Progressive programs of 1910–1920, seem to have had an effect, as did the First World War, and while the depression was an equalizing force, government policies and income transfers kept wealth inequality low from then on until it again rose sharply in the 1980s and 1990s. Many things affect the centralization of wealth, which is related to, but distinct from, wealth inequality. But we have argued that one of the most important is the appearance of large organizations.

Why did we have the surge of giant organizations at the end of the century? Because of the railroads. First, they made mass markets possible. This encouraged economies of scale, but for most industries with late-nineteenth-century technologies, this was achieved with only modest-sized firms of, say, 500 employees. The cheap, dependable, all-weather transportation that the railroads provided would have been quite consistent with a decentralized, regionalized economy with modest-sized firms—the economy we had before the railroads arrived. Goods could be made in a variety of places and inexpensively distributed locally and regionally. One four-state railroad operated this way for several years, with efficient short-haul service and innovative maintenance and shipping practices that the national railroads copied, but it was bought out by a national line. The national lines—there were six major ones by the end of the century—could make the most money by promoting long-haul transport, with low rates, and charging very high rates for short hauls. They were capital intensive and were the biggest organizations in the world, with economic and political resources that allowed them to favor a national, rather than a regional, economy. Major centers for livestock processing, food processing, steel, petroleum, and durable goods manufacturing were established, with huge organizations dominating the national market. A national railroad system needed national production centers, centralizing the economy, and since it was in private hands, centralizing wealth and power.

It seems likely that the railroads were also responsible for the massive capital needed to establish massive economic organizations. Once the roads were built, with handsome and wasteful government subsidies of course, their capital needs declined, while they themselves were rich. The investment banking houses, the banks, foreign capital, and wealthy railroad stockholders provided the funds for the massive merger movement at the end of the century. The railroads no longer needed huge amounts of capital, and were generating profits themselves, and so the capital went toward consolidating other sectors of the economy, and reducing competition. In a few short years modest-sized firms were merged into the 200 giant ones I referred to earlier, reducing competition, creating monopoly and oligopoly profits, and slowing innovation. The Philadelphia small-firm network model, innovative and socially constructive, went into decline, and the Lowell mass-production model with large, centralized, and bureaucratic firms, and large social costs for workers and communities, was ascendant (even though the textile mills themselves were in decline).

The key role of the railroads in organizing America was possible because they passed, quite quickly, into private hands with no significant regulation in the public interest. We were the only nation to allow the privatization of this immense public good. The railroads started out as quasi-governmental entities, with heavy local and state-level public investment and some public control. By the 1840s the public control was disappearing, and railroad owners began to build interstate then national lines, with federal subventions. (In order to do this, incidently, significant legal innovations were necessary, such as the ability of one firm to hold an interest in other firms, thus making mergers and giant firms possible. This controversial act was quietly achieved in Pennsylvania with a compliant legislature. Another step toward privatization involved New Jersey's liberal incorporation laws, removing the last remaining hints of public responsibility.) The country needed and desperately desired cheap transportation as it spilled westward, but in private hands, the waste, inefficiency, and corruption that attended the growth of the system is legendary. Our inventors, for example, were responsible for the major safety devices, such as automatic couplers and air brakes, but the U.S. railroads were the last to use them. The major scandal of the nineteenth century, the Credit Mobilier scandal, and the most fierce strikes of the century, concerned the railroads. Their labor policies set the antagonistic tone for all future capital-labor relations. And their bureaucratic control structure, so celebrated in organizational theory, became the model for both public and private organizations. Bureaucracy has proved to be the best unobtrusive control device that elites have ever achieved.

I have emphasized a small state with little bureaucracy that allowed private organizations to grow and exploit wage dependency. But it is a path-dependent process, with some historical accidents; there was no inevitability until the end of the century, when the path was so firm that little could, or did, change it. Had not the founding fathers had such a taste of the costs of centralized power from England and Europe, they might not have established a federated political system that allowed private organizational wealth, when it appeared, such a free reign. The country was unformed when the industrial revolution came along. Had the U.S. population of, say, 1850 been achieved in 1650, a European structure of production with guilds and trades and tenant farmers could have been in place and resisted the leveling of social institutions that industrialization, if unchecked, will produce. The United States, in contrast to Europe, had a small population with infirm traditions, and had weak, local, and regional centers and a muddled class structure. This made private economic centralization easy.

Had the Lowells and Cabots of Boston reinvested their wealth in an expanded merchant fleet instead of the power loom on remote rivers, we might have left mass-produced cheap textiles to the English to produce (and then to India; the Lowells had to get a special tariff to block Indian goods), and established a fine goods industry with small organizations, on the low-powered streams that dotted the New England coast. Had not the Irish potato famine occurred, wage dependency would not have overwhelmed the United States so quickly and easily, just when factories appeared. Had the Panic of 1837 not occurred, just as the railroads were getting underway, public investment could have been so paramount that effective governmental regulation of the railroads would have been demanded and perhaps achieved, even despite a weak federal state.

But some things were "in the cards." A vastly resource-rich, virtually unpopulated land attracted settlers who needed vast quantities of cheap goods, just when steam power permitted their production. This was a new market of unprecedented size, and because of the industrial revolution it was more likely to be filled with mass-produced goods than those of local artisans. Britain mass produced goods for the rest of Europe, which was more dominated by artisans and craftsmen, but it seems unlikely that with a market soon larger than Britain, we would have left mass production to the British.

Eventually the democratic ethos put something of a brake upon the private accumulation of wealth and power. Labor unions did what they could, despite a hostile judiciary, and an increasingly broad electorate sent messages to the federal government about corporations and private wealth during the Progressive era. Though sometimes misguided and full of bucolic idiocy, these messages often slowed centralization. So it could have been far worse — witness the imposition of Taylorism in Russia under Lenin; that was tried here but success was limited, compared to Russia. Another reason economic elites could not walk away with the whole store was that big organizations generate structural interests which can run counter to those of their masters — organizations are tools, but large ones are quite recalcitrant tools.

But it could have been far better. Look at what the United States had going for it: the first and the second industrial revolutions occurring in a nature-rich land that hardly had to be conquered; ample labor supply; no fixed class structure or nobility; no religious wars to fight or religious traditions strong enough to uphold the subjection of women; early enfranchisement; and perhaps most often unnoted, only one war of consequence, our Civil War, in contrast to our competitors. We were under the British umbrella on the high seas and used them to protect our expanding trade.

Being "far better" would have meant less human carnage in the factories and mines, less unrestrained devouring of natural resources and less pollution, and a far less steep rise in the degree of wealth and income inequality, as well as smaller, more flexible and competitive organizations, and stronger social welfare provisions by a strong federal government. (There were still orphan trains running in the 1920s, handing out kids picked up in New York and Boston to Midwestern farmers and factory owners, something really close to "wage slavery.") And, of course, we were far behind England in abolishing slavery. A weak central government waffled and quivered about slavery under the pressure of a fabulously rich Southern aristocracy running huge plantations, and of Northern textile and shipping interests — organizations all.

To sum up, a weak state allowed the private accumulation of wealth and power through the medium of big organizations. Elites developed modern bureaucracy over the century, and it was to be the means for maintaining an inequality of wealth, despite periodic reform efforts. Over the nineteenth century, the organization won the freedom to select its own officers and thus could keep public or governmental representatives off the board, even though it enjoyed public largess, and to choose its own successors, so that it could exist forever. Its owners and stockholders, who collected the profits, could not be sued for its debts or failures or accidents. Until the end of the century an employee or his or her family could not recover damages for any work-connected injury or death. The organization could control the social behavior of its employees (initially the control was crude, and legal, such that one could be fired for voting for the wrong candidate, not attending church, or not attending the right church; later the socialization of employees relied on more subtle pressures). The strongest pressure the large organizations exercised was building an economy that insured wage dependency, initially with blacklisting, then with urban work that cut employees off from a rural or small-town environment that provided other means of survival. It was hard to get people to work in factories; when they lived in large cities they had little choice. It was declared legal for the firm to pollute the environment, flood a farmer's land, and cause other negative externalities. Legally it could discriminate on the basis of gender, race, and ethnicity in hiring. The firm was ruled to be a fictitious person, so it could buy up other firms, increasing its market power, and use its resources to go into any business it wished, expanding its scope as well as scale. This was all new, and often contested since people feared centralized, uncontrolled power. But we take most of these powers for granted today. In 1820, about 20 percent of the population worked for wages and salaries; by 1900 it was 50 percent; today it is well over 90 percent, with over half of that number working for big organizations, often with the power to control the small ones. We have become a society of organizations, big ones, and it was not inevitable.

This is an *organizational* interpretation of our nineteenth-century experience. It might invite some scepticism since throughout most of the nineteenth century we were a rural rather than an industrial nation, and until late in the century there were few large organizations. Indeed, during most of the century, I have argued, production was in the hands of small- and moderate-sized firms with local and regional markets. But the explosion of big firms at the end of the century did not come from nowhere, and certainly not out of our culture, or the play of democratic politics, or the supposed efficiency of the instruments of large-scale production. It began with a mobile labor supply dependent upon wages for existence, and a series of crucial legal decisions that created instruments that could make production independent of public scrutiny and regulation and allow mergers once the railroads made mass markets available.

The natural wealth of the continent and the easy removal of its small native population, together with the industrial revolution, converged, at the end of the century, with the steel-rail girdling of the vast land into an *organizational society*. The efficiency of unobtrusive and remote controls that railroad bureaucracy fashioned penetrated all organizations, even public and nonprofit ones, and made combination the order of the day. Belatedly, the Progressive movement of the early twentieth century sought to redress the power imbalances and the costly externalities for workers and communities. But the organizational infrastructure of the nation was not to be seriously disturbed or even ideologically challenged, up to the present. A society with small- and modest-sized firms, regional rather than national markets, and with civic welfare provisions that are a right of citizenship rather than a benefit of employment—a society with wealth and power distributed widely—is now out of the question. Large bureaucratic organizations, public and private, will be our fate for the foreseeable future. It might have been otherwise.

APPENDIX

Alternative Theories Where Organizations Are the Dependent Variable

Technology. Technological interpretations argue that the technological inventions required for the production of goods and services (steam engines, steel, railroads, refrigeration, telegraphs, etc.) required and made possible large organizations, and determined their structure. Organizations are thus a dependent variable; give us a steam engine, or even a water wheel and a spinning loom, and we will organize people appropriately. The form of organization is dependent upon the technology, and has no particular further consequences of note. But extensive research has shown that most production technologies are devised and adapted to fit the existing and preferred organizational structures. However, though the current literature rightly emphasizes the "social construction" of technology, making it a dependent variable, technology can have a whopping independent effect at times. Without cheap mass transit — primarily a technological hurdle using traction engines — we would not have had, or had so soon, large organizations.

Strategy and Structure. The limited technological view is enriched and expanded by examining the connection between variations in organizational form and technology. This is the most popular and influential view among historians and social scientists. Alfred Chandler is the key theorist here, and his work is essential and monumental, but narrow (1977). Technology, he argued, was undeniably important, but worthless without an organization to exploit it, and an organization with a form that was appropriate to the technology and the demands of the market. For mass-produced goods, the organization needed to emphasize throughput speed, coordination, and integration forward to the market if it was to be efficient and prevail over other forms. In this view, organizations come closer to being an independent variable, but technology is still primary. But sampling on the dependent variable — that is, looking only at the forms that survived — is risky. We see characteristics A, B, and C in all the survivors and assume that is the explanation (e.g., multidivisional units, integration forward to marketing, high-volume production). But some failed organizations might have had A, B, and C, and we do not note that an unrecognized characteristic, D (e.g., market control), makes all the difference for survival. In general, sampling on survival favors a functionalist argument, and functionalist arguments ignore the variables of power and interests, and close off considerations of alternative developmental paths with different kinds of organizations and different consequences (e.g., smaller and more flexible units as in some European countries). Furthermore, organizations are judged strictly in terms of a narrow view of efficiency, which ignores the externalities or social costs to labor, community, and environment. Market control is mentioned but treated as a consequence rather than an intention. Thus, with Chandler, organizations are social eunuchs.

Independent of Chandler's work, "contingency theorists" in the mid-1960s elaborated schemes tying structure (typically, bureaucratic vs. flexible or decentralized) with technology (routine, nonroutine) or environment (stable, unstable). While countering the theme that there is "one best way" of organizing, and pointing to the variety of efficient structures that could exist, this theory remained a technological determinist argument, neglecting the extent to which, within limits which were obvious once they were pointed out, owners could choose a technology to suit the structure they desired, or, because of market control or market conditions, bear the cost of a mismatch between technology and structure. The limits needed to be pointed out, so the school's effect was positive, but most of the members, of which I was one, have tempered the essentially strategy-structure view with power, human relations, and ecological and other variables.

Political / Administrative. This viewpoint of "administrative theory" or "organizational administration" is not in fashion now. Here, government is the key actor for enabling and regulating business and industry and voluntary organizations. Government itself, as an organization, is understood in terms of principles of administrative rationality. David Truman, James Fessler, and, in the more modern derationalized and political version, Stephen Skowronek (1982), stand out. A particular organization is the independent variable, or a vaguely organizational system of representative government with all its elections, parties, etc. A particular organization is shaped by political processes, sometimes narrowly conceived, sometimes broadly. Organizations, per se, are means for other processes, and are not actors in themselves whereby their actions are determined by their organizational properties. Nevertheless, this school is a valuable resource, despite the failure to give privilege of place to strictly organizational variables such as the concentration of power and wealth that comes with size, and the impact of managerial control strategies upon the 90 percent of the employed population who work for managers. A good deal of what we know about the history of organizations, particularly political and governmental ones, will come from the work of this school.

Political Power. Political power is sometimes seen as based upon organizations, but more likely power is seen to be effected through organizations, the vessels that carry it. Power is really based upon family interests, dynasties, regional interests, the "growth machine" of John Logan and Harvey Molotch, (Molotch 1976, Molotch and Logan 1987), ethnicity, and religion, or upon favoritism and corruption. This is a way of talking about the commodious results of basically organizational processes, I feel, without examining the organizations themselves. Robert Caro's extraordinary account of Robert Moses in *The Power Broker* (Caro 1975), for example, could be rotated a bare five degrees to the left and be an account of the growth of a society of organizations rather than a fearful and amazed celebration of an extraordinary man. The frequent explanation for political and legal changes is "corruption," which remains a disembodied force or a property of individuals, rather than a product of organizational processes. In the "growth machine" literature, more attention might be paid to the fact that the machines (that is, organizations), run by the politicians, speculators, and real estate operators, require steady payoffs, resolution of conflicting interests, legal services, appropriate images, and so on. These are needs that are largely organizational in source and can both thwart and shape elite interests. The "machine" has its own characteristics and demands, and the organizational theorist can analyze these and their impact.

Stratification. Here, the emphasis is upon class, and organizations recede as mere signals or carriers of class. Birth, culture, socialization, class struggles, state repression, and so forth are studied with little attention to the way organizations shape them. The stratification view sees a variety of means, only one of which is organizations, used to accumulate wealth and power. Cultural variables such as education and ethnicity and religion are very important in this view, but mostly function free of organizations. Political power, exercised through influence, graft, elections, and ideology, is important, as in the political viewpoint we just considered, but the emphasis is upon class dynamics and the elite's effort to contain and control classes. Only to a limited extent do organizational variables enter, largely through the employment process. I would argue that organizations are the major independent variable for explaining modern stratification forms in the United States, that the class system was dramatically changed as the result of organizational activity, and that an important number of the cultural practices associated with classes have organizational beginnings, though, of course, not all.

Labor Process. In the most radical version of the stratification literature, class mixes with the "labor process." Here organizations are far more central than in either of the political versions, and thus this view is very useful for me. Wage dependence is a key variable; socialization is extensive and so are negative externalities. Organizations are the necessary means of domination, and there are two aspects of it. First, class processes (and ethnic, racial, and gender differences) prevent people from organizationally mobilizing their interests in the political realm, outside of the employing organization. Second, organizational processes (wage dependency, socialization, and control) keep them from mobilizing for a larger share of the surplus and a say in what is produced (e.g., goods for use rather than for profits), and for a say in the manufacturing processes themselves, where the new proletarian class status is created and reproduced.

But despite a strong emphasis upon organizations by these theorists, I still think organizations are insufficiently primary and decisive in some cases. In the labor process view, class domination and cultural variables lie behind the organizational ones, as in E. P. Thompson (1963). While appropriate prior to, say, 1850 in England and the United States, after 1850 class and culture are less independent variables. In most elite studies in this tradition, wealth is passed on through generations and is detached from the organizational source of generational wealth. Or wealth may come from land, or conquest, or even taxation and government largess, as in the political science tradition, rather than from the organizations of trade and production. Finally, organizations are too often seen as rational, responsive tools of elites, limited only by worker struggle, rather than as recalcitrant tools subject to the bounded rationality of elites and the accidents of history (Burawoy 1985).[24]

In the most virulent of the labor process theorists, organizations are generally caricatures, only the scene of exploitation, de-skilling, the extraction of surplus profit, and the commodification of life. All true to some extent, but there is more to organizations, including contributions to rising standards of living, and even the negative externalities lose their edge when we see that when workers "make their own history" they also participate in their exploitation. Organizational controls, in my view, are above all unobtrusive, and new mentalities are created to make individuals willing participants in what Marxists see as their own destruction (Burawoy 1985).[25] And organizations do produce and deliver, raising standards of living even while insuring continued inequality; their efficiency matters to all in society.

Cases are overstated, as in the de-skilling controversy. For example, I would rephrase the argument as to whether most workers were de-skilled, as the labor-process theorists have it, or up-skilled, as the economic historians and some sociologists have it, into a relative one: there was no de-skilling in *generationally* absolute terms, a specification of the conventional view, but skill requirements for most workers today, given the skills needed to survive in our complex society, are far below the skills people have, a specification of the labor process view. Surviving in an urban society requires skills that go far beyond those required of most work places. Relatively speaking, then, we do have more de-skilled employees than in the past. I would minimize the democratic chants and maximize the unobtrusive controls of organizations that shaped desires and promoted cunning ideologies of individual freedom and free-market ideology (which are more appropriate for the United States than for the English textile industry).[26] The working class was made by large organizations, once they appeared, more than it made itself, though it did that, too.

Developing a society of organizations is also more inclusive than Marxists generally perceive, with their focus upon the labor process and proletarianization. I will argue that the dynamics of large national systems are changed in ways that a focus upon exploitation and the labor process would not envision; in particular, with the dominance of large organizations, elites actually lose control because the interactions of the tightly coupled system cannot be foreseen. Still, the scholarship in this area is often stunning, the ideology agreeable, and so I am grateful for it and use it extensively.

Culture / Neoinstitutional Theory. The newest chant is culture, institutions, and institutional logics, what is being labeled as neoinstitutional theory. It veers sharply from the political and power implications of the political / stratification theorists, and should outrage them. There are organizations here, of course, and most of the practitioners of this school are card-carrying members of the organizational sections of the respective discipline of sociology, political science, history, and psychology. But here it is the institutional environment that shapes organizations, not the other way around. (One neoinstitutionalist, Lynn Zucker, does not agree with this, arguing that "organizations largely, not only on occasion, construct the institutional environment" and that "the organizational form serves as the focal defining institution in modern society" [1986].) Elites work their magic. But the magic is largely benign: custom, normative practices, absorption of values, mimicry, "isomorphism," bounded rationality and cognitive (rather than psycho-dynamic) processes, learning rather than passion. I agree with them that organizations are shaped by their environment, by branching paths in a history that is punctuated with unpredictable events such as a potato famine across the sea, or war mobilization or economic crashes. But the consequences for workers and their interests and struggles are absent from this analysis. Group interests are muted; elites mimic rather than conspire; there is no agency of power. The basic reference to the neo-institutionalist school is the work of Walter Powell and Paul DiMaggio (Powell and DiMaggio 1991). The minimization of agency is thoughtfully acknowledged, however, by DiMaggio (1988, 3–22).

While it rectifies many of the errors of the old institutionalist school and its Freudian baggage, and wisely mines the new cognitive psychology and the path-dependency arguments that labor process theorists have such trouble with, there are still problems. I find the outlines of our organizational history since 1820 simply too bold to be explained by "institutional logics" (Dobbin 1994), because the specification of just who is fashioning the logic, and what interests are behind it, are lacking or attributed to notions that I feed need to be unpacked, such as public opinion, or the normative order. Nor do I find organizations themselves theorized sufficiently: socialization is not specific to the organization but is societal in their account, the effects of unobtrusive (let alone obtrusive) controls are unexplored, the distribution of both wealth and power is unobserved, and, even worse, is sometimes of little concern in their theorizing.

This is not to say that the notion of culture—as a set of beliefs, values, frameworks for interpreting things, and ritualistic practices and categories—is not useful. It is essential; there are things worth a common label that we have come to call culture. But the notion is abstract and seductive, and can be used to suggest explanation rather than providing it. Thus, my intention is to locate the source of these cultural elements and thus give more operational content to the concept. There are occasions when no agents can any longer be found, if there ever was an identifiable set, and we must invoke ideologies, socialization, and the like. But there are cultural practices that have identifiable agents and interests behind them. Organizations provide many of these occasions.

Society of Organizations. That leaves me with this final perspective (Perrow 1991, 1996),[27] which attempts to utilize parts of all the other schemes, recognizing the importance of technology, organizational efficiency variables, the administrative state, political power and social stratification, culture, and labor processes and insurgency. But it takes organizations much more seriously, and examines more closely what is required to have large organizations that are efficient for their masters. Large organizations are seen as recalcitrant tools fashioned by particular elites; a group interest / power model modified by structural constraints of routine cooperative behavior. Some features include the following:

- *history* is path-dependent, accidental, only partially developmental
- *structure and environment* rather than entrepreneurship explain success / failure
- *technologies* are chosen to fit preferred structure / ideology
- organizations create and shape *culture*, define efficiencies in their own terms, and exploit other divisions in society
- *labor process* is shaped in part by workers' resistance and can occasionally be a key factor, but acquiescence in dependency, and trade-offs in benefits, are more often the common lot of employees
- *bureaucracy* (formalization, standardization, centralization, hierarchy) is the best unobtrusive control device that elites ever had.

NOTES

1. In nineteenth-century organizations, the surplus was substantial; there were estimates of 85 percent return on wages for some industries. Carol D. Wright, who told a Senate committee that "the factory has been a wonderful element in our civilization," went on to estimate the annual profit on each employee in industry in Massachusetts in the 1880s to be $98.00 on an annual wage of $364.00, a 27 percent surplus. See United States Education and Labor Committee (U.S. Senate, 1885), "Report on the relations between labor and capital," vol. 3, 422–25, 1885. The figure was low compared to other estimates, which ran as high as 85 percent. See Ceila Whitehead's testimony, 3: 914, in the hearings. The larger the organization, the more the surplus available to the masters.

2. Indeed, even in the twentieth century the democratic culture of the United States was slower than those of Britain and Spain in introducing democratic workplace reforms associated with the "human relations" tradition (see Guillen 1994).

3. The best historian for telling us where to dig has been Louis Galambos, starting with his seminal essay. "The Emerging Organizational Synthesis in Modern American History" (1970), and the update, "Technology, Political Economy, and Professionalization: Central Themes of the Organizational Synthesis" (1983). But Galambos also sounded the theme of this book in his 1975 volume, *The Public Image of Big Business in America, 1880–1940*, where he argues that the "single most significant phenomenon in modern American history is the emergence of giant, complex organizations," and goes on to say, "This book is based on the major premise that historians as well as sociologists should acknowledge that the process of organizational change has had a more decisive influence on modern America than any other single phenomenon" (3, 5). To that I can only say "Amen."

4. If this book were to be produced in electronic form, you could think of the italicized concepts as hypertext and click on them to see their definition, see the page numbers where they appeared, order the individual discussions by time period or industry, and even match "railroads" for example to "externalities." An index is a primitive version of hypertext.

5. Though rather obvious and consistent with much of organizational theory, the assertion that large organizations concentrate wealth and power has received remarkably little systematic attention. Theorists applaud "entrepreneurship," "small is beautiful," and market-based values (markets need numerous actors and therefore organizations must be small), but do not consider the issue of concentrated wealth and power. I look at size in the context of small-firm networks, as they have appeared in Northern Italy and several other countries, in "Small Firm Networks" (1992).

6. The classic critique of the dichotomy, placing the network form in between the ends, is Walter W. Powell's "Neither Markets Nor Hierarchy: Network

Forms of Organization" (1990). For a general criticisms of the economists' and historians' conception of the efficiencies of hierarchy and the transaction costs analysis theory with which it is associated, see Perrow's "Markets, Hierarchy and Hegemony: A Critique of Chandler and Williamson," (1981) and chapter 7 of his *Complex Organizations: A Critical Essay* (1986).

7. Burawoy, in chapter 2 of *The Politics of Production* (1985), shows how patriarchy played a key role in shaping the production system of the Lancashire textile mills, with the skilled male spinners sacrificing the interests of their women and children to retain their power over the system. Strikingly enough, when the small mills were bought up by a few big ones and large organizations appeared in the latter half of the nineteenth century, the masters were able to fold the patriarchal spinners into a larger paternalism of their own, and the spinners lost influence. This is an instance of organizations creating or sustaining *divisions*.

8. Why farm productivity increased is not important for my argument. New England can be considered either a market economy or a moral economy in the late eighteenth century. If it is considered a moral economy, the shift to market is clear as wage dependency appears. If it was already a market economy, in the sense that prices converge over a region, indicating some production for exchange rather than just for use, it was still not predominantly a market economy. Until production for exchange dominates agriculture there will not be enough agricultural surplus to feed those producing industrial goods and services for exchange. See the interesting review of recent literature on this subject by Gordon S. Wood, "Inventing American Capitalism" (1994). Wood attributes the rise in acquisitive behavior beginning in 1780 to the prospect of imitating the consumption patterns of the gentry, so easy in a weak class society. But if so, why didn't farmers produce for exchange in 1750 and 1760? He says that the Revolution released the explosion of entrepreneurial power, but he presents no evidence for the link. I prefer the ecological explanation of Charles Sellers in chapter 1 of *The Market Revolution, Jacksonian America, 1815–1846* (1991). To the gradual rise in agricultural productivity in Europe, the availability of fresh land and water transport in America was added. The rural population increased, necessitating smaller more efficient and intensive farms (rather than large "capitalist" farms with hired labor, which came later outside of New England) and the migration of excess labor.

Winifred Barr Rothenberg, in *From Market-Places to a Market Economy: The Transformation of Rural Massachusetts, 1750–1850* (1992), documents the price evidence for the rise of a market. But her interpretation is that the agricultural surplus allowed investment in manufacturing sufficient to attract a labor force. This is quite different from forcing the labor off the land because of excess supply, and thus making cheap labor available to manufactures. The difference can be neatly expressed in terms of the Lowell mills in 1820 versus 1850. In the first and for perhaps the only time in our history, the labor in a major industry could freely decide that the higher return from the mills made working there worthwhile, and yet had enough market power to force the mill owners to make the jobs worth their while. Labor's leverage lay in its alternatives, return to the farm, or other employment; it was not *wage dependent*. Here the market model works fine. But once there was a labor surplus, labor had no choice but to work in the mills. Here a *labor process* theory works best.

9. Dongyub Shin's extraordinary dissertation, "Beyond Reciprocity: The Institutionalization of an Online Interfirm Technical Cooperation Mechanism in the Computer Software Industry," Yale University, 1996, provides an unusual exception. Software professionals violate all the rational choice rules and even the more sociologically friendly "tit for tat" economistic theory of Axelrod by giving and receiving free impersonal help on technical problems in Internet web groups, producing an anonymous and vital community. One of the keys is intrinsic satisfaction chained to increasing technical expertise. Here, trust is necessary and efficient even with nonrepetitive, impersonal contacts.

10. The classic examination of the effects of wage dependency is (Keyssar 1986).

11. Braverman's work burst on an unprepared field of organizational sociology in 1973, and was very important. Labor process theorists soon criticized it for considering workers as too passive, whereas they praised the overall reorientation it gave to industrial studies. My major complaint is with the occasional evolutionary tone and Braverman's uncritical examination of the internal contracting system. He sees the persistence of crafts and subcontractors as a "transitional form" until the capitalists could gain control over the labor process, as if that development were inevitable. I will argue that it was circumstantial, and, given the right conditions, the integrated mass-production firm did not have to dominate. Braverman also sees both the subcontracting and the "putting out" or homework systems as "plagued by problems of irregularity of production, loss of materials in transit and through embezzlement, slowness of manufacture, lack of uniformity and uncertainty of the quality of the product" (63). But subcontracting and putting out made the Philadelphia textile industry highly efficient, as we shall see, and it has performed remarkably well in areas where there are small-firm networks (Perrow 1992). Long considered to be an inefficient and anomalous form by economists, subcontracting appears to have contributed essentially to the prosperity of workers in Northern Italy since the 1960s. The irony of this is well discussed by Mark Lazerson in "Organizational Growth of Small Firms: An Outcome of Markets and Hierarchies?" *American Sociological Review* 53 (1988): 330–42.

12. Chandler (1977, 67–72) dismisses the mills of the Boston Associates as examples of modern businesses in part because they did not have dispersed ownership, but were controlled by a small number of families. I would argue that dispersed ownership did not have a significant impact on either organizational form or organizational consequences until well into the twentieth century, but that centralized control over a large pool of capital was very significant.

13. H. M. Gitelman, in "The Waltham System and the Coming of the Irish" (1967), minimizes somewhat the degree of exploitation and notes the high turnover of even the more dependent Irish workers. By looking at the changing composition of the labor force over time, he shows that the decline in wages after the influx of the Irish is due to an increasing use of child labor (presumably Irish); the wages of adults even rose in some cases. He also suggests that the intensity of the work may not have increased if so many children could be

employed to perform it; the increased output is a measure of machine efficiency not necessarily greater effort. However, other scholars have adduced evidence of greater work intensity, considering that the substitution of children for adults is a measure of exploitation, and given that turnover is quite consistent with powerlessness and wage dependency.

14. Coolidge (1942) sharply distinguishes Lowell before mass immigration, from later company towns, which "were generally small. The inhabitants always formed a permanent proletariat, and the corporations owned and controlled every organization and institution in the town in a way that had not been possible earlier" (114). The possibilities for control certainly did expand with the century.

15. I am ignoring slavery, which was, of course, an extreme form of dependency. This form of wage dependency is obvious and something we do not accept today. I am dealing instead with the kinds of wage dependency that we continue to take for granted and accept. But I am also ignoring the variety of forms of contract labor and indentured labor that flourished in the 1700s in New England, and well into the 1800s in the American West. For an excellent survey, see Howard Lamar's "From Bondage to Contract: Ethnic Labor in the American West, 1600–1890," in *The Countryside in the Age of Capitalist Transformation*, ed. Steven Hahn and Johnathan Prude (Chapel Hill: University of North Carolina Press, 1985), 293–326. Despite all the rhetoric about the freedom of the frontier, Lamar points out that it is precisely on frontiers that bondage is most desirable because of the shortage of labor. The question must be asked, he says, "Was the American West and the Western frontier more properly a symbol of bondage than of freedom when it comes to labor systems?" (294). He concludes that it was a mixture, with a significant and unrecognized element of bondage along with freedom.

16. Paul McGouldrick, in his book *New England Textiles in the 19th Century: Profits and Investment* (1968), says "for the rest of the of the 19th century [after 1830], structural characteristics of the New England industry had remained substantially unchanged." There was always a healthy asset to debt ratio, new issues of stock were infrequent, the board-treasurer-agent structure remained intact, commission houses continued to handle the product. McGouldrick says that "the operation of textile mill had become so routine that a reasonably well-capitalized business having competent supervisory personnel could perform satisfactorily without stockholder surveillance. . . . [A] lack of the need to make a challenging decisions explains the passivity of the stockholders" (27; cited in Scranton 1983, 16). More recent work indicates stockholders were not always passive and some exposed corruption on the part of managers and ineffecient marketing. Thanks to Zehra Gumus-Dawes for this reference: H. Vernon-Wortzel, "Changing Patterns of Management in the Lowell Mill," in *The Textile Industry and Its Business Climate*, eds. A. Okochi and S.-I. Yonekawa (Tokyo: University of Tokyo Press, 1982).

17. Scranton was unaware of the writing of either Piore or Sabel before their 1984 volume (a circumstance conveyed to me through a personal communication), and thus Scranton's work is an important independent invention of what has become a significant intellectual tradition. Scranton drew instead on the

labor history work of the Philadelphia Social History project, David Harvey, and others. For a brief review of the Piore and Sabel legacy (one that is ignorant of Scranton's work), see Perrow, "Small Firm Networks" (1992).

18. Scranton notes that "mill operators and agents served again and again as state legislators and local government officials throughout the six decades under consideration. Indeed, the creation of local government at Lowell was twice the product of local initiative, the second time an offshoot of corporate frustration at their lack of control over the institutions setup in the mid 20s" (1983, 33–4).

19. Gumus-Dawes makes a promising beginning of this model, and, more importantly, contrasts it with the largely neglected Pocasset group, in an all-too-brief exploration of Fall River and Rhode Island mills. These stand midway in essential respects between Lowell II and the Philadelphia networks. Although the Pocasset analysis supports my position, I will not bring it into this volume (Gumus-Dawes 2000, chapter 3, n. 178).

20. Elsewhere, in a footnote, Coolidge says that in the seaports "there was a large supply of nearly destitute labor on the market of which the enterprising employer could avail himself at sweat shop wages. *This was something new, and the desire to take advantage of it shows a complete change in the attitude of the executives towards labor* [emphasis added]" from that which the Lowell executives professed. The last words, he continues, along this line were spoken in 1903 in a speech before the New England and Cotton Manufactures Association: "The most satisfactory way in which to handle any class of labor is to *have its sole connection with the mill one of work* [emphasis added] — well performed, it will mean continuous employment, poorly done, immediate discharge" (Coolidge 1942, 204).

Contrast this "interests" argument — taking advantage of available cheap labor — with Anthony F. C. Wallace, *Rockdale: The Growth of an American Village in the Early Industrial Revolution* (Wallace 1978, 293), where we have a "technological" and "strategy & structure" argument. Wallace begins by saying that the "idea that a balanced agricultural-industrial economy was possible in a nation of small rural communes was reasonable at this time [1820–1850] in American history." But with the appearance of inexpensive and efficient steam engines in the 1850s (technology), the factory could be placed in a great city with "associated savings in transportation costs . . . and accessibility to the seat of commerce" (strategy & structure). Coolidge is making a more crucially organizational one. Steam power, even more than the power loom before it, permitted the creation of a wage-dependent population that could not balance agriculture and industry as so many Rockdale inhabitants did.

21. Scranton is at odds here with Alfred D. Chandler, who dismisses the New England textile industry as having an outmoded structure. Chandler argues in *The Visible Hand: The Managerial Revolution in American Business* (1977), that the companies were run "like partnerships," and utilized management methods that "adhered to those of the mercantile world that spawned them" (67–72). If so, the mercantile world had, by then, most of the attributes of the corporate system. The fact that shares were closely held by a small elite in Boston does not gainsay the fact that the owners were remote from the business, their liability was limited in contrast to partnerships, and in contrast to partner-

ships, ownership did not dissolve with deaths or withdrawal, but was permanent. As Scranton puts it, the corporate structures of the Boston Associates were "invulnerable to individual mortality" (1983, 50).

22. The natural waterways were so plentiful and economical that one historian argued that the railroads contributed little but redundance to the economic development of the country, but that is an extreme view (Fogel 1964).

23. For details on the corruption of justices in the New York State Supreme Court, see Gordon 1988, 162–65, and for New York City magistrates, 363.

24. I would single out Michael Burawoy as the one least fitting my strictures, and indeed, his treatment of the British textile industry is a signal achievement, with a great sensitivity to what we now call "gender" issues, and a mapping of the major variables that is unmatched (state intervention in production, wage dependency, "subsumption" of labor [controlling workers' community existence], labor supply, and interfirm competition). I will have to ignore his details in my synoptic view.

25. An earlier book by Michael Burawoy, *Manufacturing Consent* (1976), notes the the extensive degree to which workers in a manufacturing plant "played games" that were unobtrusively well structured and controlled by management, and how the change from a competitive environment to one of market control eased tensions and promoted security for the workers through the "internal state" of the internal labor market. However, he persistently utilizes a labor process framework, full of "struggle" and "contradictions" that belie the extensive internalization, and indeed, the improvement for the workers.

26. See Burawoy, *The Politics of Production* (1985, 99–100), where he argues that with a "late development" history, the United States mechanized textile mills faster than Britain, and entrenched labor interests were not present to delay extensive mechanization. In addition, the British produced finer goods. This view is further substantiated by the detailed study of William Lazonic in his *Competitive Advantage on the Shop Floor* (1990, chapters 3 and 4).

27. The basic argument is laid out in Perrow 1991. A specification of the "absorption" thesis, and a discussion of its interaction with corporate downsizing, appears in Perrow 1996.

BIBLIOGRAPHY

Abolafia, Mitchel. 1996. *Making Markets: Opportunism and Restraint on Wall Street*. Cambridge: Harvard University Press.

Adams, Charles Francis, and Henry Adams. 1886. *Chapters of the Erie*. New York: Henry Holt.

Baker, Wayne E., and Robert R. Faulkner. 1993. "The Social Organization of Conspiracy: Illegal Networks in the Heavy Electricial Equipment Industry." *American Sociological Review* 58:837–60.

Baltzell, E. Digby. 1979. *Puritan Boston and Quaker Philadelphia: Two Protestant Ethics and the Spirit of Authority and Leadership*. New York: Free Press.

Berk, Gerald. 1994. *Alternative Tracks: The Constitution of American Industrial Order, 1865–1917*. Baltimore: Johns Hopkins University Press.

Berle, Adolf A., and Gardiner C. Means. 1932. *The Modern Corporation and Private Property*. New York: Macmillan.

Best, Michael. 1991. *The New Competition*. Cambridge: Cambridge University Press.

Bloch, Marc. 1961. *The Feudal Society, The Growth of Ties of Dependence*, vol. 1. Chicago: University of Chicago Press.

Bradach, Jeffrey L., and Robert G. Eccles. 1989. "Price, Authority, and Trust: From Ideal Types to Plural Forms." *Annual Review of Sociology* 15:97–118.

Braverman, Harry. 1974. *Labor and Monopoly Capital: The Degradation of Work in the Twentieth Century*. New York: Monthly Review Press.

Brown, Dee Alexander. 1977. *Hear that Lonesome Whistle Blow: Railroads in the West*. New York: Holt, Rinehart and Winston.

Burawoy, Michael. 1976. *Manufacturing Consent: Changes in the Labor Process under Monopoly Capital*. Chicago: University of Chicago Press.

———. 1985. *The Politics of Production*. London: Verso.

Buttrick, John. 1952. "The Inside Contract System." *Journal of Economic History* 12:205–21.

Caro, Robert. 1975. *The Power Broker: Robert Moses and the Fall of New York*. New York: Random House.

Chandler, Alfred Dupont, Jr. 1956. *Henry Varnum Poor, Business Editor, Analyst, and Reformer*. Cambridge: Harvard University Press.

———. 1965. *The Railroads: The Nation's First Big Business*. New York: Harcourt Brace and World.

———. 1969. *Strategy and Structure*. Cambridge: MIT Press.

———. 1977. *The Visible Hand: The Managerial Revolution in American Business*. Cambridge: Harvard University Press.

Chandler, Alfred D., and Stephen Salsbury. 1965. "The Railroads: Innovators in Modern Business Administration." In *The Railroad and the Space Program: An Exploration in Historical Analogy*, edited by B. Mazlish. Cambridge: Harvard University Press.

Chernow, Ron. 1998. *Titan : The Life of John D. Rockefeller, Sr.* New York and London: Random House.

Clawson, Dan. 1980. *Bureaucracy and the Labor Process: The Transformation of U.S. Industry, 1860–1920.* New York: Monthly Review Press.

Clinard, Marshall B., and Peter C. Yeager. 1980. *Corporate Crime.* New York: Free Press.

Cohen, Isaac. 1990. *American Management and British Labor: A Comparative Study of the Cotton Spinning Industry.* New York: Greenwood.

Coolidge, John. 1942. *Mill and Mansion: A Study of Architecture and Society in Lowell, Massachusetts, 1820–1865.* New York: Columbia University Press.

Cronon, William. 1983. *Changes in the Land : Indians, Colonists, and the Ecology of New England.* New York: Hill and Wang.

Dalzell, Robert F. 1987. *Enterprising Elite: The Boston Associates and the World They Made.* Cambridge: Harvard University Press.

Davis, Lance E., and Douglass North. 1971. *Institutional Change and American Economic Growth.* New York: Cambridge University Press.

DiMaggio, Paul. 1988. "Interest and Agency in Institutional Theory." In *Institutional Patterns and Organizations*, edited by L. G. Zucker. Cambridge: Ballinger.

DiMaggio, Paul, and Walter W. Powell. 1991. Introduction to *The New Institutionalism in Organizational Analysis*, edited by Walter W. Powell and Paul DiMaggio. Chicago: University of Chicago Press.

Dobbin, Frank. 1994. *Forging Industrial Policy: The United States, Britain, and France in the Railway Age.* New York: Cambridge University Press.

Dobbin, Frank, and Timothy J. Dowd. 2000. "The Market That Antitrust Built: Public Policy, Private Coercion, and Railroad Acquisitions, 1825 to 1922." *American Sociological Review* 65:631–57.

Dobbin, Frank, and John Sutton. 1998. "The Strength of a Weak State: The Employment Rights Revolution and the Rise of Human Resources Management Divisions." *American Journal of Sociology* 104:441–76.

Dublin, Thomas. 1979. *Women at Work: The Transformation of Work and Community in Lowell, Massachusetts, 1826–1860.* New York: Columbia University Press.

Dunlavy, Colleen A. 1992. "Political Structure, State Policy, and Industrial Change: Early Railroad Policy in the United States and Prussia." In *Structuring Politics: Historical Institutionalism in Comparative Analysis*, edited by S. Steinmo, K. Thelen, and F. Longstreth. New York: Cambridge University Press.

Edelman, Lauren. 1990. "Legal Environments and Organizational Governance: The Expansion of Due Process in the American Workplace." *American Journal of Sociology* 95:1401–40.

Edelman, Lauren, and Mark C. Suchman. 1999. "When the 'Haves' Hold Court: Speculations on the Organizational Internalization of Law." *Law & Society Review* 33:941–92.

Farnham, Wallace D. 1963. "'The Weakened Spring of Government': A Study in Nineteenth-Century American History." *American Historical Review* 68:662–80.

Fligstein, Neil. 1990. *The Transformation of Corporate Control*. Cambridge: Harvard University Press.

Fogel, Robert W. 1964. *Railroads as an Economic Force*. Baltimore: Johns Hopkins University Press.

Folsom, Burton W., Jr. 1981. *Urban Capitalists: Entrepeneurs and City Growth in Pennsylvania's Lackawanna and Leigh Regions, 1800–1920*. Baltimore: Johns Hopkins University Press.

Friedman, Lawrence M. 1973. *A History of American Law*. New York: Simon and Schuster.

Galambos, Louis. 1970. "The Emerging Organizational Synthesis in Modern American History." *Business History Review* 44 (3):279–90.

———. 1975. *The Public Image of Big Business in America, 1880–1940: A Quantitative Study of Social Change*. Baltimore: Johns Hopkins University Press.

———. 1983. "Technology, Political Economy, and Professionalization: Central Themes of the Organizational Synthesis." *Business History Review* 57:471–93.

———. 1994. "The Triumph of Oligopoly." In *American Economic Development in Historical Perspective*, edited by T. Weiss and D. Schaefer. Stanford: Stanford University Press.

Gersuny, Carl. 1976. "'A Devil in Petticoats' and Just Cause: Patterns of Punishment in Two New England Textile Factories." *Business History Review* 50:133–52.

Gitelman, H. M. 1967. "The Waltham System and the Coming of the Irish." *Labor History* 8:227–53.

Goodrich, Carter. 1960. *Government Promotion of American Canals and Railroads, 1800–1890*. New York: Columbia University Press.

Gordon, John Steele. 1988. *The Scarlet Woman of Wall Street*. New York: Weidenfeld and Nicolson.

Guillèn, Mauro. 1994. *Models of Management: Work, Authority and Organizations in Comparative Perspective*. Chicago: University of Chicago Press.

Gumus-Dawes, Zehra. 2000. "Forsaken Paths: The Organization of the American Textile Industry in the Nineteenth Century." Ph.D. diss. Sociology Department, Yale University.

Hall, Peter Dobkin. 1984. *The Organization of American Culture, 1700–1900: Private Institutions, Elites, and the Origins of American Nationality*. New York: New York University Press.

Hartz, Louis. 1948. *Economic History and Democratic Thought: Pennsylvania, 1776–1860*. Cambridge: Harvard University Press.

Harvard Law Review. 1989. Editorial, "Incorporating the Republic: The Corporation in Antebellum Political Culture." 102:1883–1903.

Hatch, Rufus. 1871. "Rufus Hatch's Circulars, 1–5." Privately published.

Hershberg, Theodore. 1981. *Philadelphia: Work, Space, Family and Group Experience in the 19th Century*. New York: Oxford University Press.

Hirschman, Albert O. 1981. *The Passions and the Interests: Political Arguments for Capitalism Before its Triumph*. Princeton: Princeton University Press.

Hofstadter, Richard. 1961 [1948]. *The American Political Tradition*. New York: Vintage Books.

Horwitz, Morton J. 1977. *The Transformation of American Law: 1780–1860*. Cambridge: Harvard University Press.

Hounshell, David A. 1984. *From the American System to Mass Production, 1800–1932: The Development of Manufacturing Technology in the United States*. Baltimore: Johns Hopkins University Press.

Huntington, Samuel P. 1968. *Political Order in Changing Societies*. New Haven: Yale University Press.

Hurst, James Willard, 1970. *The Legitimacy of the Business Corporation in the Laws of the United States, 1780–1970*. Charlottesville: University of Virginia Press.

Jackson, Robert Max. 1998. *Destined for Equality: The Inevitable Rise of Women's Status*. Cambridge: Harvard University Press.

Johnson, Paul E. 1978. *A Shopkeeper's Millennium: Society and Revivals in Rochester, New York, 1815–1817*. New York: Hill and Wang.

Kennedy, Paul M. 1993. *Preparing for the Twenty-First Century*. New York: Random House.

Keyssar, Alexander. 1986. *Out of work: The First Century of Unemployment in Massachusetts*. Cambridge: and New York: Cambridge University Press.

Lamoreaux, Naomi R. 1985. *The Great Merger Movement in American Business, 1895–1904*. New York: Cambridge University Press.

Licht, Walter. 1983. *Working for the Railroad: The Organization of Work in the Nineteenth Century*. Princeton: Princeton University Press.

Maier, Pauline. 1993. "The Revolutionary Origins of the American Corporation." *The William and Mary Quarterly* 50:51–84.

McGouldrick, Paul. 1968. *New England Textiles in the 19th Century: Profits and Investment*. Cambridge: Harvard University Press.

Mercer, Lloyd J. 1982. *Railroads and Land Grant Policy: A Study in Government Intervention*. New York: Academic Press.

Meyer, John. 1994. "Rationalized environments." In *Institutional Environments and Organizations*, edited by W. Scott and J. Meyer. Newbury Park: Sage.

Molotch, Harvey L. 1976. "The City as a Growth Machine." *American Journal of Sociology* 82:309–32.

Molotch, Harvey L., and John R. Logan. 1987. *Urban Fortunes: The Political Economy of Place*. Berkeley: University of California Press.

Montgomery, David. 1979. *Workers' Control in America: Studies in the History of Work, Technology, and Labor Struggles*. New York: Cambridge University Press.

Moore, Joseph H. 1890. *How Congressmen Are Bribed: The Colton Letters; Declaration of Huntington that Congressmen Are For Sale*. San Francisco: James H. Barry, Printer.

Nelson, William E. 1975. *Americanization of the American Law: The Impact of Legal Change on Massachusetts Society, 1760–1830*. Cambridge: Harvard University Press.

Perrow, Charles. 1981. "Markets, Hierarchy and Hegemony: A Critique of Chandler and Williamson. In *Perspectives on Organizational Design and Behavior*, edited by Andrew Van de Ven and William Joyce. New York: Wiley Interscience.

———. 1984, 1999. *Normal Accidents: Living with High Risk Technologies.* New York: Basic Books; Princeton: Princeton University Press.

———. 1986. *Complex Organizations: A Critical Essay.* 3rd ed. New York: Random House.

———. 1991. "A Society of Organizations." *Theory and Society* 20:725–62.

———. 1992. "Small Firm Networks." In *Networks and Organizations,* edited by N. Nohria and R. G. Eccles. Boston: Harvard Business School Press.

———. 1996. "The Bounded Career and the Demise of Civil Society." In *Boundaryless Careers: Work, Mobility, and Learning in the New Organizational Era,* edited by Michael B. Arthur and Denise M. Rousseau. New York: Oxford University Press.

Persons, Warren M. 1934. *Government Experimentation in Business.* New York: John Wiley.

Phillips, Ulrich B. 1906. "An American State-Owned Railroad." *Yale Review:* 259–282.

Piore, Michael, and Charles Sable. 1984. *The Second Industrial Divide.* New York: Basic Books.

Pollard, Sidney. 1965. *The Genesis of Modern Management: A Study of the Industrial Revolution in Great Britain.* New York: Cambridge University Press.

Powell, Walter W. 1990. "Neither Markets Nor Hierarchy: Network Forms of Organization." *Research in Organizational Behavior* 12:295–336.

Powell, Walter W., and Paul DiMaggio, eds. 1991. *The New Institutionalism in Organizational Analysis.* Chicago: University of Chicago Press.

Prude, Johnathan. 1983. *The Coming of Industrial Order: Town and Factory Life in Rural Massachusetts, 1810–1860.* New York: Cambridge University Press.

Redford, Arthur. 1926. *Labour Migration in England, 1800–1850.* Manchester, n.p.

Ringwalt, J. L. 1888. *Development of Transportation Systems in the United States.* New York: privately published.

Rose-Ackerman, Susan. 1978. *Corruption: A Study in Political Economy.* New York: Academic Press.

Rothenberg, Winifred Barr. 1992. *From Market-Places to a Market Economy: The Transformation of Rural Massachusetts, 1750–1850.* Chicago: Chicago University Press.

Roy, William G. 1997. *Socializing Capital: The Rise of the Large Industrial Corporation in America.* Princeton: Princeton University Press.

Roy, William G., and Philip Bonacich. 1988. "Interlocking Directorates and Communities of Interest among American Railroad Companies." *American Sociological Review* 53:368–79.

Sabel, Charles F. 1989. "Flexible Specialization and the Reemergence of Regional Economies." In *Reversing Industrial Decline?,* edited by P. Hirst and J. Zeitlin. London: Berg.

———. 1991. "Moebius-Strip Organizations and Open Labor Markets: Some Consequences of the Reintegration of Conception and Execution in a Volatile Economy." In *Social Theory for a Changing Society,* edited by J. Coleman and P. Bourdieu. Boulder, Colo.: Westview Press.

Sabel, Charles and Jonathan Zeitlin. 1985. "Historical Alternatives to Mass Production: Politics, Markets and Technology in Nineteenth-Century Industrialization." *Past and Present* 108:133–76.

———. 1997. "Worlds of Possibility: Flexible Mass Production in Western Industrialization." New York: Cambridge University Press.

Scherer, Frederick M. 1980. *Industrial Market and Economic Performance*. Boston: Houghton Mifflin.

Schivelbusch, Wolfgang. 1986. *The Railway Journey: The Industrialization and Perception of Time and Space in the 19th Century*. Berkeley: University of California Press.

Scranton, Philip. 1983. *Proprietary Capitalism: The Textile Manufacturers at Philadelpia, 1800–1885*. New York: Cambridge University Press.

———. 1989. *Figured Tapestry: Production, Markets, and Power in Philadelphia Textiles, 1885–1941*. New York: Cambridge University Press.

Seavoy, Ronald E. 1982. *The Origins of the American Business Corporations, 1784–1855*. Westport, Conn.: Greenwood.

Sellers, Charles. 1991. *The Market Revolution: Jacksonian America, 1815–1846*. New York: Oxford University Press.

Shelton, Cynthia J. 1986. *The Mills of Manayunk: Industrialization and Social Conflict in the Philadelphia Region, 1787–1837*. Baltimore: Johns Hopkins University Press.

Shenhav, Yehouda. 1999. *Manufacturing Rationality: The Engineering Foundations of the Managerial Revolution*. New York: Oxford University Press.

Simpson, Sally S. 1986. "The Decomposition of Antitrust: Testing a Multi-level, Longitudinal Model of Profit-squeeze." *American Sociological Review* 51:859–75.

Skowronek, Stephen. 1982. *Building a New American State: Expansion of National Administrative Capacities, 1877–1920*. New York: Cambridge University Press.

Somers, M. R. 1992. "Narrativity, Narrative Identity, and Social-Action: Rethinking English Working-Class Formation." *Social Science History* 16:591–630.

Summers, Mark W. 1984. *Railroads, Reconstruction, and the Gospel of Prosperity: Aid Under the Republicans, 1865–1877*. Princeton: Princeton University Press.

———. 1987. *The Plundering Generation: Corruption and the Crisis of the Union, 1849–1861*. New York: Oxford University Press.

Taylor, Alan. 1995. *William Cooper's Town: Power and Persuasion on the Frontier of the Early American Republic*. New York: Knopf.

Teece, David J. 1993. "The Dynamics of Industrial Capitalism: Perspectives on Alfred Chandler's 'Scale and Scope.'" *Journal of Economic Literature* 31:199–225.

Thernstrom, Stephan A. 1969. *Poverty & Progress: Social Mobility in a Nineteenth Century City*. New York: Simon and Schuster.

Thompson, E. P. 1963. *The Making of the English Working Class*. New York: Vintage.

Thompson, Margaret Susan. 1983. "Corruption — or Confusion? Lobbying and the Congressional Government in the Early Gilded Age." *Congress and the Presidency* 10:169–93.

Tilly, Charles. 1998. *Durable Inequality*. Berkeley: University of California Press.

Tucker, Barbara M. 1984. *Samuel Slater and the Origins of the American Textile Industry, 1790–1860*. Ithaca: Cornell University Press.

United States Education and Labor Committee and U.S. Senate. 1885. "Report on the Relations Between Labor and Capital."

Ure, Andrew. 1836. *The Cotton Manufacurer of Great Britain Systematically Investigated*, vols. 1 and 2. London, n.p.

Useem, Michael. 1996. *Investor Capitalism: How Money Managers Are Changing the Face of Corporate America*. New York: Basic Books.

Vance, James E., Jr. 1995. *The North American Railroad: Its Origin, Evolution and Geography*. Baltimore: Johns Hopkins Univeristy Press.

Vogel, David. 1978. "Why Businessmen Distrust Their State: The Political Consciousness of American Corporate Executives." *British Journal of Political Science* 8:45–78.

Wallace, Anthony F.C. 1978. *Rockdale: The Growth of an American Village in the Early Industrial Revolution*. New York: Knopf.

Ware, Caroline F. 1931. *The Early New England Cotton Manufacture: A Study in Industrial Beginnings*. Boston: Houghton Mifflin.

Warner, Sam Bass, Jr. 1968. *The Private City: Philadelphia in Three Periods of its Growth*. Philadelphia: University of Philadelphia Press.

Wilentz, Sean. 1984. *Chants Democratic: New York City and the Rise of the American Working Class, 1788–1850*. New York: Oxford University Press.

Williamson, Jeffrey G., and Peter H. Lindhert. 1980. *American Economic Inequality: A Macroeconomic History*. New York: Academic Press.

Williamson, Oliver. 1975. *Markets and Hierarchy: Analysis and Antitrust Implications*. New York: Free Press.

———. 1985. *The Economic Institutions of Capitalism: Firms, Markets, Relational Contracting*. New York: Free Press.

Wood, Gordon S. 1994. "Inventing American Capitalsim." *New York Review of Books*, June 9, pp. 45–49.

Zeitlin, Maurice. 1974. "Corporate Ownership and Control: The Large Corporation and the Capitalist Class." *American Journal of Sociology* 79:1073–1119.

Zucker, Lynne G. 1986. "Production of Trust: Institutional Sources of Economic Structure, 1840–1920." *Research on Organizational Behavior* 8:53–111.

INDEX

absorption of society, 15

Adams, Charles Francis, Jr., 145, 155, 176, 188–89

Adams, Henry, 145

administrative theory, 18, 230

Albro, Martin, 189

American exceptionalism, 217

Appleton, Nathan, 71

attorneys. *See* lawyers, as the shock troops of capitalism

Awkwright, Richard, 50

Baltzell, Digby, 83

Bank of Lexington, 46–47

Berk, Gerald, 180, 182, 184, 186–87, 190–97, 209

Berle, Adolf A., 206

Best, Michael, 27

Bloch, Marc, 27

Boston Associates: capital of, 82–84, 239n12; as corporate capitalism, 81; as corporate organization, 33; hierarchy in mills owned by, 29; labor control, factories as, 66–67; Lowell mills, investors in, 64; market control and profits, 69–70; power loom, development of, 67–68; risk diversification through multiple sites, 85; structural adaptation and, 77–79; structural factors and unskilled labor, 71–73; technology, stealing of, 65. *See also* Lowell textile mills

Bradach, Jeffrey, 23

Braverman, Harry, 67, 239n11

Britain: early iron production firm, 67; railway development in, 96–100, 102–3, 108–9; textile production in, 49–50, 54

Buck, Solon, 190

Burawoy, Michael, 13, 242nn24–26

bureaucracy: divisionalization, 13, 161–62; implications of, 3; as unobtrusive control device, 19, 163, 228, 233, 235. *See also* organizations

Calhoun, John C., 47

capital: availability of in Boston and Philadelphia, 82–84; centralization of markets, 183–86; the corporate form and, 198–99; hierarchy and, 29; initial capitalization, significance of, 70; mechanization and, 52–53; and the rise of organizational power, 218–21; scale economies, employment of without, 37–38

capitalism: centralization and corporate power, 204–7; corporate and corruption, 200–201; in France, 106; as independent variable, 6–7, 201, 205–7, 218, 220–21; investment and, 35; large corporations and, 131; logic of in textile production, 72–73; organizations and, 6–7; running dogs/shock troops of, 26, 43–47; steam power, development of, 97–98

Carey, Matthew, 52

Carnegie, Andrew, 215

Caro, Robert, 231

Centeno, Miguel, 6

centralization of surpluses, 12, 69. *See also* profits

centralization of wealth and power. *See* concentration of wealth and power

Chandler, Alfred DuPont, Jr.: Boston Associates as modern business, 239n12; the contract system, 167–68; corporations, explaining the dominance of, 201–2; corruption, 145–46, 149, 157; as historian of business and industry, 17; holding company, Pennsylvania Railroad perfection of, 211; labor, lack of attention to, 174, 178; model of mass production, 69; privatization of U.S. railroads, 117, 133, 137; railroads, administration and management, 161–67, 171–72, 195, 196–97; railroads, significance of, 111–13, 115; regionalism, 190; scale economies, 37; Standard Oil monopoly, 190; structure of the New England textile industry, 241n21; as theorist of limited technological view, 229–30

charters, 33

Chernow, Ron, 190

Chicago Great Western Railroad, 195–96

child labor, 54–55, 74–75, 79–80, 90–91
class: Boston Associates and, 73; conflict, 62–63; railway system and, 99; working, 61–62. *See also* labor process theory
Clawson, Dan, 168
Clay, Henry, 46–47
Cohen, Isaac, 61
Colton, David D., 146
community: basic form of, 24, 30; Lowell textile mills and, 75–76; market *vs.* hierarchy continuum and, 23–25, 29–30; *vs.* corporate interests, 129–31
competition, reduction of through holding companies, 209–12
concentration, 3–4; of capital markets, 183–86; fear of, 33–34; inability of weak state to prevent, 31; railroad bankruptcies leading to, 209; of wealth and power (*see* concentration of wealth and power)
concentration of wealth and power, 1, 3, 15; adaptation and organizational structure, 79; corporations and, 31–32, 36, 43–44; and inequality in the United States, 223; limited in decentralized organizations, 27–28; mass-production firms as model for, 111; and organizational forms and regulation, 17; prefactory, 53; profits and, 9; railroads and, 112–13, 144, 178–79; United States compared to other nations, 16–17. *See also* corporations
contingency theory. *See* strategy and structure theory
contracting out, 166–71, 215–16, 239n11. *See also* outworkers; small-firm networks
Cook, James, 194
Cook, William W., 207–8
Cooke, Jay, 204
Coolidge, John, 65, 240n14, 241n20
Cooper, William, 34–35
corporate liberalism, 192–95
corporations: the anti-charter movement, 135–36; capital, institutional structure, and the growth of, 204–7; corruption and, 200–201; and the courts (*see* courts; Supreme Court, U.S.); fear of, 33–35; holding companies, reduction of competition through, 209–12; limited

liability and, 207–9; needs of, 35–36; origins of, 31–33, 36–40, 68; railroads and the development of, 196–99, 201–3; unique development of American, 217–20; *vs.* community interests, 129–31
corruption: corporate capitalism and, 200–201; costs of, 142–43; evidence of, 144–51, 156–57; government control of railroads and, 127, 143–44; interpretation of, 147–48, 151–56; organizational interests and, 128, 141–42, 153–54, 158–59; private railroad ownership and, 118–19; railroad development and, 114, 116, 138; reactions to, 123
courts: agency theory, 177; corporations as natural entities, 209; federal regulation of railroads, prevention of, 134; holding company, acceptance of, 210; large corporations, promoting interests of, 44–45; railroad safety and, 177–78; support for private railroad owners, 133, 135; Supreme Court (*see* Supreme Court, U.S.). *See also* lawyers, as the shock troops of capitalism
Crocker, Charles, 146
Cronon, William, 32
Cullom, Shelby, 191
cultural theory: critique of analysis based on, 125–26; emergence of the corporate form, 32; incorporation, explanation of, 38–40; as independent variable, 9–10; investment of Philadelphia elite, 83; labor militancy, 59–60; Lowell textile mills, 76; models of production, 93–94; organizations, 19, 233–34; railroad development, 114, 124–27, 155–56; railroads and mechanization, 100; state-supervised pooling, opposition to, 189. *See also* neoinstitutional theory

Dalzell, Robert, 70–73
Dartmouth College, 41, 181, 219
Davis, Lance, 103, 115–16
debts, 41–42
Democracy in America (Tocqueville), 64
density, 3–4
DiMaggio, Paul, 208, 234
discrimination. *See* divisions
divisions: divisionalization in railroad administration, 161–62; in the Lowell

mills, 73–75, 95; patriarchy in the Lancashire textile mills, 238n7; use of by organizations, 13, 49

Dobbin, Frank: comparative study of railroads, 102, 104–8; contracting out as an ethos, 170; corruption, 153–56; discrimination cases of 1867, 212; divisions and employment rights, 13–14; neoinstitutionalism, 117–19, 123–27; public ownership, 132–34; stabilizing thesis, 201

Dowd, Timothy J., 201

Drew, Daniel, 167

Dublin, Thomas, 73–74

Dunlavy, Colleen A., 110, 132–33

Durable Inequality (Tilly), 13

Eccles, Robert, 23

economic development: American, 16–17, 19–20, 217–28; incorporation and, 36–40; legal revolution and, 40–47; regional *vs.* national, 186–87 (*see also* railroads, geographical scope of); toward hierarchy and networks, 28–31; toward markets, 25–28

Edelman, Lauren, 15

education, and organizational needs, 56–57, 78

efficiency: corporations, explaining the dominance of, 201–2; of discrimination, 73; of noncorporate firms, 198; railroad administration and, 165–73; railroad development and, 113, 115–17, 136–37

eminent domain, 45

employees. *See* labor

Enterprising Elite (Dalzell), 71

environment: concern for health of, 32; potash extraction, 34–35

evangelical Christianity, organizations and, 60–61

externalities: adaptation and creation of, 79; court decisions regarding, 45; of the flexible production system, 90–92; for the labor and mill towns, 77; limited in decentralized organizations, 28; of long-haul unitary railroad cars, 188; in Manayunk, 55; of mass production, 94, 111–12; needs of corporations and, 35–36; networks of small firms compared to large organizations, 58; of organizations, 1–2, 14–15; of railroads, 99,
138–39, 178; of small organizations, 5–6

factories: labor and wage dependency, 221; labor control in, 48–50, 66–67; mechanization, 51–53; railroads and the development of, 111–13; technology and the first, 66–67; workhouses, 50–51. *See also* Lowell textile mills; Manayunk textile mills

family model of textile production, 79–81

farm productivity, 238n8

Farnham, Wallace D., 138, 143

Federalist party, 24, 43, 45–46

Fessler, James, 230

Field, David Dudley, 140

Figured Tapestry (Scranton), 92–93

flexible production. *See* Kensington textile production

Fligstein, Neil, 201

Folsom, Burton, 156

Ford, Henry, 78

Forging Industrial Policy (Dobbin), 102

France: horses *vs.* coal, 97–98; railroad development and the state, 102–8

Franklin, Benjamin, 49

Friedman, Lawrence, 37

Galambos, Louis, 38, 237n3

Gallatin, Albert, 46

Gallman, R. E., 203

Georgia, Western and Atlantic Railroad, 119–22

Gersuny, Carl, 80

Gitelman, H. M., 71, 74–75, 239–40n13

Goodrich, Carter, 117–19, 123, 134

Gordon, John Steele, 145

Gould, Jay, 116, 145, 154, 189

government: corruption and railroad development, 114, 123, 127, 141–44, 154–56; European, 8; federal and private economic power, 28, 68; federal support for railroads, 137–39; federal *vs.* state in the regulation of corporations, 42–43; limited to avoid concentration, 33; participation in by mill operators, 241n18; regulation of railroads (*see* railroads, ownership and regulation of); state and democratic pressures to regulate corporations, 42–43; states and capital availability, 83;

government (*cont.*)
　weakness of federal, 143–44. *See also*
　state, the
Grange laws, 188–91
Granovetter, Mark, 113
Gras, N. S. B., 67
Great Western Railroad, 195–96
Guardians of the Poor, 50–52
Gumus-Dawes, Zehra, 65, 68–70, 72, 83

Hadley, Arthur Twining, 188
Hall, Peter Dobkin, 33–34
Hamilton, Alexander, 49, 76
Hartz, Louis, 38, 117, 129–33, 132, 135–
　37, 148
Hatch, Rufus, 145
hierarchy: basic form of, 24, 30; commu-
　nity and, 23–25; economic development
　and, 28–31; expense of, 28–29; in the
　Lowell textile mills, 75–76; *vs.* markets,
　22–23. *See also* mass-production
　techniques
Hirschman, Albert, 32
historical institutionalism, 113–14, 117–
　19, 122–23
Hofstadter, Richard, 38
Hopkins, Mark, 146
Horwitz, Morton J., 44, 177–78
Hounshell, David A., 37
Huntington, Collis P., 146
Huntington, Samuel P., 152–53
Hurst, J., 37

ICC. *See* Interstate Commerce
　Commission
immigration, 50, 58, 61, 240n14
incorporation, 36–40. *See also*
　corporations
indexes, as hypertext, primitive version of,
　237n4
inequality: bifurcation of wealth in the
　1830s, 63; in income and wealth, 223
　(*see also* wealth); industrial capital and,
　64; large organizations and, 16. *See also*
　concentration of wealth and power
inflation, 170
institutional economics, 17, 25
institutionalism: historical, 113–14, 117–
　19, 122–23; new economic, 110; politi-
　cal science, 17–18. *See also* neoinstitu-
　tional theory

institutional logics, 124–27. *See also* orga-
　nizational logic
interests: critique of analysis based on,
　124–25; as explanation of incorpora-
　tion, 38–40; organizational (*see* organi-
　zational interests); private railroad
　ownership, 118–19; representation by
　lawyers, 44–47; structural (*see* struc-
　tural interests)
Interstate Commerce Commission (ICC):
　lack of regulation by, 128–29; railroad
　rates, 192–93; railroads, regional *vs.*
　national, 180, 186, 216; railroad safety,
　177
Irish, discrimination against and exploita-
　tion of, 74–75, 239–40n13

Jackson, Robert Max, 13
Jacksonian party, 63
Jefferson, Thomas, 76, 134
Johnson, Andrew, 204
Johnson, Paul, 60
Joyce, Patrick, 57

Kennedy, Paul, 15
Kensington textile production: adaptation
　and organizational structure, 78–79; de-
　cline of, 92–93; dispersed capital of, 38;
　externalities of flexible production, 90–
　92; flexible mass production, 85–86; in-
　stability of partnerships in, 33; labor re-
　lations, 90–91; mechanization, labor,
　and capital, 52–53; networks and trans-
　actions costs, 88–90; as Philadelphia
　model, 81–82; public facilities, 58;
　small-firm network model, decline of,
　224; small-firm networks and skilled la-
　bor, 72; small-firm networks of, 29–30,
　222; small-scale operations, structural
　implications of, 86–88
King, Richard, 194
Knights of Labor, 62

labor: child, 74–75, 79–80, 90–91; con-
　tracting out, 166–71, 215–16, 239n11;
　control of, 48–50, 66–67; the courts
　and, 44–45; discipline of, 55–56; divi-
　sions, exploiting social and ethnic (*see*
　divisions); employees working for large
　organizations, percentage of, 1; exploi-
　tation of, 54–55, 69; imprisonment of,

80; living and working conditions, 57–58; mechanization and, 51–53; outworkers, 48, 51, 91; railroads and, 173–79; regulation in workhouses, 50–51; and the rise of organizational power, 218, 221–22; skilled in small-scale operations, 87; strikes and responses, 58–63, 90–91; surplus, development and, 24–25; unskilled and structural interests at Lowell, 71–73; working class *vs.* working classes, 61–62. *See also* labor process theory; socialization; wage dependence

Labor and Monopoly Capital: The Degradation of Work in the Twentieth Century (Braverman), 67

labor process theory, 18–19, 231–33; class and the Boston Associates, 73; improvement for workers, 242n25; innovation and adaptation, 78; labor surplus, in conditions of, 239n8; strikes, importance to, 71; technology and the first factories, 67

LaFollette, Robert, 193

Lamoreux, Naomi, 182

lawyers, as the shock troops of capitalism, 43–47

Lehigh Navigation Company, 129–32, 135

Licht, Walter, 164, 167, 169–70, 173–78

limited liability, 207–9

Lindert, Peter, 223

Locks and Canal Company, 69

Logan, John, 231

loom, waterpowered, 65–68

Lowell, Francis Cabot, 67–68, 71

Lowell, Robert, 219–20

Lowell textile mills: ascendancy of mass-production model at, 224; charter for, 37; concentrated capital of, 38; to 1846 (*see* Lowell I textile mills); 1846 to century's end (*see* Lowell II textile mills); as first modern business, 75–77; hierarchy in, 29; mechanization, labor, and capital, 52–53; paternalistic controls, 57; structural adaptation and, 77–79. *See also* Boston Associates

Lowell I textile mills: defined, 64; divisions at, 73–74; labor recruitment, 68–69; site selection, 68

Lowell II textile mills: child labor at, 74–75; defined, 64; divisions at, 74–75; living and working conditions at, 71–72; mass production at, 81; wage dependence, establishment of, 70–71

Manayunk textile mills: concentration of wealth and power, 53–55; exploitation of labor, 54–55; Guardians of the Poor workhouse, 50–51; inflexibility of production, 84–85; labor control and the origin of factories, 48–50; labor discipline, 55–56; labor militancy, 58–63; mechanization, labor, and capital, 52–53; the new aristocrats of, 64; paternalistic controls, 56–57; public facilities and living conditions, 57; wage dependence, 62

Market Revolution, The (Sellers), 33

markets: basic form of, 24, 29–30; community and, 23–25; control of by the Boston Associates, 70; economic development and, 25–28, 31; Lowell textile mills and, 75; shift to in New England, 238–39nn8–9; *vs.* hierarchy, 22–23

Marshall, John, 41

Marx, Karl, 12, 61

mass-production techniques: externalities of, 94; historical circumstances and the dominance of, 225–26; Lowell and Manayunk as among the first to use, 69–70; in Lowell textile mills, 77, 81, 224; in the Slater model, 81; slow development of, 222. *See also* hierarchy; technology

McCallum, Daniel, 163

McGouldrick, Paul, 240n16

Means, Gardiner C., 206

mechanization, 51–53, 100. *See also* technology

Mercer, Lloyd J., 115, 137–38

Merrimack Manufacturing Company, 92

Meyer, John, 13

Miller, George, 190–91

Mizruchi, Mark, 201

Molotch, Harvey, 231

monopoly, railways and, 98–99, 190

Montgomery, David, 60

Morgan, J. P., 195–96, 201, 209, 216

Mulcahy, Michael, 194

nationalization, of railroads. *See* railroads, geographical scope of

Nelson, William E., 44

neoinstitutional theory: corporations, explaining the dominance of, 202–3; explanatory weakness of, 212; incorporation, explanation of, 38–40; Lowell textile mills, 76; organizations and, 18–19, 233–34; railroad development, 114, 123–27. See also cultural theory

networks: characteristics of, 25; development of, 29–31; economic development and, 31; market vs. hierarchy continuum and, 23; small-firm (see small-firm networks); trust in, 23

new economic institutionalism, 110

New Jersey, holding company, acceptance of, 210–11

noncorporate forms of organization, 32

noneconomic organizations, 2, 7–8

North, Douglass, 103, 115–16

organizational administration theory, 230

organizational interests: concentration of wealth and power and, 44–45; emergence of the corporate form and, 43; independent power, suppression of, 104–5; labor and, 241n20; labor militancy and, 60; of the Lehigh Navigation Company, 131; and the nationalization of railroads (see railroads, geographical scope of); political process, distinguished from, 185; railroad administration and, 165–66; railroad development and, 111–13, 123, 127–29, 133–41, 148–51, 153–54, 158–59; and railroad development in Britain, 108–9; and railroad development in France, 105–8; and railroad development in Prussia, 110; religion and, 60–61. See also structural interests

organizational interpretation: of American economic development, 16–17, 19–21, 217–28; of the emergence of the corporate form, 36–40; of labor militancy, 58–60; of structural adaptation at Lowell, lack of, 77–79. See also society of organizations

organizational logic: Lowell textile mills and, 72; railroad development and, 102–4, 110–11, 122–23

organizations: capitalism and, 7; contemporary size of, 1; corporate form of (see corporations); dependent variable, treated as the (see theories); divisions, benefits of, 49; impact of large, 1–3; impacts of, 12–15; as independent variable, 10–12; noncorporate forms of, 32; noneconomic, 2, 7–8; size, dynamics of, 4–6; society of (see society of organizations); weak state and, 217–19

outworkers, 48, 51, 91. See also contracting out

Passions and the Interests, The (Hirschman), 32

Pennsylvania: anti-investment legislation, 134–36; bank regulation and capital availability, 83; Lehigh Navigation Company, 129–31; nationalization of railroads, 194; oil industry monopoly, 190; opposition to railroads, 139–40; Philadelphia (see Philadelphia); state ownership of railroads, 132–33

Pennsylvania Railroad Company, 205, 210–11

pension plans, in the railroad industry, 178

Persons, Warren M., 119

Philadelphia: capital, availability in, 82–84; county government, functions of, 56; early-nineteenth-century, 27; Germantown, conditions in, 58; Kensington textile production (see Kensington textile production); Manayunk textile mills (see Manayunk textile mills); poverty rate, early 1820s, 55

Philadelphia model. See Kensington textile production

Phillips, Ulrich B., 120–22

Piore, Michael, 77

Plundering Generation, The (Summers), 44

politics: class conflict in, 62–63; corporations, explaining the dominance of, 203; emergence of the corporate form and, 43; nationalization of railroads and, 181–82, 184–85; political distinguished from organizational process, 185; power and organizations, 18, 231

Pollard, Sidney, 67

Poor, Henry Varnum, 139, 149, 167–69, 172, 174

Powell, Walter W., 23, 208, 234

power: concentration of (*see* concentration of wealth and power); organizations and, 8–10; political, 18; wealth and, 9

Power Broker, The (Caro), 231

Preparing for the Next Century (Kennedy), 15

privatization, of railroads. *See* railroads, ownership and regulation of

profits: of the Boston Associates, 69–70; and concentration of wealth, 9, 12; contracting out and, 170–71; wage surplus returns, 237n1

Proprietary Capitalism (Scranton), 48, 77, 81

Prude, Jonathan, 26–27, 60

Prussia, railroad development, 110, 132

Public Image of Big Business in America, 1880–1940, The (Galambos), 237n3

Puritan Boston and Quaker Philadelphia (Baltzell), 83

railroads: administration of (*see* railroads, administration of); competition, reduction through holding companies, 209–12; corporate form, emergence of, 196–99, 201–3; corruption and (*see* corruption); the courts and privatization of, 42; development in Britain, 108–9; development in France, 104–8; development in Prussia, 110; federal government support for, 137–39; Georgia's Western and Atlantic, 119–22; management *vs.* stockholders, 205–6; national *vs.* regional (*see* railroads, geographical scope of); opposition to, 139–41; organizational logic and development of, 102–4, 110–11; and the organization of America, 223–25; private ownership of (*see* railroads, ownership and regulation of); rates and freight charges, 188–90, 192–93; regulation of (*see* railroads, ownership and regulation of); safety issues, 176–78; significance of, 111–13, 115, 182–83; technology and, 96–101, 111–12

railroads, administration of, 160; authority, lines of, 163–65; the Chicago Great Western Railroad, 195; contracting out, 166–71; divisionalization, 161–62; finance office, 162–63; inevitability of path taken, 165–66, 171–73; informa-tion and the head office, 163; labor issues, 175–79; management style and labor relations, 173–75; predatory tactics, 171–73

railroads, geographical scope of, 179–89; capital market concentration and, 183–86; debate over, 187–91; organizational *vs.* political interpretation, 180–83, 192–94; regionalism, viability of, 195–96; regionalization *vs.* nationalization, 186–87

railroads, ownership and regulation of, 113–15, 157–59; anti-investment legislation, 134–37; the corruption argument, 114, 141–44 (*see also* corruption); the efficiency argument, 113, 115–17; government regulation, attempts at, 102, 110, 118–19, 127–28; initial government control of, 126–27; the institutionalist argument, 113–14, 117–19, 122–23; the neoinstitutionalist argument, 114, 123–27; the organizational interest argument, 127–29, 133–41, 148–51, 153–54, 158–59; state ownership, 119–22, 132–34

Railway Journey, The (Schivelbusch), 96

Redford, Arthur, 49

regulation, of railroads. *See* railroads, ownership and regulation of

religion, organizations and, 60–61

Republican party, 24, 43, 46, 76–77

Ringwalt, J. L., 150–51

Ripka, Joseph, 84–85, 91

Roberts, Wade, 194

Rockdale (Wallace), 60

Rockefeller, John D., 190

Rothenberg, Winifred Barr, 238n8

Roxborough. *See* Manayunk textile mills

Roy, William, 113, 182, 197–205, 207–12

Sabel, Charles, 77, 93

Salsbury, Stephen, 161–63

Sanders, Elizabeth, 187

Schivelbusch, Wolfgang, 96–101

Schlesinger, Arthur, 60

Schneiberg, Marc, 194

Scott, Thomas, 146, 211

Scranton, Philip: Globe Mill, 48; as independent representative of an intellectual tradition, 240–41n17; innovation, lack

Scranton, Philip (*cont.*)
  of in Lowell, 77; living conditions for labor, 57–58; Philadelphia textile industry, 27, 81–83, 85–93; structure of New England textile industry, 241–42n21
Seavoy, Ronald E., 115, 136–37
Sellers, Charles: labor surplus theory, 25; marketization of the United States, 43; partnerships and joint-stock companies, 33; shock troops of capitalism, 43, 208; South Carolina planters, 47; Webster, description of, 41
Shelton, Cynthia, 48–52, 54–56, 58–64
Shin, Dongyub, 239n9
Shopkeepers Millenium (Johnson), 60
Skocpol, Theda, 192
Skowronek, Stephen, 189, 192, 230
Slater, Samuel, 29, 65, 71, 79–80
Slater model of textile production, 79–81
slavery, 226, 240n15
small-firm networks: in early-nineteenth-century America, 26–27; organizational size, role of, 4–6; in Philadelphia (*see* Kensington textile production). *See also* contracting out
Smith, Adam, 97, 109
Smith, Conyers, 88
Smith, Herbert Knox, 208
socialization: of employees and customers, 1; labor control in Manayunk, 55–57; needs of corporations and, 36; organizations and, 13; of workers in the workhouse, 51
Socializing Capital: The Rise of the Large Industrial Corporation in America (Roy), 197
society, absorption of, 15
society of organizations: anticipated in the eighteenth century, 67; creation of, 3; manufactures, early prejudice against, 76; in mid-nineteenth-century America, 175; as theory of American economic development, 19, 227–28, 234–35. *See also* organizational interpretation
Springfield armory, 29–30
Standard Oil, 190
Stanford, Leland, 146
state, the: in Britain, 102–3, 108–9; in France, 102–8; large organizations and, 33; railroads and, 102–4, 142–44; weak, implications of, 31, 217–19

Stickney, A. B., 195–96
Strategy and Structure (Chandler), 164
strategy and structure theory: innovation and adaptation, 78; labor and, 241n20; organizations and, 18, 230; technology and the first factories, 67
stratification theory, 18, 231
structural interests: adaptation at Lowell, lack of, 77–79; of big organizations, 226; of bureaucracies, 104–5; family control and inflexibility, 85; Lowell textile mills and, 71–73, 95; needs of corporations and, 35; organizations and, 13–14; small-scale operations and, 86–88
Suchman, Mark C., 15
Summers, Mark, 44, 156–57
Supreme Court, U.S.: corporations, explaining the dominance of, 203; decisions supporting corporations, 40–43, 219; and the nationalization of railroads, 180–81, 186, 192–93, 216
surpluses. *See* profits
Sutton, John, 13–14
system accidents, 15

tariffs, 70, 77, 94, 220
Taylor, Alan, 26, 34
technology: adaptation and organizational structure, 77–79; corporate form, development of and, 43; and the emergence of the corporate form, 37; in a flexible production network, 87–88; labor and, 241n20; loom, waterpowered, 65–68; looms, improvements in, 77; organizations and, 17–18, 18, 218, 229–30; railroads and, 96–101, 111–12. *See also* mass-production techniques
Teece, David, 171
telegraph system, 99
textile production: British, 49–50, 54; decline of, 92–94; in the large factories of Manayunk (*see* Manayunk textile mills); in the mass-production factories of Lowell (*see* Lowell textile mills); the Slater model of, 79–81; in the small-firm networks of Kensington (*see* Kensington textile production)
theories: administrative or organizational administration, 18, 230; cultural (*see* cultural theory); labor process (*see* labor

process theory); neoinstitutional (*see*
neoinstitutional theory); political power,
18, 231 (*see also* politics); society of organizations (*see* society of organizations); strategy and structure (*see*
strategy and structure theory); stratification, 18, 231; technology, 17–18, 229–
30 (*see also* technology)
Thernstrom, Stephan, 175
Thiers, Adolphe, 106
Thompson, E. P., 52, 232
Thompson, Margaret Susan, 152–53
Tilly, Charles, 13
Tocqueville, Alexis de, 63–64, 104–5
transactions cost economics, 22
transportation: railroads (*see* railroads);
waterways, 100–101, 129–31
Truman, David, 230
trust, in networks, 23
Tucker, Barbara M., 60–61

unions, evolution of big labor, 179

Vance, James, 96–97, 100
Vanderbilt, Cornelius, 141, 145, 154
variables, independent and dependent,
65–66
Visible Hand, The (Chandler), 37, 164, 174
Vogel, David, 143

wage dependence: factories, development
of and, 221; lack of among farmers'
daughters, 68–69; lack of associated
with hand looms, 66; lack of in early
nineteenth century, 26–27; Lowell, establishment of at, 70–71, 238–39n8;
mass-production firms as model for,

111; organizations and, 12; property
and avoiding, 39; slavery, ignoring of,
240n15; and the working class, emergence of, 61–62
Wallace, Anthony F. C., 26, 55, 60,
241n20
Ware, Carolyn, 76, 79–80
Warner, Sam Bass, 27
Washington, George, 34
Watt, James, 96
wealth: accumulation of and structural organization, 88; concentration of (*see*
concentration of wealth and power); inequality in during the nineteenth century, 223; organizations and, 10; power
and, 9; shares of the very rich during
the nineteenth century, 203
wealth and power: benefits of deconcentration, 169; concentration of (*see*
concentration of wealth and power)
Weber, Max, 12
Webster, Daniel, 41, 219
Whig party, 63
White, Josiah, 130
Wilentz, Sean, 60
Williamson, Jeffrey, 223
women: benefits of employment, 49; and
divisions at Lowell, 73–74; employment
of, 54; recruitment at Lowell, 68–69
Women at Work (Dublin), 73
Wood, Gordon S., 238n8
workhouses, 50–51, 67
working class, 61–62
Wright, Carol D., 237n1

Zimny, Mark, 144
Zucker, Lynn, 233